# Computer Applications for Paralegals, 2nd Edition

## Using MS Office Suite and Windows to Prepare Professional Documentation

Barb Asselin

Asselin Group Online Publisher
R.R. #2, 449 Flat Rapids Road
Arnprior, ON Canada K7S 3G8

www.AsselinGroup.com

Copyright © 2020 Barb Asselin
Reprinted December 2020

All Rights reserved. No part of this book may be reproduced or used in any way or form or by any means whether electronic or mechanical, this means that you cannot record or photocopy any material ideas or text or graphics that are provided in this book.

# Table of Contents

Table of Contents ................................................................................................. iii
Preface .................................................................................................................. 11
    Chapter Features ........................................................................................... 12
        Learning Outcomes ................................................................................. 12
        Hands-On Demonstration ....................................................................... 12
        Video Demonstration .............................................................................. 12
        Practice Exercises ................................................................................... 12
        Chapter Summary ................................................................................... 13
    Online Resources ........................................................................................... 13
    Acknowledgements ....................................................................................... 13
Chapter 1: Paralegal Firm Configuration ........................................................... 15
    Learning Outcomes ...................................................................................... 15
    Overview of Paralegal Firm ......................................................................... 15
    Paralegals' Professional Corporation .......................................................... 16
    Chart of Paralegals and Staff ....................................................................... 18
    Chart of Administration Department .......................................................... 19
    Chapter Summary ......................................................................................... 19
Chapter 2: File Management ............................................................................... 21
    Learning Outcomes ...................................................................................... 21
    Physical Files ................................................................................................. 21
        From Folders to Boxes ............................................................................ 21
        File Organization ..................................................................................... 23
        Location of Files ...................................................................................... 23
        Filing ......................................................................................................... 24
    Electronic Files ............................................................................................. 25

Windows ..........................................................................................26
    Creating a New Folder.................................................................27
    Navigating Windows Using the Left-Hand Task Pane ......................30
    Displaying Windows Content in the Right-Hand Task Pane ..............31
Chapter Summary..............................................................................32
Exercises ...........................................................................................33
    Exercise 2.1 ................................................................................33
    Exercise 2.2 ................................................................................34
    Exercise 2.3 ................................................................................34
    Exercise 2.4 ................................................................................35
    Exercise 2.5 ................................................................................36
    Exercise 2.6 ................................................................................37

## Chapter 3: Outlook..........................................................................39
Learning Outcomes ............................................................................39
Overview ...........................................................................................39
Calendar ............................................................................................40
    Creating an Appointment............................................................41
    Viewing Your Calendar ...............................................................49
    Printing Your Calendar ...............................................................49
Contacts ............................................................................................50
    Creating a New Contact .............................................................51
    Contact Options .........................................................................52
    Contact Views ............................................................................53
    Printing your Contacts ................................................................54
Tasks .................................................................................................54
    Creating a New Task ..................................................................54
    Printing Your Tasks ....................................................................56
Chapter Summary..............................................................................57

Exercises ........................................................................................................ 58
    Exercise 3.1 ............................................................................................ 58
    Exercise 3.2 ............................................................................................ 59
    Exercise 3.3 ............................................................................................ 60
    Exercise 3.4 ............................................................................................ 62
    Exercise 3.5 ............................................................................................ 63
    Exercise 3.6 ............................................................................................ 64

## Chapter 4: PowerPoint ........................................................................... 67

Learning Outcomes ................................................................................. 67
Overview .................................................................................................. 67
Creating a Presentation .......................................................................... 67
Slide Layouts ........................................................................................... 69
New Slide ................................................................................................. 70
Design ...................................................................................................... 71
    Customizing the Design ......................................................................... 72
Adding Text ............................................................................................. 72
Customizing Bullets ................................................................................ 75
Headers and Footers ............................................................................... 77
Adding Content ....................................................................................... 80
    Tables ...................................................................................................... 80
    Charts ...................................................................................................... 83
    Smart Art Graphics ................................................................................. 88
    Pictures ................................................................................................... 90
    Videos ..................................................................................................... 91
    More Content ......................................................................................... 93
Notes ........................................................................................................ 97
Transitions ............................................................................................... 97
Animations .............................................................................................. 99

Saving Different Formats ............................................................................ 100
Viewing Your Presentation ........................................................................ 101
Printing Your Presentation ........................................................................ 102
Chapter Summary ....................................................................................... 103
Exercises ....................................................................................................... 104
    Exercise 4.1 ............................................................................................. 104
    Exercise 4.2 ............................................................................................. 106
    Exercise 4.3 ............................................................................................. 108
    Exercise 4.4 ............................................................................................. 111
    Exercise 4.5 ............................................................................................. 114
    Exercise 4.6 ............................................................................................. 117

Chapter 5: Excel ............................................................................................. 121
    Learning Outcomes ................................................................................. 121
    Overview .................................................................................................. 121
    Creating a Spreadsheet ........................................................................... 121
        Data ..................................................................................................... 122
    Formulas .................................................................................................. 125
        Basics .................................................................................................. 125
        Auto-Sum and Adding ..................................................................... 125
        Anatomy of a Formula ..................................................................... 126
        Copying a Formula ........................................................................... 127
        Calculating Tax ................................................................................. 128
        Totaling Columns and Rows ........................................................... 129
    Formatting ............................................................................................... 130
        Adding Rows and Columns ............................................................ 130
        Borders ............................................................................................... 131
        Shading and Fonts ............................................................................ 131
    Tables ........................................................................................................ 132

Sorting and Filtering ................................................................................. 134

Conditional Formatting.............................................................................. 138

Charts........................................................................................................ 142

Statistics.................................................................................................... 148

Functions................................................................................................... 150

Pivot Tables .............................................................................................. 156

Other Things to Note................................................................................. 162

    Freezing Rows or Columns ................................................................. 162

    Hiding and Un-hiding Data................................................................... 163

    Show Formulas .................................................................................... 164

    Absolute Cell Reference ...................................................................... 165

Printing ...................................................................................................... 167

Chapter Summary ..................................................................................... 169

Exercises................................................................................................... 170

    Exercise 5.1 ......................................................................................... 170

    Exercise 5.2 ......................................................................................... 171

    Exercise 5.3 ......................................................................................... 172

    Exercise 5.4 ......................................................................................... 173

    Exercise 5.5 ......................................................................................... 174

    Exercise 5.6 ......................................................................................... 176

Chapter 6: Word ............................................................................................ 178

Learning Outcomes................................................................................... 178

Overview................................................................................................... 178

Correspondence........................................................................................ 180

    Full Block Letters ................................................................................. 182

    Modified Block Letters......................................................................... 184

    Modified Block Letters with Indentation .............................................. 186

    Multi-Page Letters ............................................................................... 187

| | |
|---|---|
| Envelopes and Labels | 190 |
| Merging | 192 |
| Step 1 | 194 |
| Step 2 | 195 |
| Step 3 | 196 |
| Step 4 | 199 |
| Step 5 | 204 |
| Step 6 | 204 |
| Memos | 206 |
| Multi-Page Memos | 208 |
| Fax Cover Sheets | 210 |
| Templates | 213 |
| Reports | 216 |
| If Your Copy and Paste Doesn't Work | 220 |
| Using a Cover Page Template | 220 |
| Typing the Body of Your Report | 222 |
| Styles | 233 |
| Tables | 235 |
| Editing | 239 |
| Proofreading | 239 |
| Find and Replace | 240 |
| Compare, Comment, and Track Changes | 242 |
| Saving | 245 |
| Printing | 247 |
| Chapter Summary | 248 |
| Exercises | 249 |
| Exercise 6.1 | 249 |
| Exercise 6.2 | 250 |

- Exercise 6.3 ............................................................................................................. 251
- Exercise 6.4 ............................................................................................................. 251
- Exercise 6.5 ............................................................................................................. 252
- Exercise 6.6 ............................................................................................................. 253
- Exercise 6.7 ............................................................................................................. 255
- Exercise 6.8 ............................................................................................................. 255
- Exercise 6.9 ............................................................................................................. 256
- Exercise 6.10 ........................................................................................................... 257

## Chapter 7: Combining Software ............................................................................. 259
- Learning Outcomes ................................................................................................ 259
- Overview .................................................................................................................. 259
- Embedding Into Word ............................................................................................ 261
- Embedding Into PowerPoint ................................................................................. 265
- Embedding Into Excel ............................................................................................ 268
- Chapter Summary .................................................................................................. 271
- Exercises ................................................................................................................. 272
  - Exercise 7.1 .......................................................................................................... 275
  - Exercise 7.2 .......................................................................................................... 275
  - Exercise 7.3 .......................................................................................................... 275

## Conclusion ................................................................................................................ 277

## Summary of Templates ........................................................................................... 279
- Chapter 1 ................................................................................................................. 279
- Chapter 6 ................................................................................................................. 279

## Summary of Instructional Videos .......................................................................... 281
- Chapter 2 ................................................................................................................. 281
- Chapter 3 ................................................................................................................. 281
- Chapter 4 ................................................................................................................. 281
- Chapter 5 ................................................................................................................. 282

Chapter 6 ............................................................................................... 282
Chapter 7 ............................................................................................... 283
Also by Barb Asselin ............................................................................. 284
Notes ...................................................................................................... 285

# Preface

Working as a successful Paralegal for either yourself, a law firm, a paralegal firm, the government, or private industry, requires an individual to possess many skills, not the least of which is the ability to use a variety of software programs to properly draft, create, and format documentation.

*Computer Applications for Paralegals* introduces students to many of the software programs of the MS Office Suite and acts as a guide through the proper use of each program to generate accurate, ready-for-delivery documentation.

The primary goals of this text are:

- To discuss the importance of both physical and digital file management and demonstrate proper digital file management principles
- To demonstrate how MS Outlook can be used to maintain an accurate client base, juggle multiple deadlines and time commitments, as well as keep an accurate schedule
- To demonstrate how MS PowerPoint can be used to deliver a meaningful presentation to co-workers, peers, industry professionals, and clients
- To demonstrate how MS Excel can be used to generate accurate cost projections and analyses, maintain accounting records, and perform other mathematical calculations to assist in the day-to-day business of the law or paralegal firm, governmental agency, or corporate entity
- To use MS Word to quickly and accurately create a variety of office documentation such as correspondence, memos, fax cover sheets, professional business reports, court documents, merges, and agreements, and
- To combine the MS Office software programs into one cohesive, inclusive, multi-media report or presentation.

The text sets out a fictional paralegal firm together with its partners and employees in a firm hierarchy, so that each student can see how they will interact with others in the firm, depending on the task and area of law. The members of the firm will become the senders and recipients of various documentation prepared in the exercises and examples in the text. In this manner, students will feel as if they've experienced a "hands-on" and realistic approach to the work they would be asked to do in an actual firm.

The skills taught in this text are transferable, so that as students enter the work force, they will be able to confidently begin their new employment as valuable members of the team.

## Chapter Features

### Learning Outcomes

At the beginning of each chapter, a list of the chapter's desired employability skills is listed.

### Hands-On Demonstration

The main content of each chapter is a hands-on demonstration of the software used. There are a multitude of graphics that the student can use to mimic the demonstration. The goal is that each student will follow the given instructions and work alongside the demonstration to generate the exact document created in the text.

### Video Demonstration

Each chapter contains a link to video training, in case the student requires additional instruction on a certain topic. Look for this symbol to let you know that an instructional video is available on a particular topic:

There is an instructional video for students on this topic at:
Webpage: http://www.asselingroup.com/paralegals
Password: paralegals

### Practice Exercises

Following the demonstration portion of each chapter, practice exercises are given to allow the student to practice the chapter's newly learned skills.

## Chapter Summary

At the end of each chapter, a summary of the learned skills is given, so that the student may check to ensure they have successfully navigated and learned each item.

## Online Resources

A private webpage is available to all users of this text. It contains links to the video tutorials, practice exercise documents, and precedents. The webpage is available here:

    Webpage:    http://www.asselingroup.com/paralegals

    Password:    paralegals

## Acknowledgements

Author Barb Asselin, MBA, thanks her husband and two daughters for their ongoing support and encouragement in her writing endeavors, and for providing her with never-ending motivation to succeed.

# Chapter 1: Paralegal Firm Configuration

## Learning Outcomes

In this chapter, students will:

- Discover the configuration of the paralegal firm that will be used throughout the text
- Learn how to access the private webpage that accompanies the text
- Find the letterhead templates to be used in generating professional legal correspondence in the exercises that accompany the text

## Overview of Paralegal Firm

The examples and exercises in this text refer to a fictional paralegal firm, **Paralegals' Professional Corporation**. The firm practices in the following areas of law:

- Landlord and Tenant Tribunal
- Small Claims Court
- Employment Law
- Provincial Offences
- Summary Convictions
- Immigration Law

The firm is comprised of a Managing Partner, an administrative department, plus a variety of legal professionals including paralegals, law clerks, and legal assistants.

Your role in this firm will be as a paralegal who specializes in the landlord and tenant area of law. However, you may be required to create documentation for the other paralegals in the firm when they are away from the office or overloaded with work.

# Paralegals' Professional Corporation

As you create the documentation in either the demonstration portion of this book or the exercise portion of this book, you can use one of the following satellite offices of **Paralegals' Professional Corporation**:

- Kingston Office

    Paralegals' Professional Corporation
    1 Paralegal Private
    Kingston, Ontario
    K2K 2K1

- Toronto Office

    Paralegals' Professional Corporation
    1 Paralegal Private
    Toronto, Ontario
    M2K 2K2

- Ottawa Office

    Paralegals' Professional Corporation
    1 Paralegal Private
    Ottawa, Ontario
    K2K 2K2

- Sault Ste. Marie Office

    Paralegals' Professional Corporation
    1 Paralegal Private
    Sault Ste. Marie, Ontario
    P2K 2K1

- Thunder Bay Office

    Paralegals' Professional Corporation
    1 Paralegal Private
    Thunder Bay, Ontario
    P2K 2K2

- London Office

    Paralegals' Professional Corporation
    1 Paralegal Private
    London, Ontario
    N2K 2K2

Alternatively, your professor may choose to create a custom office for your class. To do so, simply change the city to your city, and change the first letter of the postal code to the first letter of your postal code.

**ONLINE**: Note that letterhead precedents are provided to you on our private webpage, as follows:

    Webpage:    http://www.asselingroup.com/paralegals

    Password:    paralegals

# Chart of Paralegals and Staff

The individual paralegals and staff are detailed in the organizational chart shown below.

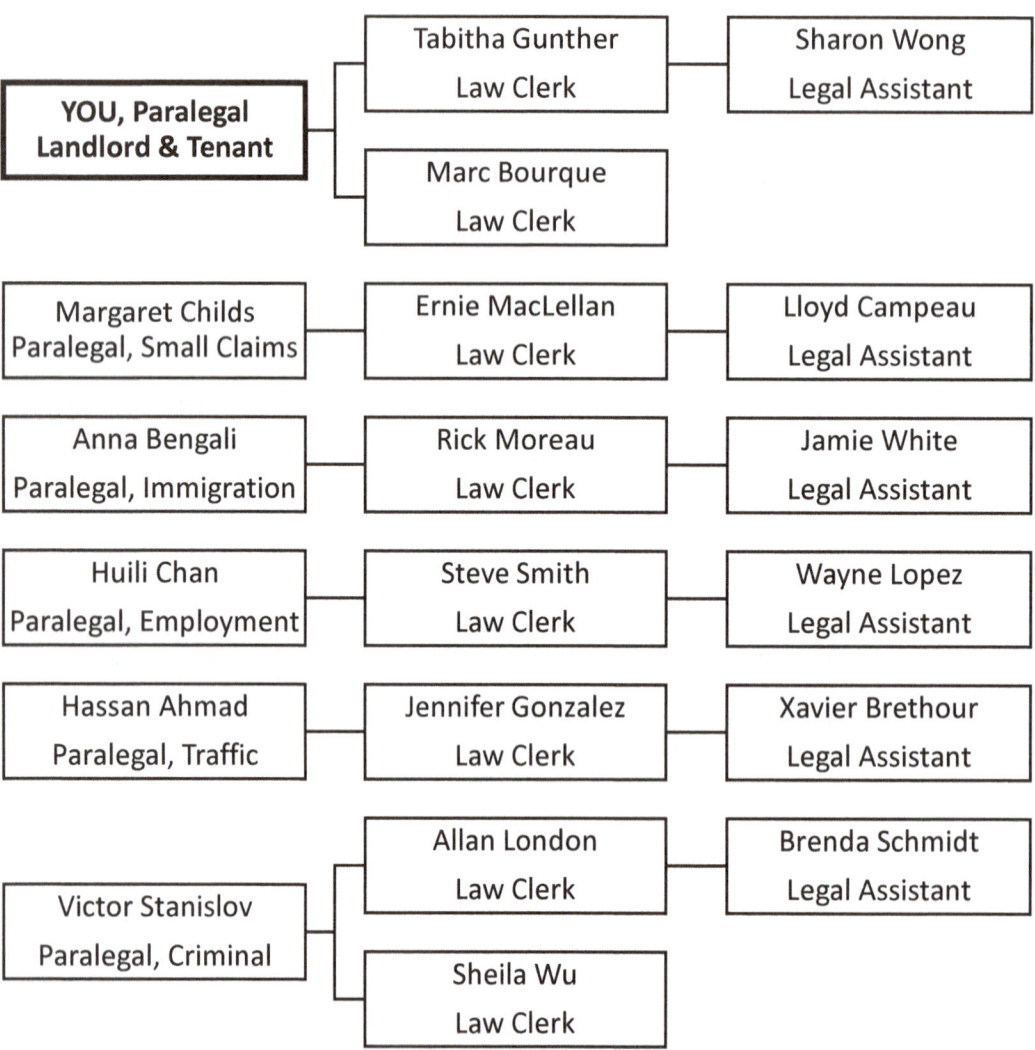

# Chart of Administration Department

The Managing Partner and the employees in the administration department are detailed in the organizational chart shown in Figure 1.2.

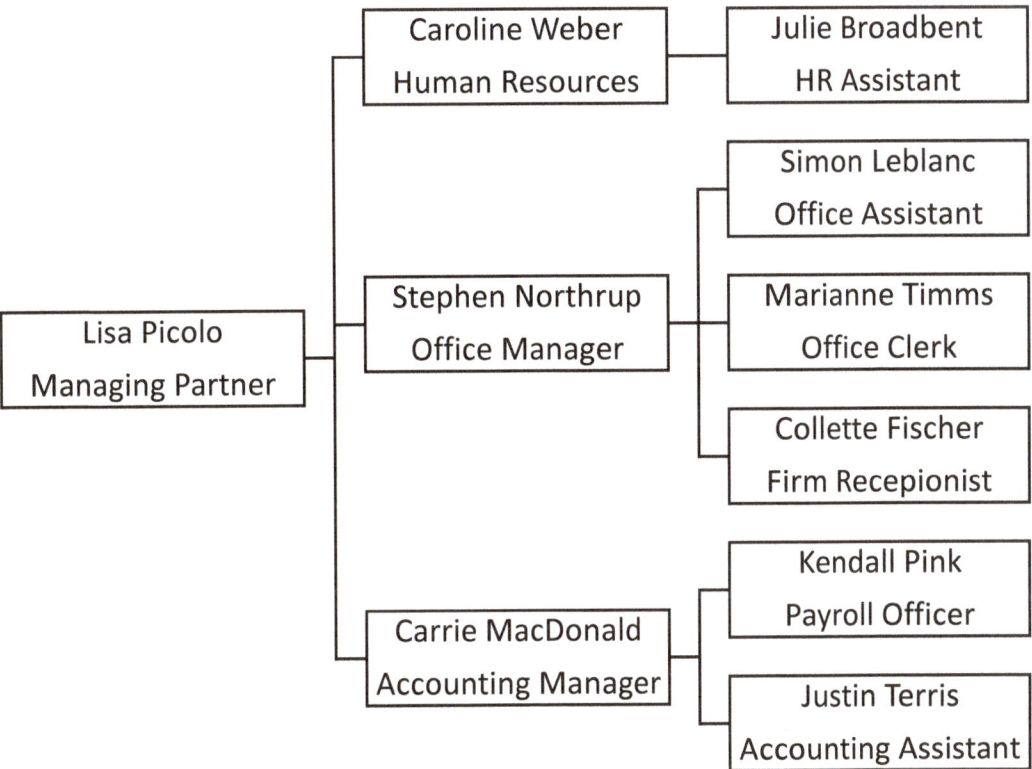

# Chapter Summary

In this chapter, students discovered how the firm used in the text's exercises is set up and their place in the firm. Students found out how to access the supporting documentation, videos, and precedents that will allow them to succeed in their course through a private webpage.

# Chapter 2: File Management

## Learning Outcomes

In this chapter, students will:

- Discuss the importance of an organized file management system, for both physical and digital files
- Discuss various ways to organize the interior of a file
- Learn how to create an electronic file management system using Windows

## Physical Files

Physical files always start with the introduction of a new client. The client is met by the paralegal and the new file opening sheet is given to the support staff member in charge of opening new files.

### From Folders to Boxes

Each new file begins in a legal-sized file folder. There is a tab on the open side of the folder that is used to display information about each individual file.

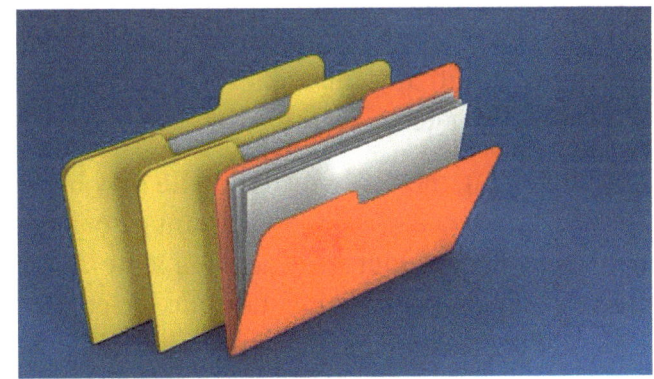

Usually, the staff member in charge of opening the file will print a couple of labels. The labels will include the client's name, last name first, or company, as well as the file number and the reference line of the file.

Labels may also include information on the responsible paralegal and file opening date. Here is an example of a file label:

> ASSELIN, Barb                                      File No. 19826-20
>
> RE:    Asselin v. Short
>           Small Claims (damaged vehicle)
>
> Responsible Paralegal: Margaret Childs     Opened: May 30, 2020

As the firm works on a client's file, it will grow in size. Each time a letter or a memo or a document is prepared and sent to someone on behalf of a client, a copy is kept in the file folder. Each time a letter or a memo or a document is received by someone on behalf of a client, it is kept in the file folder. If the contents of a file are sufficient to warrant placing an elastic band around the file in order to keep it shut, the firm will use an expandable document folder to keep the file inside.

At this point, the contents of the file may be divided into segments such as correspondence, pleadings, accounts, documents, medical reports, etc. These are called sub-folders and new file folders will be used for the sub-folders. The original file folder will become the correspondence file and will contain all letters and memos regarding a file in chronological order from oldest to newest.

Each sub-folder will be a legal-sized file folder labelled to properly reflect which file it belongs to and what its contents are, in case someone removes a sub-folder in order to complete some work on the file.

If a file that has been "upgraded" to an expandable file folder becomes too large for the new folder, the firm will transfer the contents of the folder to a document box. The box will be labelled appropriately with the file name and number on the outside of the box in black marker. The inside of the document box will be organized using file folders and expandable file folders and will be divided up according to the contents of the file. For example, a client who is the owner of several apartment buildings will likely need a document box that will contain a variety of file folders such as:

- Individual files for each tenant issue
- Individual files for small claims court actions where no remedy is available through the Landlord and Tenant Board, and
- Individual files for each apartment building's/unit's rent increases.

## File Organization

The original file folder should be organized so that any document can be found quickly. Here are some best practices for keeping a neat and tidy file:

- On the inside cover of the file, tape the file opening information, which will include information such as the client's contact information, the opposing party, the opposing party's paralegal and contact information, the file number, the date the file was opened, and the responsible paralegal
- On the inside back cover of the file, consider taping a large envelope with the flap cut off and use the envelop to hold documents relating to the file, so that they are not loose in the file folder, and
- Consider keeping all letters, memos, invoices, and notes on a "correspondence brad" or within a clip of some kind, organized with the most recent item on the top and the oldest item on the bottom.

## Location of Files

Now that we know how to organize our files, it is important to know how to store them.

Each firm is different in its storage of files. Each paralegal or law clerk may have the files they are working on in their offices. Or, there may be a centralized location for each department, such as the immigration law department, where all of the files are kept and you would go to the centralized location in your department to take the files you need to work on.

Alternatively, the entire firm may have a centralized file management system where all of the files are kept, regardless of the area of law.

Some firms require you to sign out a file when you remove it from the filing system, so that if someone else is looking for the same file, it will be clear where that file can be located.

Regardless of where the individual files are located, they should be filed in accordance with standard filing rules.

If your firm files its files numerically, they will be stored from lowest to highest by file number. This is not a common practice because you would have to memorize each file's file number in order to find it.

More likely, your firm will store its files alphabetically. They may be further divided by area of law and stored alphabetically within each area of law. The alphabetized system works like this:

- Numbers come before letters (i.e., 12345 Ontario Inc. is filed before ABC Realty)
- Nothing comes before something (i.e., A Plus Bakery is filed before Arthur Air Conditioning)
- Personal names are filed last name first, then first name (i.e., Barb Asselin would be filed under A for Asselin. If there are two clients with the last name of Asselin, Barb Asselin would be filed before Jacqueline Asselin), and
- Company names are filed as written (Barb Asselin Bakery Inc. would be filed under B for Barb since Barb is the first name in the company name).

## Filing

Now that we know how to file our files and how to organize the interior of our files, it is very important to keep these files as up to date as possible. If you or a law clerk or co-worker is working on a file, that person will be able to work more efficiently if the file has all of the outstanding filing inside it. This means that each person in your firm should make an effort to do their filing on a daily basis.

If you receive or send an email on a file, you should print it out and file it in the file right away. If you receive correspondence or a courier or a fax on a file that needs to be reviewed by someone in the firm, consider attaching the correspondence to the file and giving it to the individual so that it can easily be filed once the letter is reviewed.

It is very difficult to work on a file that is incomplete. For example, if you are drafting a document for a client on a small claims court matter, it will be nearly impossible to complete if the notes that the paralegal took while meeting with the client are on the paralegal's desk buried under a stack of papers.

## Electronic Files

We know how important it is to keep our files properly filed and to keep our filing up to date. It is equally important to file our electronic documents where they can easily be retrieved.

All of the computers in your firm are likely networked together, which means that each person working on a computer has access to all of the documents on the network. There can be many, many documents stored on a firm's network.

Let's do a quick math exercise to see how many documents could be stored in your firm's computer...

Let's suppose that you work for a mid-sized paralegal firm. There are 10 employees in total: three paralegals, three legal assistants, two law clerks, one office manager, and one receptionist.

In any given month, you may work on 30 files (probably more).

Each file may generate 20 documents (probably more). This is a total of 600 files you could generate in a month.

If everyone in your firm has the same workload, then your firm could generate 6,000 electronic files in a month.

Over the course of a year, your firm could generate 72,000 electronic documents. These documents are all found on the network drive for your firm and are accessible from your computer.

Also, the day you started working at this firm was probably not its first day of business, so let's assume your firm was in business for 10 years before you started working there (see how I'm keeping the math easy?).

This means that, over the past 10 years, the employees at your firm could have generated at least 720,000 electronic files, all of which are on your computer's network drive and accessible by you.

So.....if you created a document for a client five years ago and the client suddenly has a similar problem and you need to update that original document, what will you do?  Will you re-type the 10-page document?  Or, will you find it on your computer and simply revise it?

Of course, the quickest way to complete this client's new document would be to find the document on your computer and make the necessary changes.  Will you be able to find it?  What if someone else created the original document and that person is no longer with your firm?  Will you still be able to find it?

Having an electronic system of organizing client and precedent files is critical to being a productive employee.  There will likely be a system in place wherever you are hired to work.  You will be responsible for saving all of your newly created documents in the correct place, so that:

- You can find them again to revise, if necessary
- Someone else can find your documents to revise or reprint if you are away, or
- You can find someone else's documents if they are away.

## Windows

Windows is a program that allows us to organize our files however we see fit. By creating folders, we can create an organized system so that items are easy to find.

Let's create a system for this textbook, using Windows...

# Computer Applications for Paralegals 27

## Creating a New Folder

 There is an instructional video for students on this topic at:
Webpage: http://www.asselingroup.com/paralegals
Password: paralegals

First, open Windows on your computer by clicking on the file folder icon, either on the bottom taskbar of your computer:

Or in the Start menu of your computer:

Or on your desktop.

Next, create a folder called **Computer Applications for Paralegals**. There are a few ways to do this:

1. Click on the New folder icon at the top left of your Windows screen

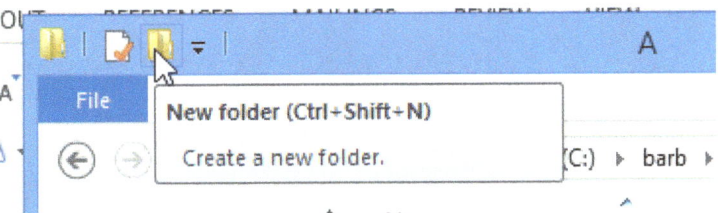

2. Press Ctrl + Shift + N, or
3. Right-click in the right-hand side of your Windows screen and then click New > Folder

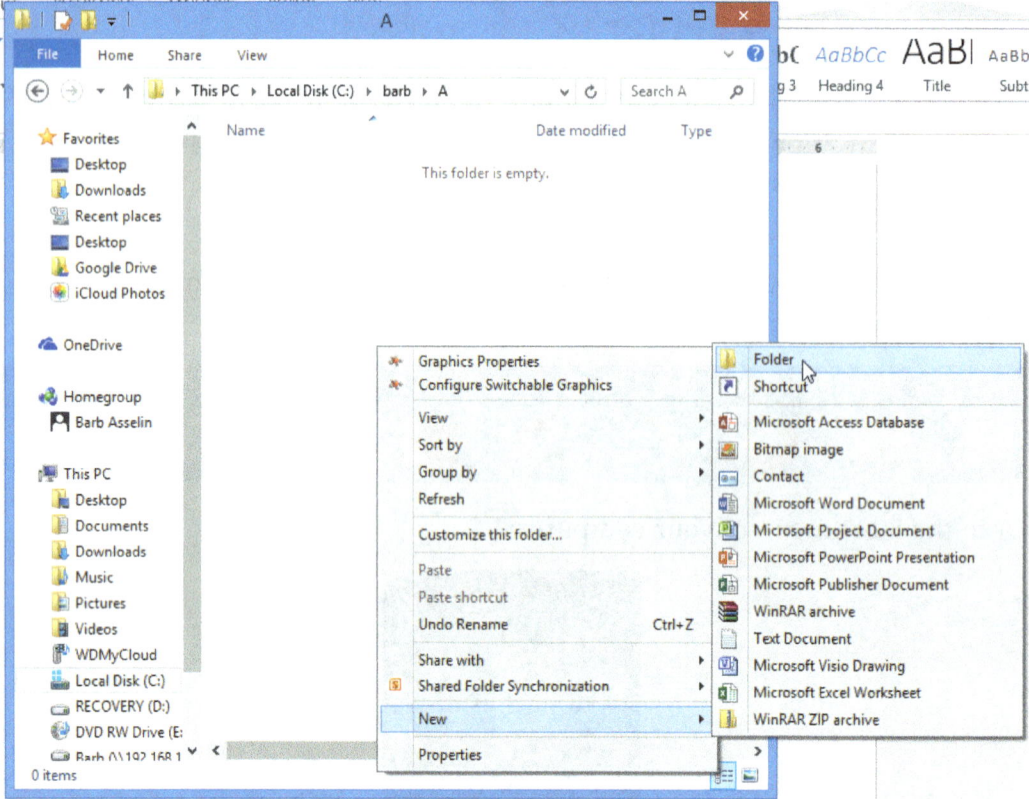

Once you have a new folder, it should be active, or dark blue with the curser flashing after the new folder icon.  If you ended up pressing Enter and your new folder is called New Folder, right-click on the name and choose Rename and call it ***Computer Applications for Paralegals***.

# Computer Applications for Paralegals

29

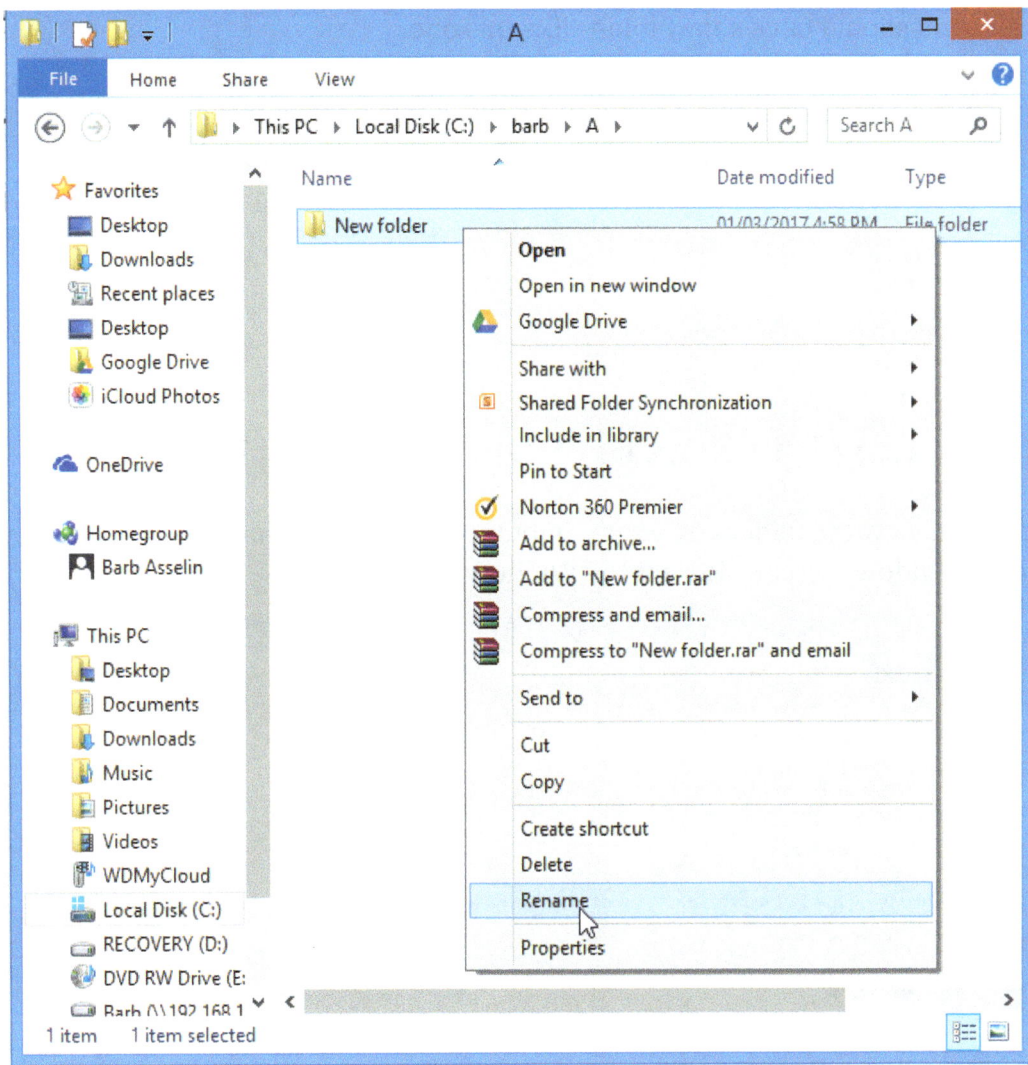

Now you should have a new folder like this one:

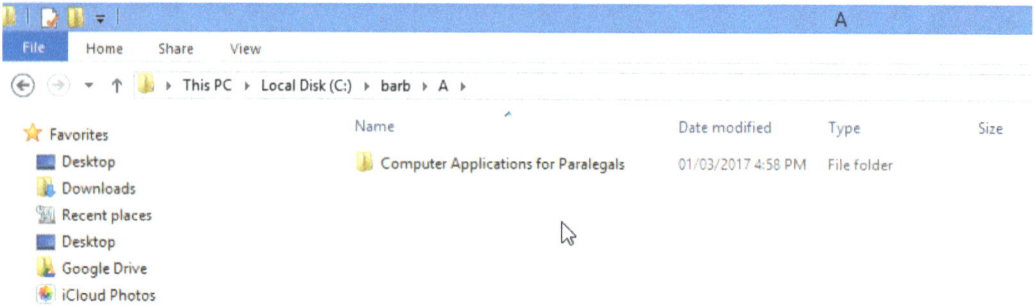

## Navigating Windows Using the Left-Hand Task Pane

You can view the folders on your computer using the left-hand task pane of your Windows screen. Here is my Windows screen:

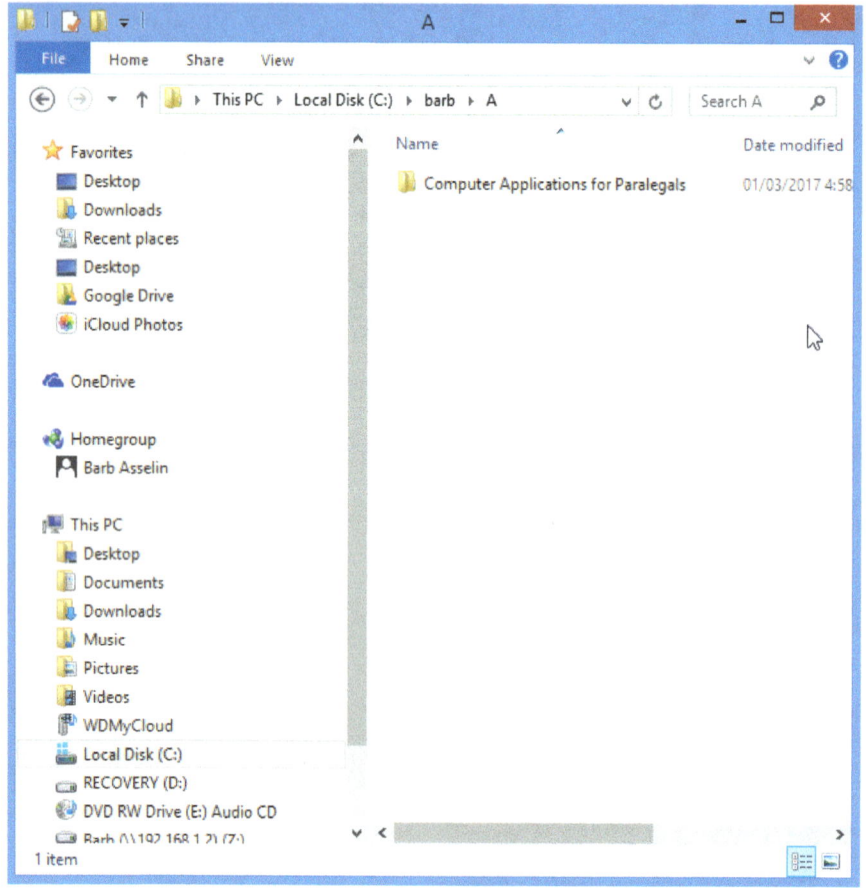

Note that your Windows screen will probably look different from mine. The left-hand task pane will be divided up into sections. The top section has commonly used area links such as Desktop, Downloads, and Photos. You may or may not have a middle section. The bottom section will be your computer and all of the various drives on it. You can see on mine, it is called This PC and contains links to the contents on the Desktop, Documents, Downloads, Music, Pictures, and Videos. After Videos, you will see all of the different drives on your computer. I have a C:/ drive (my laptop), a D:/ drive (for recovery), an E:/ drive (DVD), and a Z:/ drive (external hard drive). You may have a USB drive and/or a network drive.

Notice the symbols beside the various drives and location links. These are "expand" and "collapse" icons. The expand icon ▷ 📁 Desktop can also be a "+" sign and means that the folder includes other folders and can be expanded. If you click on the expand icon, the folder will expand to show any folders inside that folder.

The collapse icon ◢ 🖥 This PC can also be a "-"sign and means that the folder is already expanded to its fullest. If you click on the collapse icon, the folder will minimize itself.

## Displaying Windows Content in the Right-Hand Task Pane

If you click on any of the folders in the left-hand task pane, the contents of that folder will display in the right-hand task pane of Windows. You will see any folders contained in that upper folder as well as any documents. Here is an example of the contents of one of my folders:

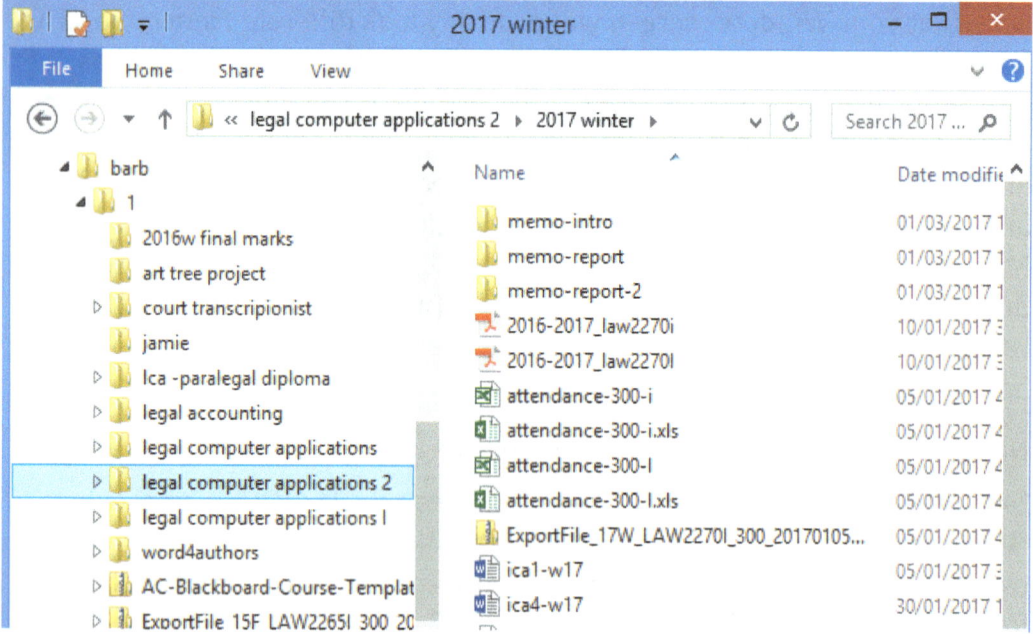

Notice that I have selected the folder *legal computer applications 2* (it is selected on the left) and that the contents of that folder are displayed on the right. Inside that folder are some other folders at the top and, below the folders, you can see some other documents displayed alphabetically. They are a variety of PDFs, Excel documents, zipped folders, and Word documents.

Congrats! You are now ready to create your own system of folders with the practice exercises at the end of this chapter.

## Chapter Summary

In this chapter, students learned the importance of an organized file and filing system for physical files, as well as some best practices for organizing files. Students also learned how to create a new file folder in Windows so that they can create and maintain an efficient digital filing system.

# Exercises

## Exercise 2.1

Open Windows and create the following series of folders:

1. Create a folder called ***Computer Applications for Paralegals***
2. Inside ***Computer Applications for Paralegals***, create the following folders:
    a. ***Chapter 1 Paralegal Firm***
    b. ***Chapter 2 File Management***
    c. ***Chapter 3 Outlook***
    d. ***Chapter 4 PowerPoint***
    e. ***Chapter 5 Excel***
    f. ***Chapter 6 Word***
    g. ***Chapter 7 Integration***
3. Inside each of the seven folders listed in number two above, create the following folders:
    a. ***Exercises***
    b. ***Templates***
4. Go to the private webpage for this textbook and download the letterhead precedent for your geographic region
5. Save the letterhead precedent to your ***Chapter 1 Paralegal Firm > Templates*** folder
6. Open the hierarchy of the ***Computer Applications for Paralegals*** folder in Windows on the left-hand side of your screen
7. Ensure that every folder you just created is displayed on the left, by clicking on all of the expand icons in your folder
8. Display the contents of the ***Chapter 1 Paralegal Firm > Templates*** folder on the right-hand side of your Windows screen
9. Maximize the window if necessary and show your professor once you have completed this exercise

## Exercise 2.2

Open Windows and create the following series of folders:

1. Create a folder called *Paralegal*
2. Search the Internet to find your college's website and search the website until you find your program
3. Inside the *Paralegal* folder, create a folder for each semester of your program (i.e., *Semester 1*, *Semester 2*, etc.)
4. Inside each of the semester folders created in number three above, create a folder for each course in each semester
5. Inside each of the course folders listed in number four above, create the following folders:
    a. *Admin*
    b. *PowerPoints*
    c. *Assignments*
    d. *Precedents*
6. Go to the website for this course and download your Course Outline posted by your professor
7. Save the Course Outline to your *This Course > Admin* folder
8. Open the hierarchy of the *Paralegal* folder in Windows on the left-hand side of your screen
9. Ensure that every folder you just created is displayed on the left, by clicking on all of the expand icons in your folder
10. Display the contents of the *This Course > Admin* folder on the right-hand side of your Windows screen
11. Maximize the window if necessary and show your professor once you have completed this exercise

## Exercise 2.3

Open Windows and create the following series of folders:

1. Create a folder called *Your Name Paralegal Firm*
2. Inside *Your Name Paralegal Firm*, create the following folders:
    a. *Employment*
    b. *Immigration*
    c. *Landlord and Tenant*

Computer Applications for Paralegals

      d. *Precedents*
      e. *Provincial Offences*
      f. *Small Claims*
      g. *Summary Convictions*
3. Inside each of the seven folders listed in number two above (except the **Precedents** folder), create the following folders:
    a. *A-E*
    b. *F-J*
    c. *K-O*
    d. *P-T*
    e. *U-Z*
4. Go to the private webpage for this textbook and download the letterhead precedent for your geographic region
5. Save the letterhead precedent to the **Your Name Paralegal Firm > Precedents** folder
6. Open the hierarchy of the **Your Name Paralegal Firm** folder in Windows on the left-hand side of your screen
7. Ensure that every folder you just created is displayed on the left, by clicking on all of the expand icons in your folder
8. Display the contents of the **Your Name Paralegal Firm > Precedents** folder on the right-hand side of your Windows screen
9. Maximize the window if necessary and show your professor once you have completed this exercise

## Exercise 2.4

Open Windows and create the following series of folders:

1. Create a folder called **Immigration Law**
2. Inside **Immigration Law**, create the following folders:
    a. *A-E*
    b. *F-J*
    c. *K-O*
    d. *P-T*
    e. *U-Z*
    f. *Precedents*
3. Create the following folders inside the appropriate alphabetized folders:

       a. *Barnes*
       b. *Ghaza*
       c. *Li*
       d. *Smith*
       e. *Virtolli*
4. Create the following folders inside each client folder listed in number three above:
       a. *Accounts*
       b. *Correspondence*
       c. *Pleadings*
       d. *Research*
5. Go to the private webpage for this textbook (details on page 13) and download the letterhead precedent for your geographic region
6. Save the letterhead precedent to your ***Immigration Law > Precedents*** folder
7. Open the hierarchy of the ***Immigration Law*** folder in Windows on the left-hand side of your screen
8. Ensure that every folder you just created is displayed on the left, by clicking on all of the expand icons in your folder
9. Display the contents of the ***Immigration Law > Precedents*** folder on the right-hand side of your Windows screen
10. Maximize the window if necessary and show your professor once you have completed this exercise

## Exercise 2.5

Open Windows and create the following series of folders:

1. You have decided to pursue a Criminology degree in your spare time in the evenings
2. Using your search engine of choice, find a Canadian University with a Criminology degree (if there is no university with such a degree near you, choose University of Ottawa's Major in Criminology degree)
3. Create a folder called ***Criminology***
4. Inside ***Criminology***, create the following folders:
       a. *Level 1*
       b. *Level 2*
       c. *Level 3*

Computer Applications for Paralegals 37

      d. *Level 4*
5. Using the Criminology program that you found during your research, create folders inside each level folder in number four above – note that you will create one folder for each course in your researched program
6. Create the following folders inside each course folder that you created in number five above:
      a. ***Admin Documents***
      b. ***Assignments***
      c. ***Instructions***
      d. ***Lectures***
7. Go to the private webpage for this textbook (details on page 13) and download the PDF document, "Acceptance to Criminology Program"
8. Save the acceptance letter PDF to your ***Criminology*** folder (not in any particular level folder, just in the ***Criminology*** folder)
9. Open the hierarchy of the ***Criminology*** folder in Windows on the left-hand side of your screen
10. Ensure that every folder you just created is displayed on the left, by clicking on all of the expand icons in your folder
11. Display the contents of the ***Criminology*** folder on the right-hand side of your Windows screen
12. Maximize the window if necessary and show your professor once you have completed this exercise

## Exercise 2.6

Open Windows and create the following series of folders:

1. Create a folder called ***Landlord and Tenant***
2. You have accumulated a lot of new clients, both landlords and tenants, and you need to organize your files
3. Inside ***Landlord and Tenant***, create the following folders:
      a. ***Landlords***
      b. ***Tenants***
      c. ***Tribunal Information***
4. Create the following folders inside the ***Landlords*** and ***Tenants*** folders:
      a. ***Clients***

    b. *Precedents*
    c. *Research*
5. Create the following folders inside each of the **two** the *Clients* folders listed in number four above:
    a. *A-E*
    b. *F-J*
    c. *K-O*
    d. *P-T*
    e. *U-Z*
6. Go to the private webpage for this textbook and download the letterhead precedent for your geographic region
7. Save the letterhead precedent to your *Landlord and Tenant > Tribunal Information* folder
8. Open the hierarchy of the *Landlord and Tenant* folder in Windows on the left-hand side of your screen
9. Ensure that every folder you just created is displayed on the left, by clicking on all of the expand icons in your folder
10. Display the contents of the *Tribunal Information* folder on the right-hand side of your Windows screen
11. Maximize the window if necessary and show your professor once you have completed this exercise

# Chapter 3: Outlook

## Learning Outcomes

In this chapter, students will:

- Review the importance of the use of a program such as Outlook in a busy law office
- Learn how to use the calendar feature to organize their day
- Learn how to use the contacts feature to keep track of clients, co-workers, peers, industry professionals, and personal contacts
- Learn how to use the task feature to prioritize their workload and keep track of deadlines

## Overview

Outlook is part of the Microsoft Office Suite and allows you to communicate with others through email, as well as manage your time properly so as to avoid missing important deadlines.

Time management is a very important part of life in a paralegal firm, whether you are working for yourself or for someone else. Many areas of law are time-sensitive and missing a deadline can mean an impending lawsuit by a disgruntled client. You definitely want to avoid that!

There are four applications in Outlook, which are:

- Email
- Calendar
- Contacts, and
- Tasks.

This textbook will delve into three of the four applications. Since you are likely already an "expert" in email, this textbook will focus on the remaining three applications of calendar, contacts, and tasks.

When you launch Outlook, it will automatically open to your email application. There is a quick way to navigate through the four different applications. Notice the following icons at the bottom left of your screen:

You can use these "hot keys" to jump from one application to another. You can probably guess which one is which.

- The envelope is your email
- The icon with the rectangle at the top and the dots below it is your calendar
- The icon with two individuals is your contacts, and
- The clipboard icon with a checkmark inside it is your tasks.

Click on the calendar icon to jump to the calendar application.

# Calendar

The calendar application allows you to keep track of:

- Personal appointments
- Appointments with clients
- Interoffice meetings, and
- Meetings outside the office.

You can keep track of such appointments for both yourself and your boss or partner, or any other individual whose calendar you have access to.

You may also use the calendar portion of Outlook to schedule departmental meetings of selected individuals within your organization, without having to spend time speaking with each individual to determine when they are free. This can save you a great deal of time.

Before we start learning how to effectively use Outlook, let's make sure we are all viewing the program in the same configuration.

To start, make sure the ribbon is displayed at the top of your screen. If is not already displayed, click on the Home tab at the top left, which will display the ribbon. Then, move your curser to the far right and click on the push pin icon to pin the ribbon in place.

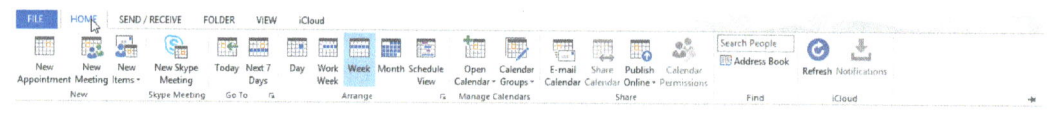

# Computer Applications for Paralegals

Next, make sure the left-hand navigation task pane is displayed.

If yours is not displayed, click on the chevron (small arrow-type icon) that is directly under the File tab.

By clicking on the chevron, you will display the left-hand task pane.

It will remain displayed until you click on the chevron again, which will hide the left-hand task pane.

Next, click on the **File** tab and then click on the **Day** item in the Arrange grouping. Your screen should look like this:

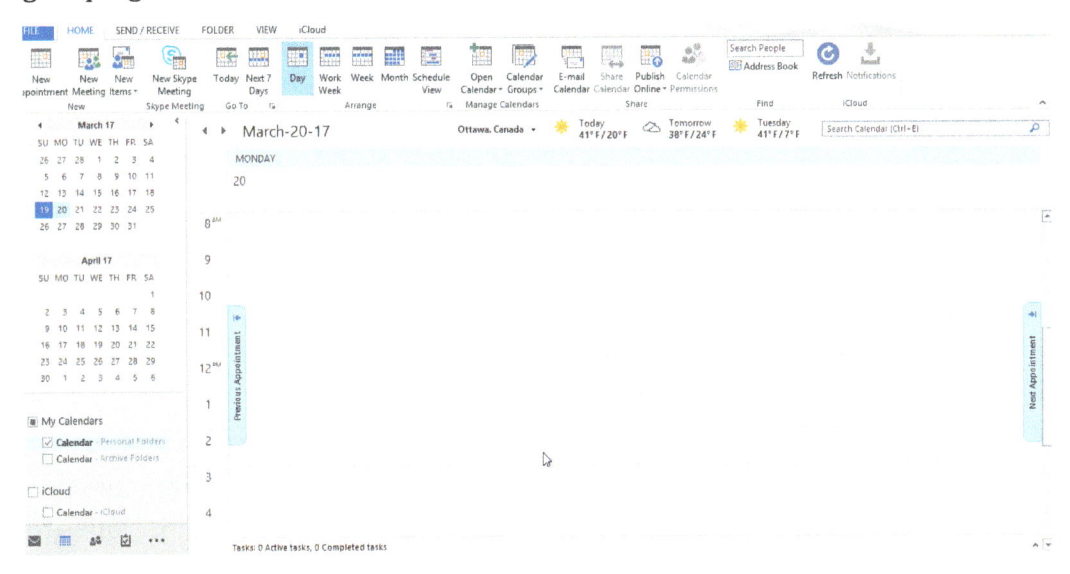

## Creating an Appointment

There is an instructional video for students on this topic at:
Webpage:    http://www.asselingroup.com/paralegals
Password:   paralegals

There are a few different ways to add an appointment to your calendar:

- Click on New Appointment at the top left of the Home tab on the ribbon

- Double-click anywhere in your calendar (on the right side of the screen), or
- Click CTRL-N

Whichever way you choose, you will end up with the following screen:

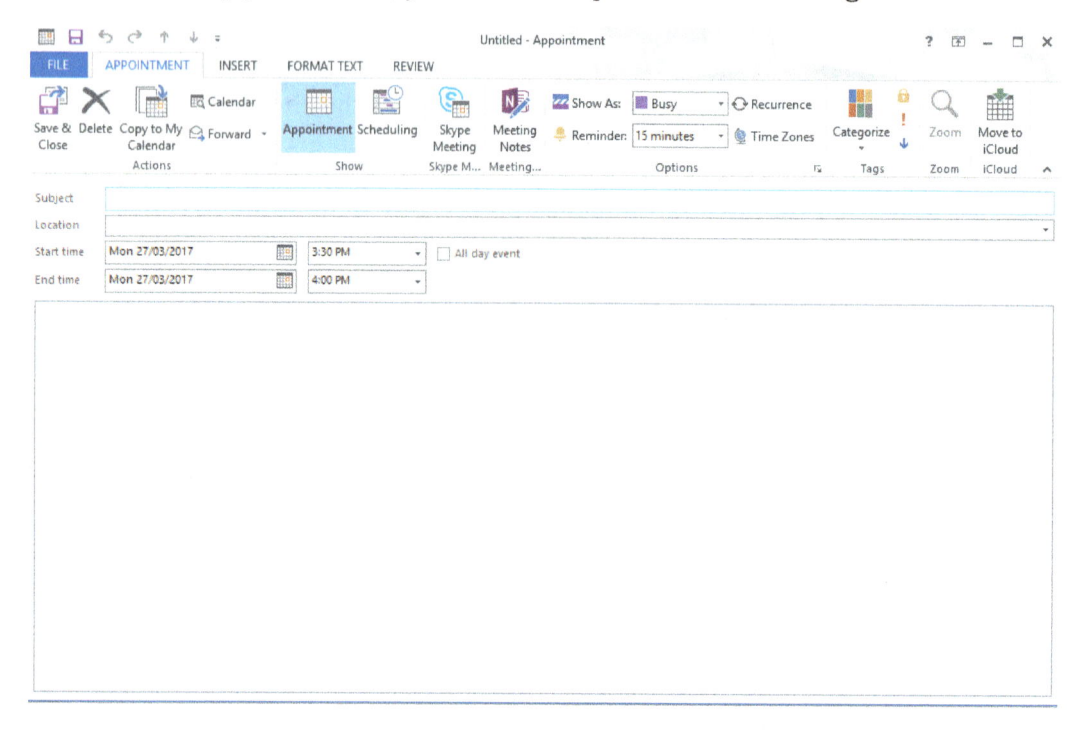

**Subject:** In this field, enter a short phrase that is meaningful to you, such as, "Meeting with Mr. Smith" or "Meeting with Ms. Jones to sign documents" or "Staff meeting" or perhaps an acronym such as "MW Law Clerks"

**Location:** In this field, enter where the meeting will take place. You may be meeting in a specific office or room at you place of business, or you may be meeting at a location outside of your place of business.

**Start Time:** Here, you can choose the day and time of the start of this appointment.

Computer Applications for Paralegals 43

**End Time:** Here, you can choose the day and time of the end of this appointment. Note that if you choose to check the "All day event" box, it will show your appointment as taking place from 12:00 a.m. to 11:59 p.m.

In the blank box at the bottom of the screen, you can add more details about the appointment, however, any information in this field will not show on your calendar in the daily, weekly, or monthly formats.

When you are finished setting up your appointment, click "Save & Close". Your appointment will show on your main screen in the time frame you selected. It will also show the day of your appointment as bold in the mini calendar on the left-hand task pane of your screen.

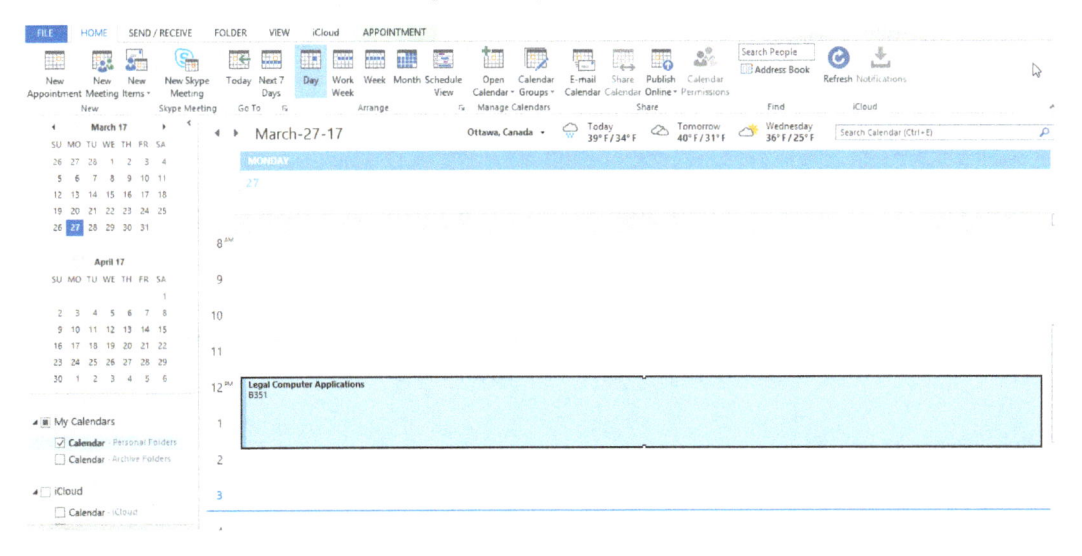

There are ways to further customize your appointments. Simply double click on an appointment and make any of the following changes or additions:

**Scheduling:** By clicking on the Scheduling option on the Appointment ribbon, you can add other members of your company to an appointment by selecting them from the given list. Note that this option may not be available to you at your school because your computers are not networked together in the same manner as they would be in a paralegal firm or other company.

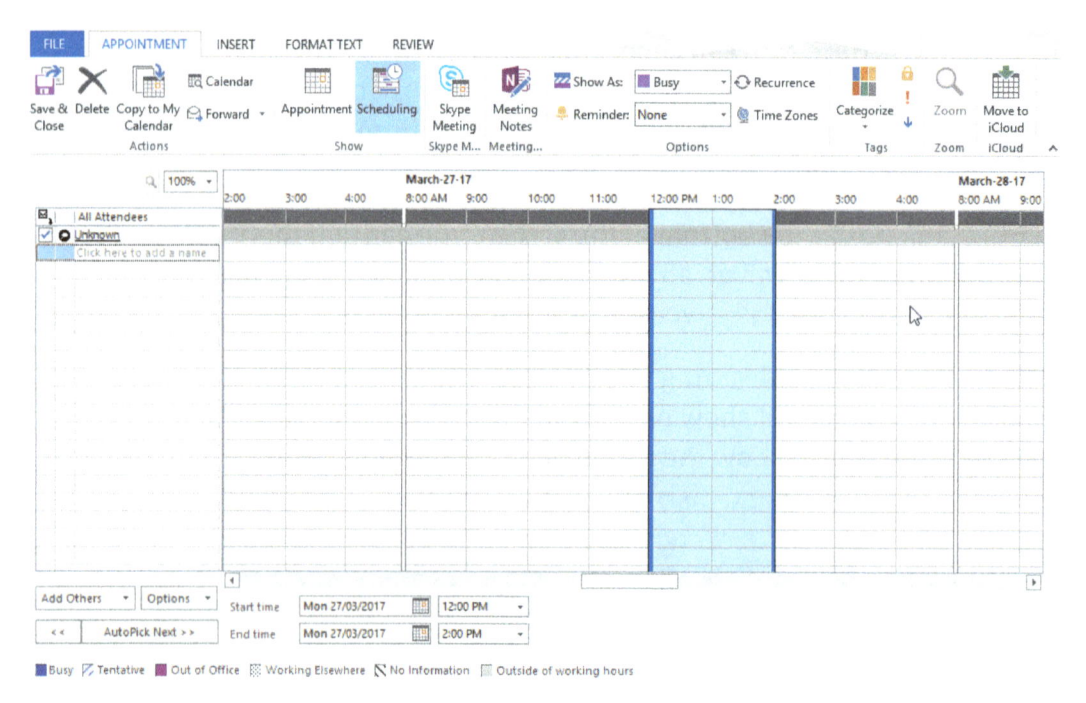

**Recurrence:** You can make your appointment a recurring appointment by clicking this button on the Appointment ribbon. There are many options that allow you to set an appointment as daily, weekly, bi-weekly, monthly, semi-monthly, annually, and more.

Computer Applications for Paralegals 45

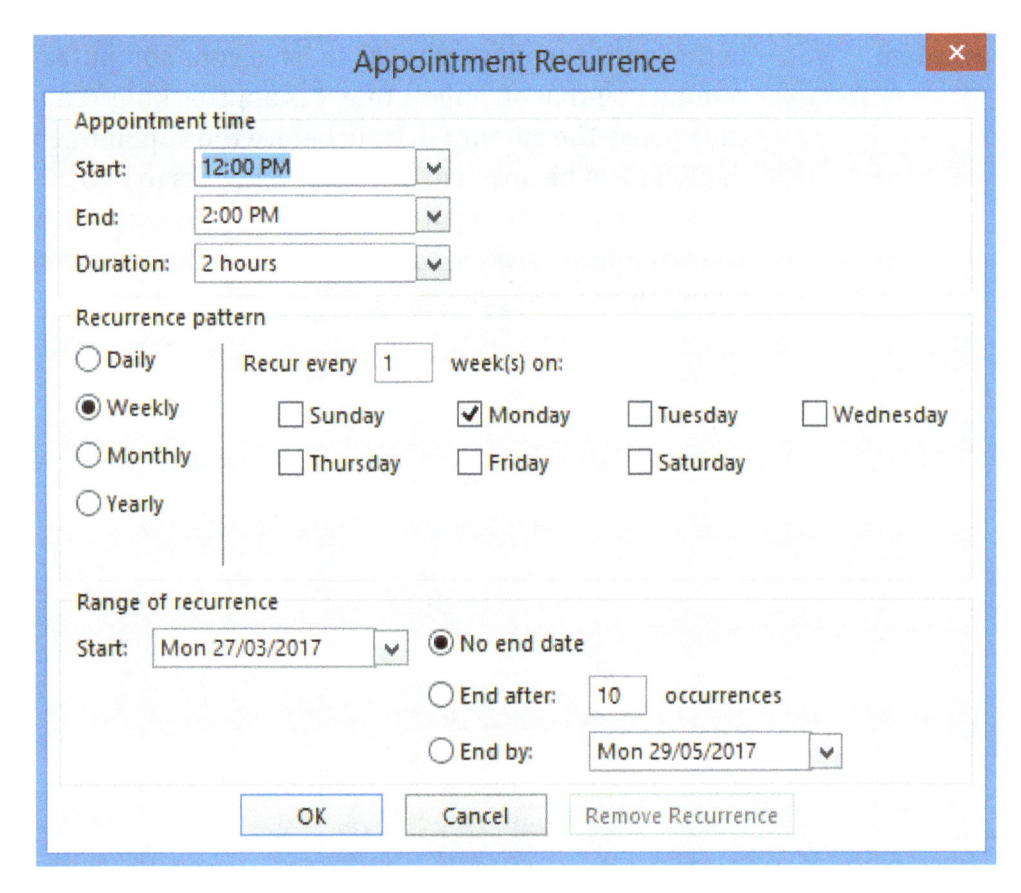

**Show As:** The Show As option allows you to choose how your appointment will be viewed by others if you mark your appointment as private. It can show as: Free, Working Elsewhere, Tentative, Busy, or Out of Office.

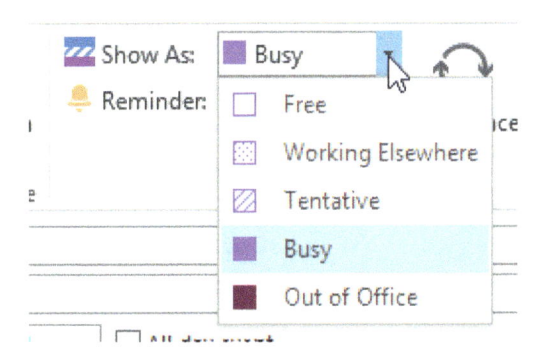

**Reminder:** In this option, you can choose to have your computer remind you that an appointment is approaching. You can choose the amount of time before the appointment that you will be notified, from zero minutes to two weeks and everything in between. You can even have your computer make a sound to let you know that your appointment is approaching.

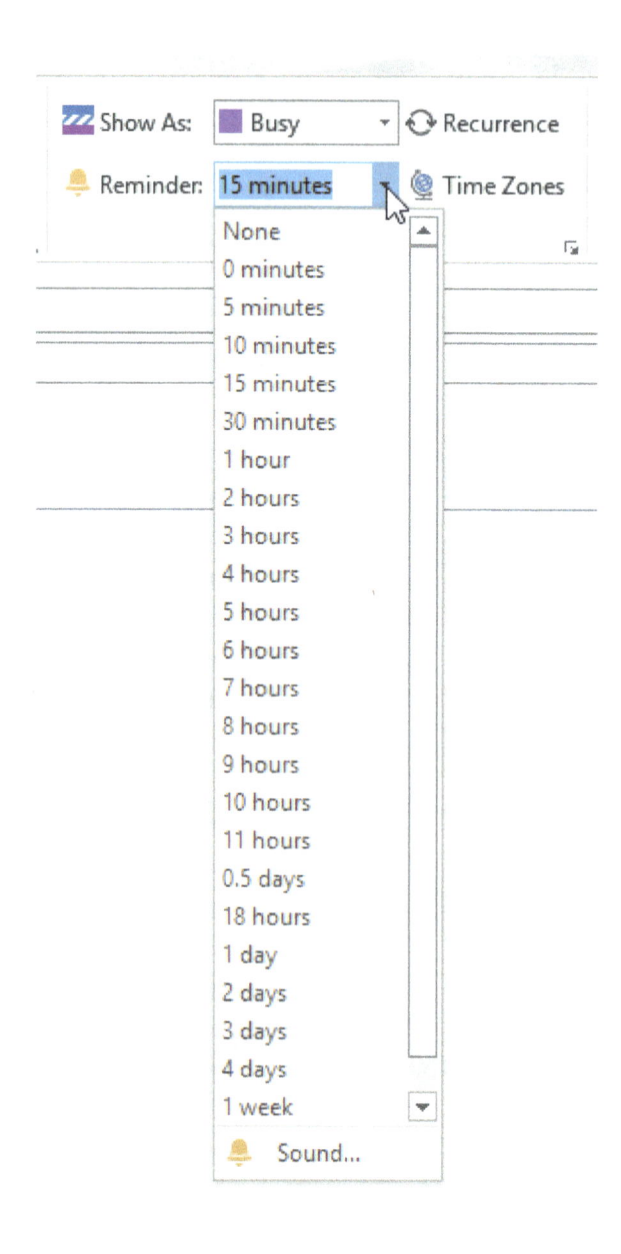

**Category:** With this option, you can categorize your appointments. For example, you may choose to set a different color for each area of law appointment. You may have your meetings with employment law clients red and your small claims court clients green. Or, you may choose to have your client appointments yellow and your meetings with co-workers blue.

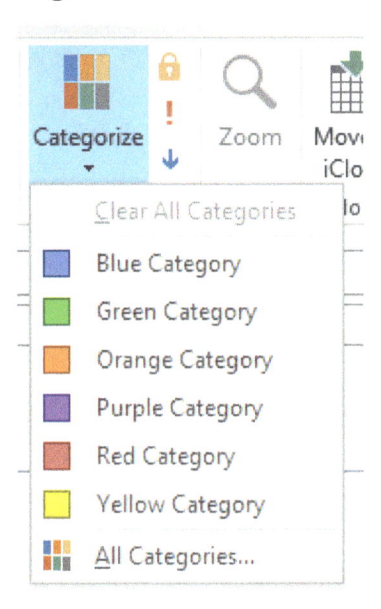

By clicking on all categories at the bottom of the list, you can even customize your categories so that they are areas of law instead of colors. Or, you could have categories such as: clients, personal, admin, or co-workers.

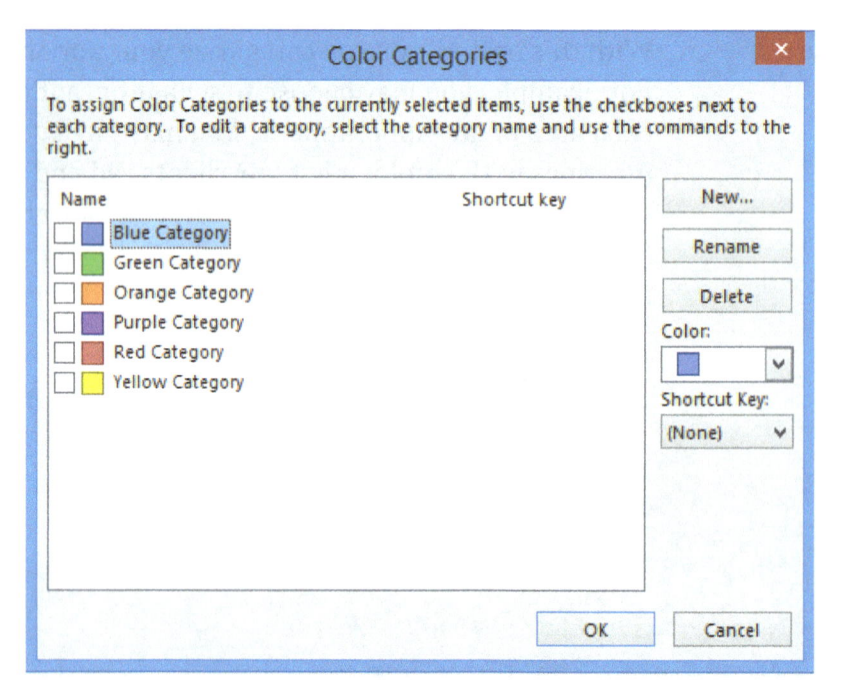

**Lock:** The lock symbol is found in the Tags grouping and allows you to mark your appointment as private. That way, other people viewing your calendar from within your firm, will only see that you are busy or out of the office (or whichever designation you choose) instead of the details of your appointment. This option is most often used when an individual has a private meeting with a doctor, etc.

**Importance:** The importance option is also found in the Tags grouping. You can select either the exclamation mark to show that an appointment has high importance, or you can choose the down arrow symbol to show that an appointment has a low importance.

Computer Applications for Paralegals 49

**Delete:**  The delete option is the large X found next to the Save & Close button. It allows you to delate an appointment that is no longer necessary.

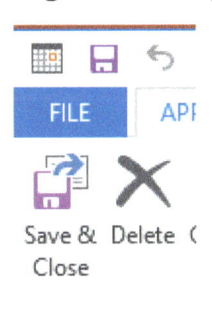

**Reschedule:**  Rescheduling an appointment is easy. Simply double-click on the appointment that needs to be changed. Then, go to the day and time options for that appointment. Change the day to the correct day and change the time options, if necessary. Click Save & Close and your appointment will now show on your calendar for the new day and time specified.

## Viewing Your Calendar

There are many ways to view your calendar. They are all found in the Go To and Arrange groupings.

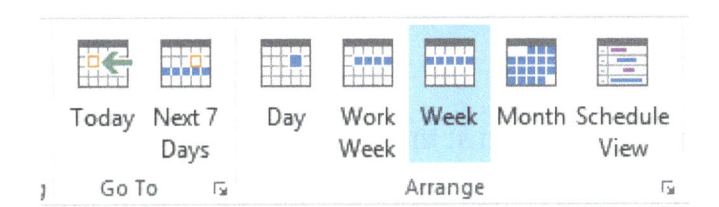

As you can see, you can view your day, your week, your work week, your month, or a schedule view that includes others in your firm.

## Printing Your Calendar

To print your calendar, go to File > Print.

You will see a preview of your calendar for the view you have selected.

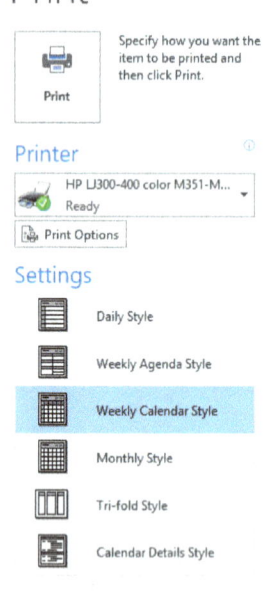

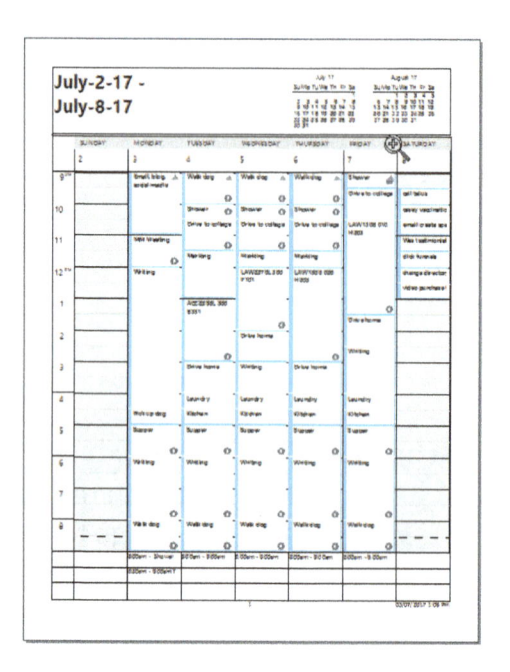

You can also print in different styles. The styles are similar to the views that are available, only these ones are for printing only. They include daily style, weekend agenda, weekly calendar, monthly, trifold, and calendar. Try looking at each style in the preview box on the right to see which one you prefer. Or perhaps you prefer not to print your schedule and simply view it on your computer screen.

## Contacts

By clicking on the contact icon at the bottom left of your screen, you will be taken to the contacts area of Outlook. You can keep track of contacts in a variety of different areas, such as:

- Clients
- Work colleagues
- Personal contacts
- Process servers
- Judges
- Tribunal and court offices, and
- Much, much more.

Computer Applications for Paralegals								51

## Creating a New Contact

> There is an instructional video for students on this topic at:
> Webpage:	http://www.asselingroup.com/paralegals
> Password:	paralegals

To create a new contact, you can:

- Click on the Home tab and either click on New Contact or New Item > Contact
- CTRL-N after clicking on the contact hot key, or
- CTRL-SHFT-C.

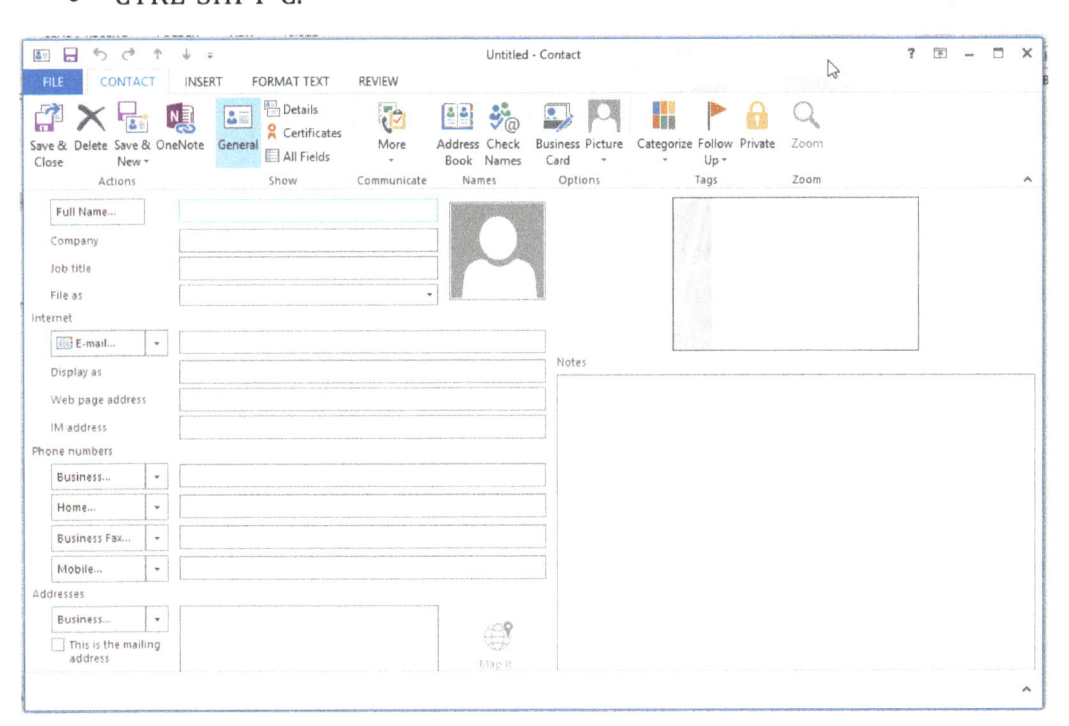

The new contact dialogue box opens up and allows you to fill in the details of your new contact in a "fill-in-the-blank" style of form. Simple click in the empty box after each item and fill in the necessary information.

There are two sections, however, where it is better to approach the data entry in a different manner. For the Full Name and Address fields, it is better to click on the actual instruction box instead of the empty box.

When you click on the Full Name field, the following dialogue box opens up:

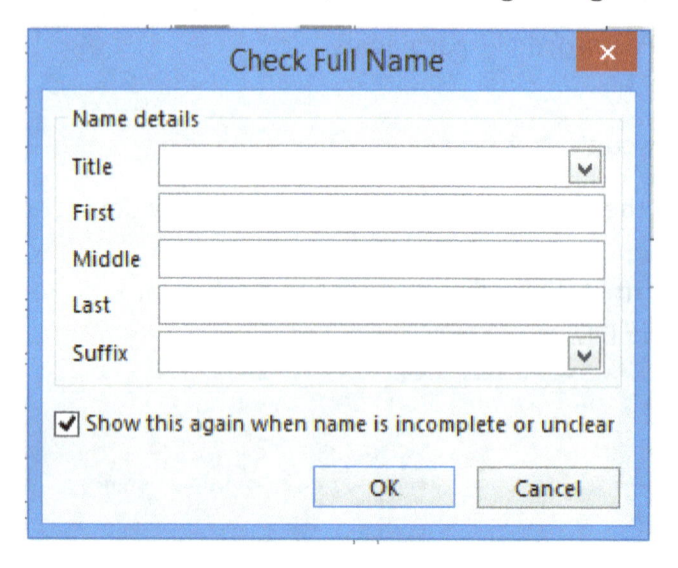

This allows you to enter the first and last name separately. This is helpful as each person may enter an individual's name in a different way. Some people may enter the first name first while others may enter the last name first. By using this form, there will be no question as to which name is the first name and which one is the last name.

## Contact Options

You can add a variety of additional information about your contacts as well.

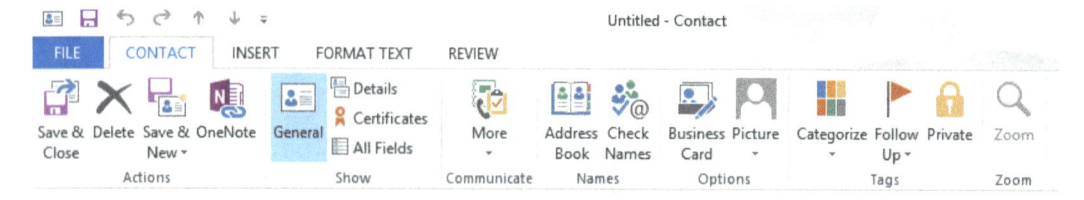

Notice how the General option is selected in the above graphic. You can also select the Details option to add information such as birthday, partner's name, anniversary, employer, and more.

The Categories option allows you to categorize each contact in any way you like. For example, you could categorize your client contacts by area of law, or you could categorize your contacts in general, with tags such as clients, personal, work, peers, etc.

You can click on the red flag near the far right of New Contact ribbon to give yourself notification to follow up with a particular contact in a certain time period, such as tomorrow, next week, or next month.

Clicking on the lock symbol allows you to mark a contact as private. Doing so prevents others in your network from viewing your private contact.

Once you are finished entering information about a contact, click the Save & Close button on the far left of the New Client ribbon.

To amend a contact's information, simply double-click on that contact to re-open the contact's form and make the necessary changes.

## Contact Views

You can view your contacts in four different ways:

- **People** – this view shows your contacts in alphabetical order by either last name or company name
- **Business Card** – this view shows your contacts with all of the entered information (for example, if you had entered more than one address for a contact, both addresses would show)
- **Card** – this view shows your contacts with a condensed view of their information (this option would only show the preferred address for a contact instead of all entered addresses), and
- **List** – this view shows your contacts in a further condensed list with one contact showing per row (you can also sort your contacts in this view alphabetically by any of the fields, such as by company name – this would give you an alphabetical list of all contacts who work for the same company).

## Printing your Contacts

To print your contacts, click on File > Print.

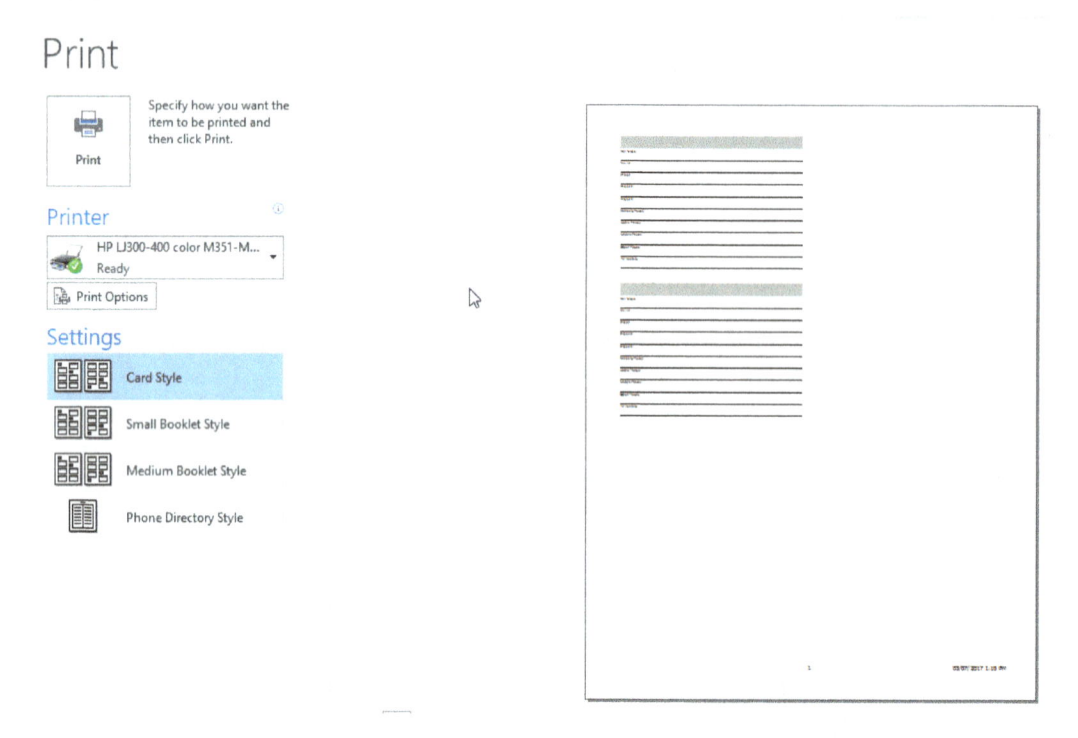

The options available to you for printing are: card style, small booklet style, medium booklet style, and phone directory style. If you choose to print, try selecting each option and viewing it in the preview box on the right to see which one you like the best.

# Tasks

Click on the task icon in the quick launch toolbar to go directly to tasks.

Tasks are similar to appointments, but with less options and information.

## Creating a New Task

There is an instructional video for students on this topic at:
Webpage:     http://www.asselingroup.com/paralegals
Password:    paralegals

Computer Applications for Paralegals 55

To enter a new task, do one of the following:

- Go to tasks using the quick launch icon and press CTRL-N
- Go to tasks using the quick launch icon and click New Task
- Press CTRL-SHFT-K, or
- Go to tasks using the quick launch icon and click New Item > Task.

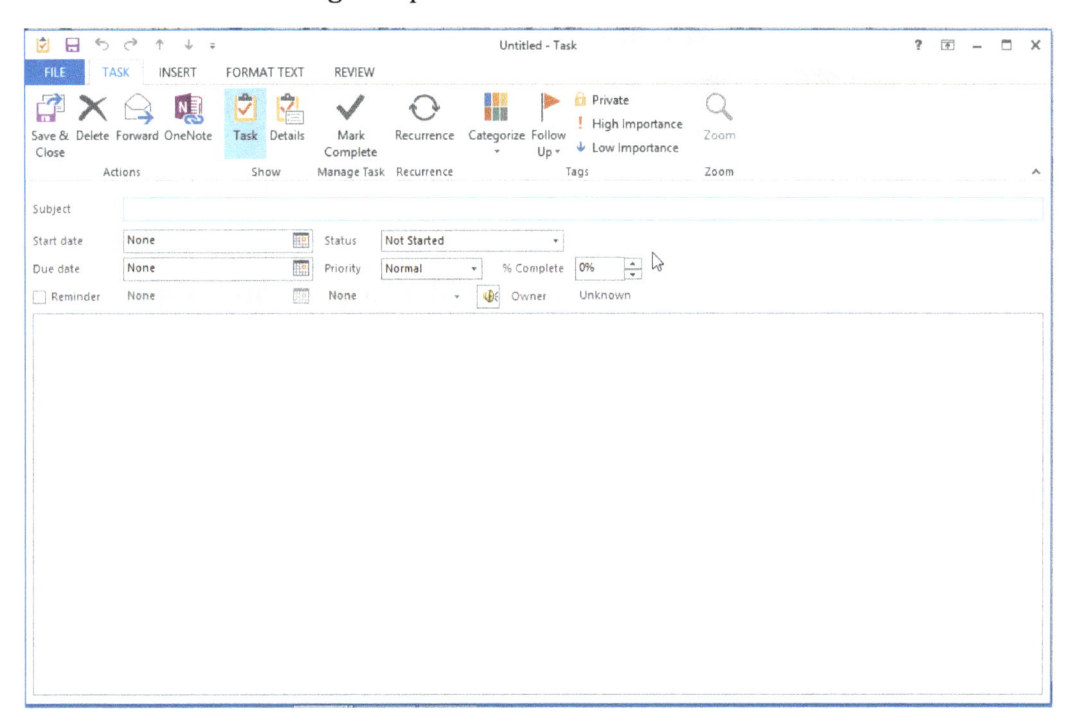

| **Subject:** | Enter the title of your task, or a brief description |
| **Start/End Date:** | Enter the day you will start your task and the day it must be completed, if applicable |
| **Reminder:** | You can add a reminder to yourself to do any task that you create |
| **Status:** | Set the status of your task – options include: Not Started, Completed, In Progress, Waiting on Someone Else, and Deferred |
| **Priority:** | Set the priority of your task – either Low, Normal, or High |

**% Complete:** Indicate how complete your task is, from 0 to 100 percent

As you can see, you can be as organized as you want with your tasks. Not all of these options are necessary. Just select the ones that apply to your situation and leave the rest.

The New Task ribbon offers additional features for customizing your tasks:

**Save & Close:** For when you are done setting up your task

**Delete:** In case you created a task in error

**Forward:** Forward your task to another individual

**Details:** Enter even more information about your task

**Mark Complete:** For when your task is completed

**Recurrence:** You can create a recurring task, similar to creating a recurring appointment in your calendar

**Category:** You are able to categorize your task, just as you can with your appointments and contacts

**Follow Up:** Give yourself a reminder to follow up with your task after a certain time frame

**Private:** Mark your task as private so that others cannot see it

**Importance:** Set either a high or low importance to your task

## Printing Your Tasks

To print your tasks, go to File > Print.

The only option available is to print a list of your tasks in table style. However, if you re-visit your calendar application and go to the print feature, you will see that there are a couple of options that allow you to see both your calendar and your tasks in the same printout.

- The Daily Style prints your current day and shows your tasks on the right hand side of your day. This is a helpful feature as it allows you to

see how much available time you have in a day so that you can determine which tasks you have time to complete.
- The Tri-Fold Style prints a sheet divided into three sections. On the left is your current day. In the middle are your tasks, and on the right is a snapshot of your week's appointments. This option is another good planning tool for individuals who prefer a paper version of their schedule and a checklist for their tasks.

## Chapter Summary

In this chapter, students learned the importance of using software such as Outlook and how it can help keep you organized. Students were shown how to create and maintain a working calendar, an up-to-date list of contacts, and a complete to-do list.

# Exercises

## Exercise 3.1

Enter the following items into Outlook:

1. Your department (Landlord and Tenant law) has received a couple of new clients and you have the following meetings to add to your calendar for next Monday:
   a. 9:00 a.m. meeting with yourself (add your name so that you know this is your assignment when it prints)
   b. 9:30 a.m. meeting with Gord Tapp of Silverhouse Investments Inc. (90 minutes)
   c. 11:00 a.m. meeting with Darla Abercrombie regarding her new rental property (60 minutes)
   d. 12:30 p.m. departmental lunch to celebrate boss's birthday (90 minutes)
   e. 3:00 p.m. personal meeting outside of the office (mark as private – 60 minutes)
   f. 4:00 p.m. weekly departmental meeting to discuss workload (recurring appointment every Monday for eight weeks – 30 minutes)
2. Add the following tasks:
   a. Open Silverhouse file
   b. Open Abercrombie file
   c. Prepare meeting minutes
   d. Draft documents for Silverhouse
   e. Draft documents for Abercrombie

Computer Applications for Paralegals 59

3. Add the following new contacts:

| Silverhouse Investments Inc. | Darla Abercrombie |
| Work Address: | Home Address: |
| 123 Silver Street | 25 Forest Ridge Road |
| Ottawa, Ontario | Ottawa, Ontario |
| K7S 3G8 | K2P 2K1 |
| Attention: Gord Tapp, President | Work Address: |
| Home Address: | 1 Darla Drive |
| 74 Tapp Blvd. | Ottawa, Ontario |
| Ottawa, Ontario | K8G 3H9 |
| K1P 6K8 | Home telephone: 613-555-9999 |
| Home telephone: 613-555-4444 | Work telephone: 613-555-8888 |
| Work telephone: 613-555-6666 | |
| Work fax: 613-555-6667 | |

4. Add yourself (first and last name only) to your contacts
5. Add three more contacts of your choice, giving two addresses to each contact.
6. Print the following to hand in to your professor:
    a. Calendar of next Monday in daily format
    b. List of contacts showing all details

## Exercise 3.2

Enter the following items into Outlook:

1. You are helping out the Immigration law department this week and they have received a couple of new clients. Add the following to your calendar for next Tuesday:
    a. 9:00 a.m. meeting with yourself (add your name so that you know this is your assignment when it prints – mark as private)
    b. 9:30 a.m. weekly departmental meeting to discuss workload (recurring appointment for six weeks – 30 minutes)
    c. 10:00 a.m. attend court on Lisa Marshall file (3 hours)
    d. 1:30 p.m. daily training of new law clerk for Immigration law department (recurring appointment for four occurrences – 90 minutes)

  e. 3:00 p.m. appointment with new client Joshua Tavarez (60 minutes)
2. Add the following tasks:
  a. Open Marshall file
  b. Open Tavarez file
  c. Prepare training manual for new law clerk
  d. Arrange follow up appointment for Marshall file
  e. Pick up court order on Marshall file
3. Add the following new contacts:

| | |
|---|---|
| Lisa Marshall<br>Work Address:<br>909 – 1200 Marshall Street<br>Ottawa, Ontario<br>K2J 8F4<br>Home Address:<br>1 Parliament Private<br>Ottawa, Ontario<br>K1F 4L9<br>Home telephone: 613-555-1212<br>Work telephone: 613-555-2323<br>Work fax: 613-555-2324 | Joshua Tavarez<br>Home Address:<br>1 Tavarez Terrace<br>Ottawa, Ontario<br>K8F 3J7<br>Work Address:<br>90 Bank Street<br>Ottawa, Ontario<br>K2P 3J7<br>Home telephone: 613-555-9797<br>Work telephone: 613-555-9696 |

4. Add yourself (first and last name only) to your contacts
5. Add three more contacts of your choice, giving two addresses to each contact
6. Print the following to hand in to your professor:
  a. Calendar of next week in weekly format
  b. List of contacts showing all details

# Exercise 3.3

Enter the following items into Outlook:

1. You are working in the Small Claims court department this week while their paralegal is on holidays. They have received a couple of new clients and you have the following meetings to add to your calendar for next Wednesday:
  a. 9:00 a.m. meeting with yourself (add your name so that you know this is your assignment when it prints)

      b. 9:30 a.m. personal meeting with your doctor outside the office (mark as private – 60 minutes)
      c. 11:00 a.m. meeting with Ani Tourian regarding her new file (60 minutes)
      d. 12:00 p.m. weekly lunch with the other paralegals for moral support (recurring appointment to occur for the next eight weeks – 60 minutes)
      e. 2:00 p.m. meeting with Mark and Kathy MacKenzie on their new file (60 minutes)
      f. 3:30 p.m. meeting with law clerk, Ernie MacLellan, to discuss workload (60 minutes)
2. Add the following tasks:
      a. Open Tourian file
      b. Open MacKenzie file
      c. Prepare update for meeting with law clerk
      d. Request research on Tourian file
      e. Request research on MacKenzie file
3. Add the following new contacts:

| Ani Tourian<br>Work Address:<br>99 Bank Street<br>Ottawa, Ontario<br>K1Y 7R4<br>Home Address:<br>74 Tourian Crescent<br>Ottawa, Ontario<br>K1L 4H7<br>Home telephone: 613-555-2121<br>Work telephone: 613-555-2323<br>Work fax: 613-555-2123 | Mark and Kathy MacKenzie<br>Home Address:<br>1 Kathy Crescent<br>Ottawa, Ontario<br>K4L 7F5<br>Work Address:<br>1000 – 120 Slater Street<br>Ottawa, Ontario<br>K2P 9Y6<br>Home telephone: 613-555-7777<br>Work telephone: 613-555-6666 |
|---|---|

4. Add yourself (first and last name only) to your contacts
5. Add three more contacts of your choice, give each contact two addresses
6. Print the following to hand in to your professor:
      a. Calendar of next Wednesday in daily format
      b. List of contacts showing all details

# Exercise 3.4

Enter the following items into Outlook:

1. You are helping out in the Provincial Offences department this week. They have received a couple of new clients and you have the following meetings to add to your calendar for next Thursday:
    a. 9:00 a.m. meeting with yourself (add your name so that you know this is your assignment when it prints – mark as private)
    b. 9:30 a.m. meeting with human resources to discuss your holidays (30 minutes)
    c. 10:30 a.m. meeting with Alan McDonald regarding his outstanding traffic tickets (60 minutes)
    d. 12:00 p.m. departmental lunch to celebrate your birthday (90 minutes)
    e. 2:00 p.m. meeting with Silvia Faour regarding her upcoming court date (60 minutes)
    f. 4:00 p.m. daily departmental meeting to discuss workload (recurring appointment every day for seven occurrences – 30 minutes)
2. Add the following tasks:
    a. Open McDonald file
    b. Open Faour file
    c. Prepare meeting minutes
    d. Find Brigitte Faour's previous file in storage room
    e. Request research on Faour file
3. Add the following new contacts:

| Alan McDonald | Brigitte Faour |
|---|---|
| Work Address: | Home Address: |
| 999 Old Orchard Lane | 986 Kippen Road |
| Ottawa, Ontario | Ottawa, Ontario |
| K9A 3G7 | K3L 2K8 |
| Home Address: | Attention: Silvia Faour, Executrix |
| 7 – 35 Rapids Road | Work Address: |
| Ottawa, Ontario | 1 Silva Street |
| K8A 2H6 | Ottawa, Ontario |
| Home telephone: 613-555-7171 | K4J 7H7 |
| Work telephone: 613-555-9292 | Home telephone: 613-555-6868 |
| Work fax: 613-555-9293 | Work telephone: 613-555-5757 |

4. Add yourself (first and last name only) to your contacts
5. Add three more contacts of your choice, giving each contact two addresses
6. Print the following to hand in to your professor:
    a. Calendar of next Thursday in weekly format
    b. List of contacts showing all details

## Exercise 3.5

Enter the following items into Outlook:

1. You are working in the Employment department this week. They have received a couple of new clients and you have the following meetings to add to your calendar for next Tuesday:
    a. 9:00 a.m. meeting with yourself (add your name so that you know this is your assignment when it prints)
    b. 9:30 a.m. personal meeting with your Managing Partner, Lisa Picolo to discuss your annual performance review (mark as private – 60 minutes)
    c. 11:00 a.m. meeting with Greg Neill regarding his new file (90 minutes)
    d. 1:00 p.m. weekly lunch date with your best friend (recurring appointment to occur for the next six weeks – 60 minutes)
    e. 3:00 p.m. meeting with John and Caroline Chapman to swear their affidavits on their new file (30 minutes)
    f. 4:00 p.m. meeting with Lisa Picolo (Managing Partner), to discuss workload (60 minutes)
2. Add the following tasks:
    a. Open Neill file
    b. Open Chapman file
    c. Prepare update for meeting with Lisa
    d. Print two copies of each affidavit on the Chapman file
    e. Order Neill file from offsite storage to ensure no conflict with new file

3. Add the following new contacts:

| Greg Neill<br>Work Address:<br>902 Arnprior Avenue<br>Ottawa, Ontario<br>K9J 6K3<br>Home Address:<br>111 Redwood Road<br>Ottawa, Ontario<br>K9Y 4F2<br>Home telephone: 613-555-7089<br>Work telephone: 613-555-7088<br>Work fax: 613-555-7087 | John and Caroline Chapman<br>Home Address:<br>10 Chapman Crescent<br>Ottawa, Ontario<br>K4I 1F7<br>Work Address:<br>7 Air Avenue<br>Ottawa, Ontario<br>K1K 4H2<br>Home telephone: 613-555-2431<br>Work telephone: 613-555-2432 |
|---|---|

4. Add yourself (first and last name only) to your contacts
5. Add three more contacts of your choice, give each contact two addresses
6. Print the following to hand in to your professor:
    a. Calendar of next Tuesday in daily format
    b. List of contacts showing all details
    c. List of all tasks

# Exercise 3.6

Enter the following items into Outlook:

1. You are working in the Small Claims department this week. They have received a couple of new clients and you have the following meetings to add to your calendar for next Monday:
    a. 9:00 a.m. meeting with yourself (add your name so that you know this is your assignment when it prints)
    b. 9:30 a.m. team meeting to plan a surprise retirement party for Anna Bengali (mark as private – 60 minutes)
    c. 11:00 a.m. meeting with Sharon Nesbitt regarding her new file against ABC Inc. (90 minutes)
    d. 1:00 p.m. weekly lunch with law clerk, Tabitha Gunther (recurring appointment to occur for the next seven weeks – 60 minutes)

e. 3:00 p.m. meeting with Ray Small, President of Small Enterprises Ltd. on their new file (60 minutes)
   f. 4:00 p.m. team meeting to discuss workload (60 minutes)
2. Add the following tasks:
   a. Open Nesbitt file
   b. Open Small Enterprises Ltd. file
   c. Prepare update for team meeting
   d. Order conflict search on Nesbitt file
   e. Order conflict search on Small Enterprises Ltd.
3. Add the following new contacts:

| Sharon Nesbitt<br>Work Address:<br>111 Sharon Street<br>Ottawa, Ontario<br>K8D 3D6<br>Home Address:<br>99 Design Drive<br>Ottawa, Ontario<br>K9J 4J8<br>Home telephone: 613-555-6666<br>Work telephone: 613-555-6667<br>Work fax: 613-555-6668 | Small Enterprises Ltd.<br>Attention: Mr. Ray Small, President<br>Work Address:<br>900 – 1 Small Street<br>Ottawa, Ontario<br>K6G 4G6<br>Work telephone: 613-555-0001<br>Work fax: 613-555-0002 |
|---|---|

4. Add yourself (first and last name only) to your contacts
5. Add three more contacts of your choice, give each contact two addresses
6. Print the following to hand in to your professor:
   a. Calendar of next Monday in daily format
   b. List of contacts showing all details
   c. List of all tasks

# Chapter 4: PowerPoint

## Learning Outcomes

In this chapter, students will:

- Learn how to create a presentation that appeals to all types of audiences
- Add text to their presentations
- Customize the presentation's design
- Add various forms of content to a presentation
- Print and save a presentation in a variety of ways, and
- Learn how to give a presentation in front of an audience.

## Overview

PowerPoint software allows you to create a professional looking presentation with just a few clicks of the mouse. With many built-in design features and graphic options, creating an interesting slide show that appeals to all types of audiences is not difficult.

## Creating a Presentation

There is an instructional video for students on this topic at:
Webpage: http://www.asselingroup.com/paralegals
Password: paralegals

To create a new presentation, simply open the software and a blank presentation should be on your screen.

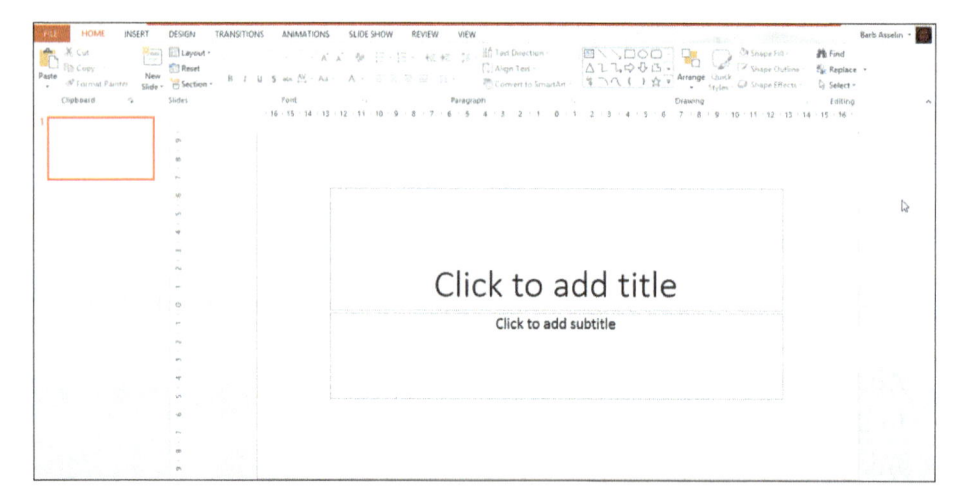

If you already have the software open, and a blank presentation is not visible, click on File > New and select Blank Presentation.

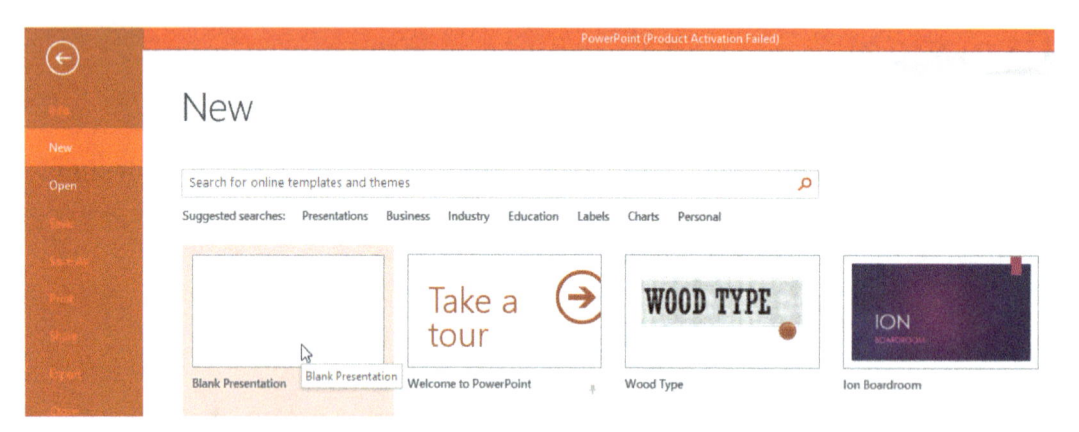

You will see that the screen is split into a few different sections:

- The ribbon is across the top of the screen and allows you to select one of many tabs, which will change the selections available on the ribbon
- The left-hand task pane, which shows you mini versions of your slides, and
- The main screen, which displays a full-sized version of the current selected slide.

On the main screen, you will see a blank title slide with two places to add text: the title and the subtitle. To add a title and subtitle to your slide, simply follow the instructions on your screen. Click in the title text box and type in the title of your presentation. Then, click in the subtitle text box and type in the subtitle of your presentation.

Computer Applications for Paralegals 69

## My Presentation

Barb Asselin

## **Slide Layouts**

The example shown above is a layout called Title Slide. To see the other layouts that are available, click on the Home tab and then click on the down arrow beside the Layout option on the left.

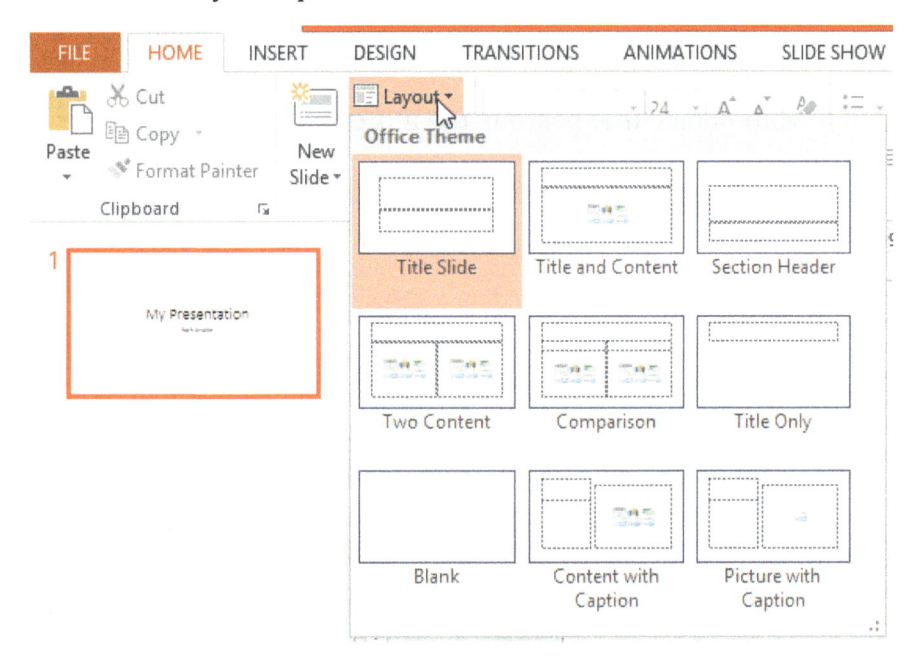

The different layouts are:

- Title Slide is usually the first slide in a presentation
- Title and Content is a standard design that contains an area for the slide title as well as an area for the content of slide, which can either be text or content (something more visual than text)
- Section Header is a layout that can be used as an introduction to a new section of slides and is often used in longer presentation
- Two Content allows you to have a title as well as two sections of content (note that of these two content sections, one is usually text while the other is usually something more visual such as a photo)
- Comparison is a layout that is best used when comparing two sets of data and has sections for a title, two large areas of content, as well as titles for each of the areas of content
- Title Only allows you to enter your title information and then design your own slide layout with textboxes and other types of content
- Blank is a layout without even a title section – it is a completely blank canvas waiting for your custom layout, and
- Content with Caption and Picture with Caption are the final two layouts that are specifically for either a picture or other forms of content such as a chart or a table, with additional sections for information and a caption.

With each new slide, simply drop down the arrow beside Layout and choose the layout of your choice that best fits the information that you are proposing for a particular slide.

# New Slide

You can create a new slide in a number of different ways:

- Click on the current slide in the left-hand task pane and press ENTER,
- Click on New Slide on the Home tab
- Click CTRL-M, or
- Click on the down arrow beside New Slide and select your layout of choice

Computer Applications for Paralegals 71

If you use any of the first three options listed above, you will automatically get a new slide with the Title and Content layout. The last option above will allow you to input a new slide with the layout of your choice.

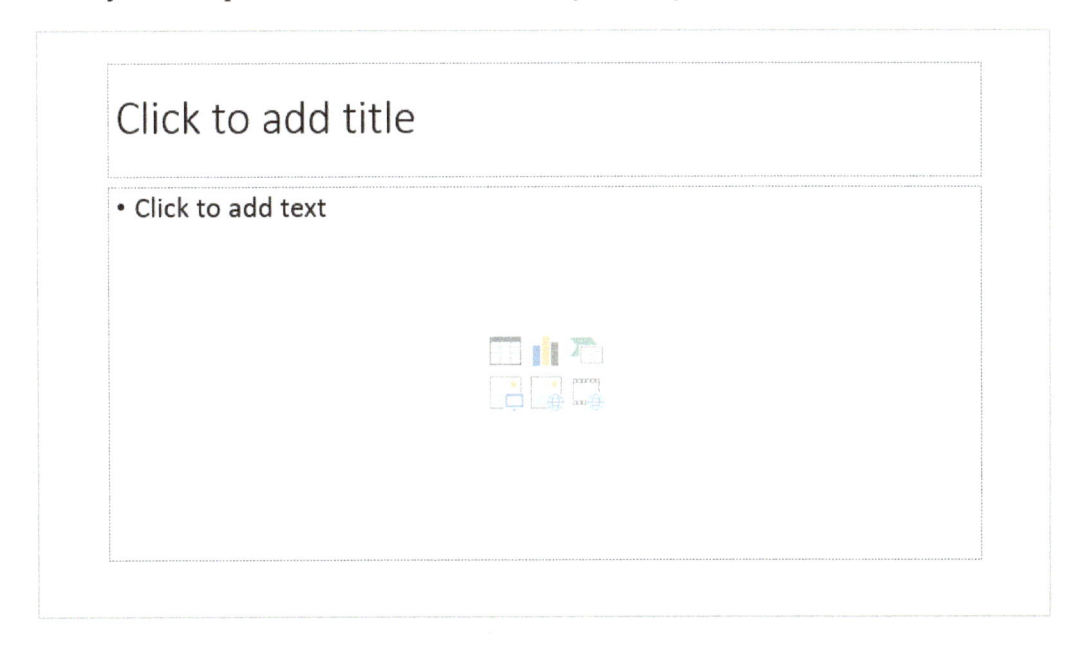

## Design

It's a good idea to choose a design when you are starting a new presentation, so that as you add different elements, you can create them to match the color scheme of the design you have chosen.

To choose a design, click on the Design tab at the top of your screen. You will see a few design options, or themes, on the ribbon. If you drop down the arrow at the bottom right of the Themes grouping, you will see more choices.

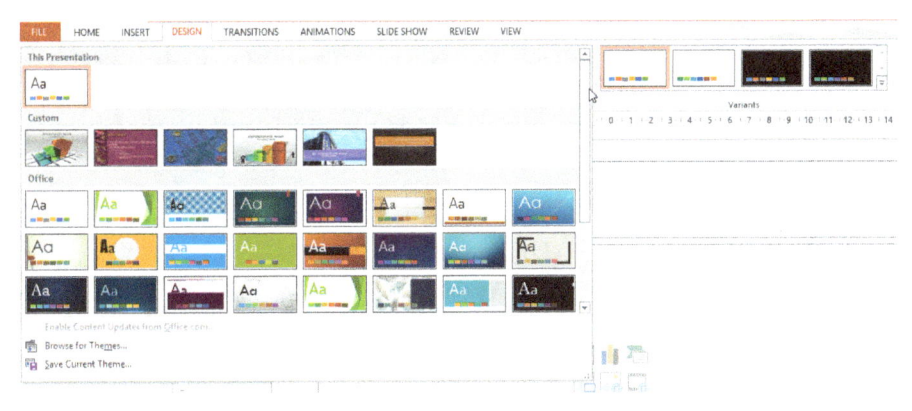

There are still more design choices available online. By clicking on the Browse for Themes option at the bottom of the available themes, you can view the free themes that are available on Microsoft.com.

## Customizing the Design

Once you have chosen a theme, you can further customize it. There are four quick variants available for each theme. The variant grouping is on the Design tab beside the Themes grouping.

In the example below, I have chosen the Main Event theme. You can see what the Title Slide and the Title and Content layouts look like on the left side of the image. You can also see the four variants. In this case, they are red, gold, green, and blue.

On the bottom right of the Variants group, you can drop down the expand arrow to further customize your design with additional color schemes, fonts, effects, and background styles.

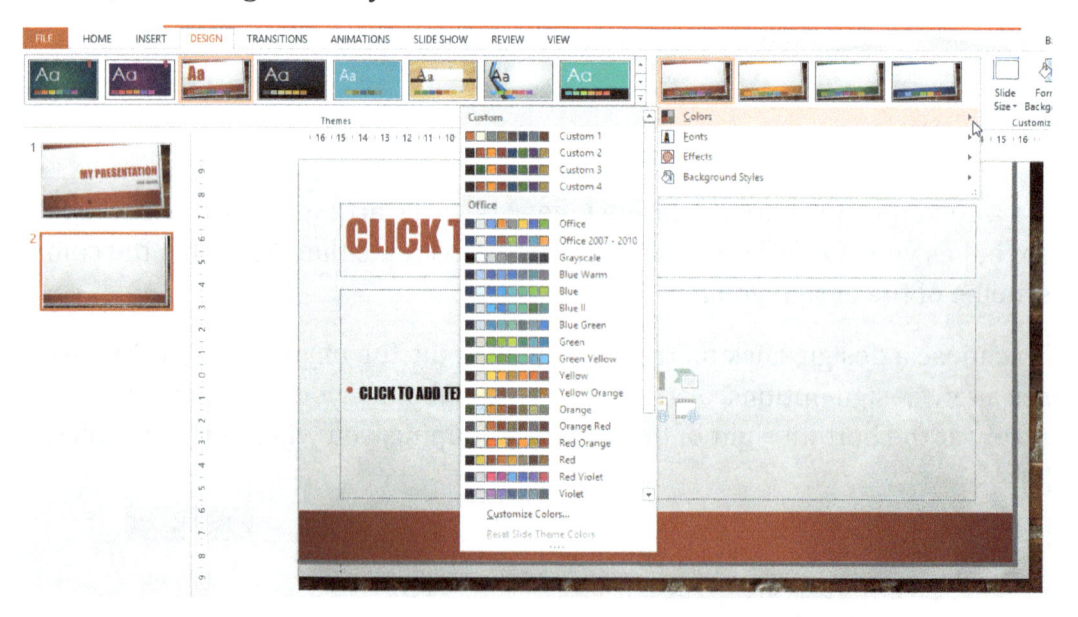

## Adding Text

Adding text to a slide is easy. If you were able to add a title and a subtitle to your title slide, you already know how to do it.

Next, add a second slide to your presentation using the Title and Content layout. Add a title to the top section.

Next, click in the main section of the slide and type some text. You will note that it automatically gives you a first-level bullet at the left edge of the text box.

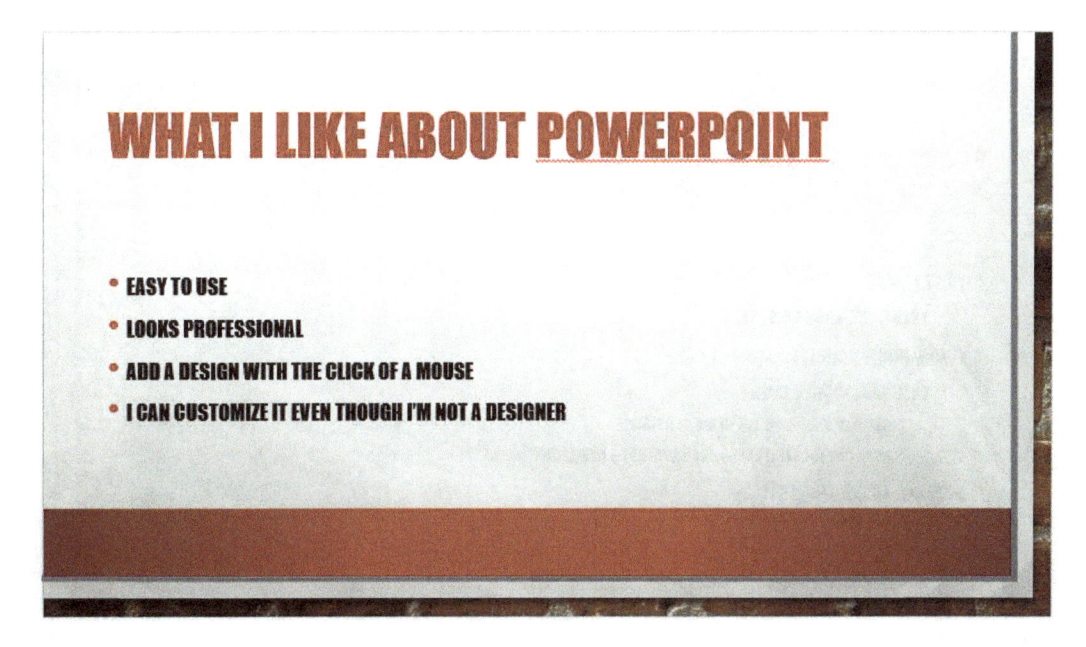

When adding text to your presentation, try not to put too much text on each slide. Your goal should be to include the basics on your slide and elaborate more during the spoken part of your presentation. A good rule is the "7 x 7 rule", which is a loose rule that indicates that a slide shouldn't have more than seven words per bullet and that it shouldn't have more than seven bullets per slide. If you end up with more than this amount of text on a slide, you will notice that the font automatically reduces in size so that the text will fit in the text box. The smaller the font size, the harder it will be for your audience to read it. Plus, if you have a lot of text, your audience will be too busy reading the slide and not watching or listening to you!

There are many levels of bullets. You can access them using the TAB (increasing the indent) and SHIFT-TAB (decreasing the indent) buttons on your keyboard. Alternatively, you can use the increase and decrease indent icons in the Paragraph grouping on the Home tab.

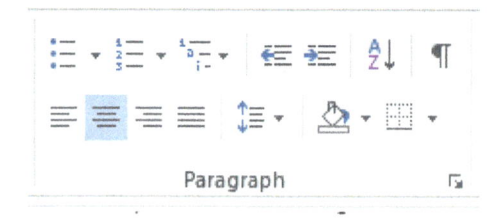

Try using some first, second, and third-level bullets.

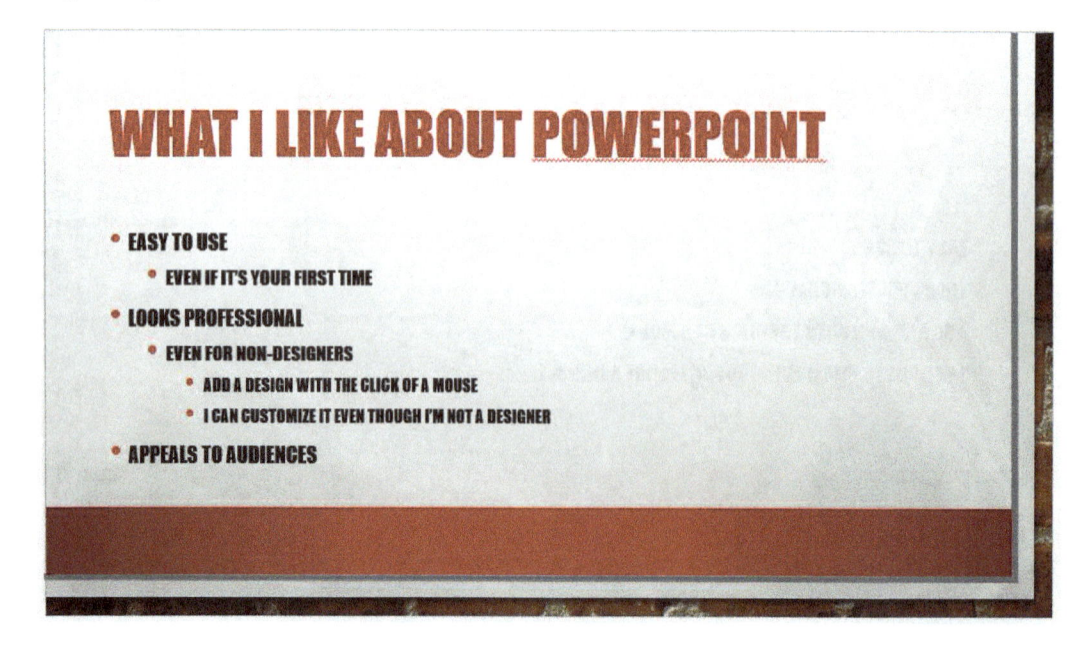

**WHAT I LIKE ABOUT POWERPOINT**

- EASY TO USE
    - EVEN IF IT'S YOUR FIRST TIME
- LOOKS PROFESSIONAL
    - EVEN FOR NON-DESIGNERS
        - ADD A DESIGN WITH THE CLICK OF A MOUSE
        - I CAN CUSTOMIZE IT EVEN THOUGH I'M NOT A DESIGNER
- APPEALS TO AUDIENCES

Computer Applications for Paralegals 75

# **Customizing Bullets**

> There is an instructional video for students on this topic at:
> Webpage: http://www.asselingroup.com/paralegals
> Password: paralegals

Each theme has its own pre-designed bullets however, you can customize them to another predesigned bullet, a graphic of your choice, or a symbol. You can also control the size and color of the bullet or symbol.

To customize your bullets, go to the View tab and click on the Slide Master option. Notice that a new tab called Slide Master has opened on the ribbon. You will see many slide layout options in the left-hand task pane. Click on the scroll bar and scroll it all the way to the top. The top mini slide in the left-hand task pane will be slightly larger than all of the others.

Click on the larger slide so that your bullet customizations will affect all of the slides in your presentation. If you only want your customization to affect certain layouts of slides in your presentation, then click on the smaller slide that reflects the layout you are looking for.

Once you click on the slide you want (the example uses the top, larger slide), you can customize the template in a variety of different ways. You can change the font type and size and color for either the title or the body of the slide.

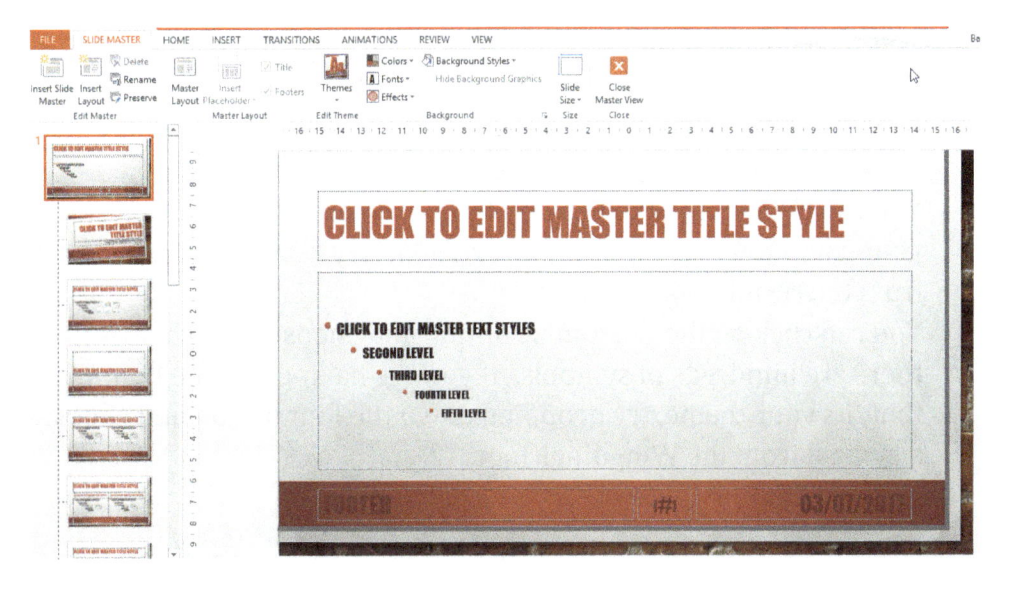

The body of the slide shows the current bullet and font selections for this theme. To change the first-level bullet, right-click in the first-level text and choose Bullets > Bullets and Numbering.

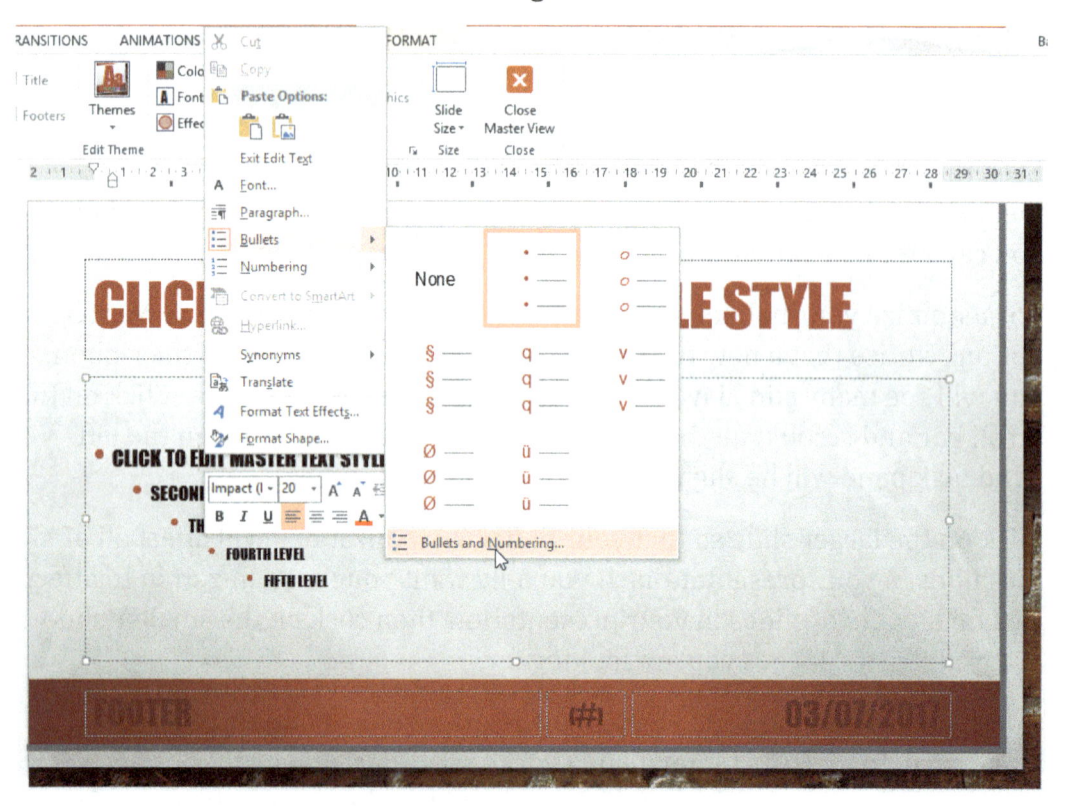

You have many options at this point:

- You can choose either no bullet or one of the other five bullet options
- You can change the size of the bullet, which is represented as a percentage based on the size of the text
- You can change the color of the bullet
- You can click on the Picture option and either choose a graphic from your computer, or search for a particular keyword and then choose from the resulting graphics, or
- You can click on the Customize option and choose a symbol. Note that there are hundreds of symbols. If you are having trouble finding one that fits your theme, try dropping down the font option and choosing a symbol from the Wingdings font.

Computer Applications for Paralegals

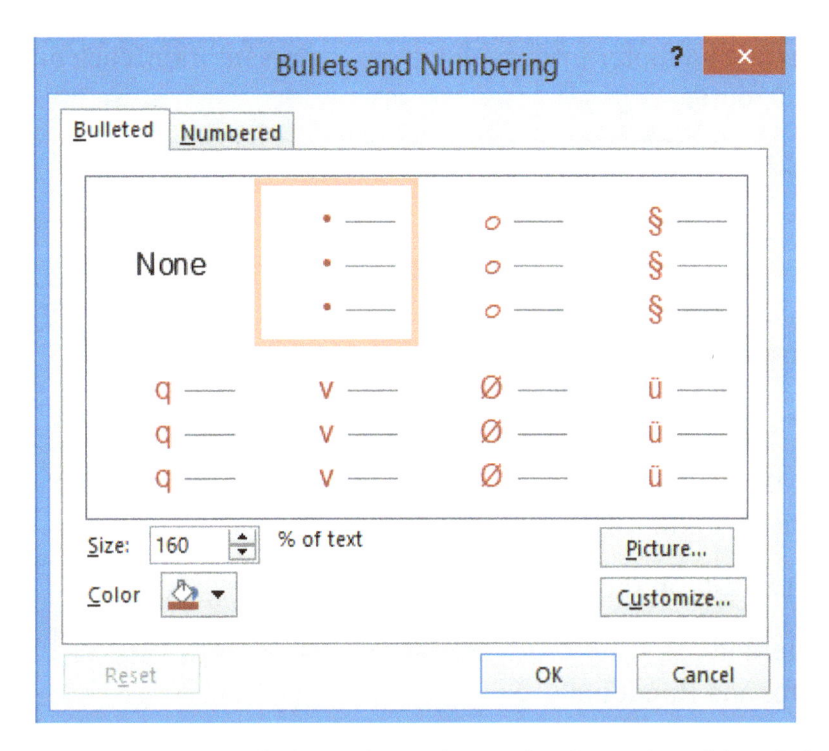

To close the Slide Master, click on the red X at the far right of the Slide Master tab.

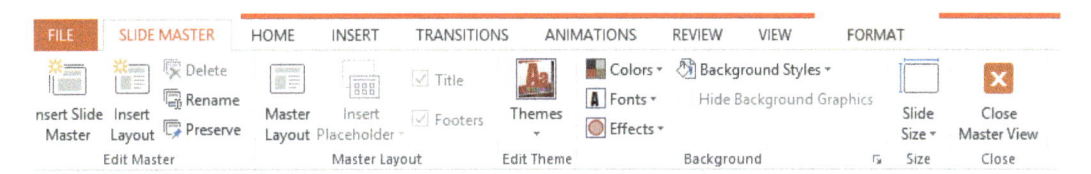

## Headers and Footers

There is an instructional video for students on this topic at:
Webpage: http://www.asselingroup.com/paralegals
Password: paralegals

Headers and footers add some "housekeeping" pieces of information to your presentations, such as date, page, slide number, name, title of presentation, or company name. There are two types of headers and footers:

- A footer that add information to your slides, and
- A header and footer that adds information to your handouts.

To add header and footer information to your presentation, click on Insert > Header and Footer.

A dialogue box will open up allowing you to add information to either the slides or the handouts of your presentation.

There are two tabs at the top of the dialogue box:

- Slide, and
- Notes and Handouts.

You will see a preview box on the top right of the box. The preview box will show you where each of the components of the header or footer will go when you activate.

To activate a component of the header or footer, click the check box beside each one. As you click each check box, the preview box will fill in the area where that piece of information will go, depending on the theme of your presentation.

I suggest that you always check the box "Don't show on title slide" as the information in the footer will likely already be on your title slide, or it will be obvious that it is slide one, for example. The footer will clutter up the design of your title slide.

Computer Applications for Paralegals 79

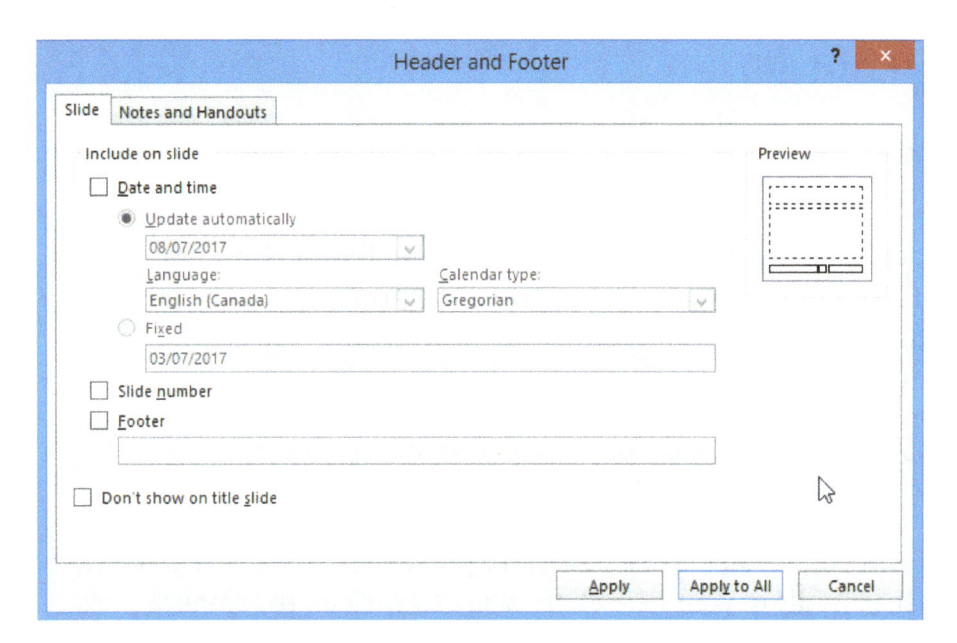

When you click on the Notes and Handouts tab, the options will change and so will the preview box.

You will have four options to choose from. The preview box shows where each of the four options will appear. You can see from the preview box that the page is portrait orientation and that your slides show inside the page.

The example shows two slides per page and the header and footer information appear on the top, bottom, right, and left corners of the page.

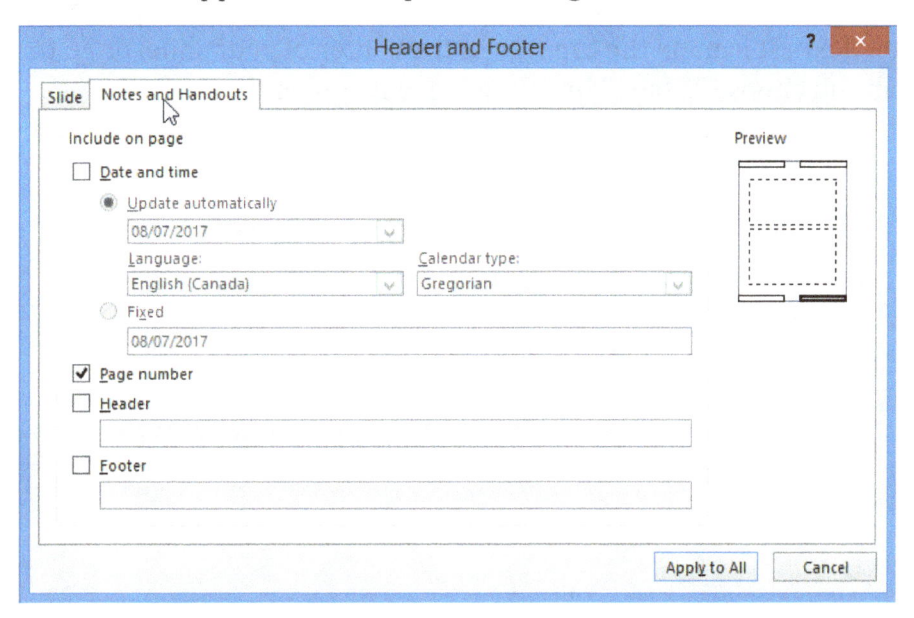

# Adding Content

Adding content is different from adding text. Content includes more visual items such as tables, charts, graphics, and more.

A good presenter will include more than just text in their presentation. Your goal should be to appeal to all different types of learners who may be in your audience. Some learners will prefer to read text, some will prefer to look at graphics or charts, and some will prefer to listen to some audio or watch a video. By including all kinds of media and content, you will have a better chance of getting your point across to your entire audience.

All of the content items listed below can be found on the Insert tab of your software. However, if you make a new slide, you will see six of the items as symbols in the middle of your new slide. You can click on the symbol directly, or you can access each of the items from the Insert tab.

## Tables

There is an instructional video for students on this topic at:
Webpage:     http://www.asselingroup.com/paralegals
Password:    paralegals

Tables are a good way to show data to your audience. After inserting a new slide, click on the first icon on the top row in the center of your slide, or go to the Insert tab and choose Table. The following will appear:

Computer Applications for Paralegals 81

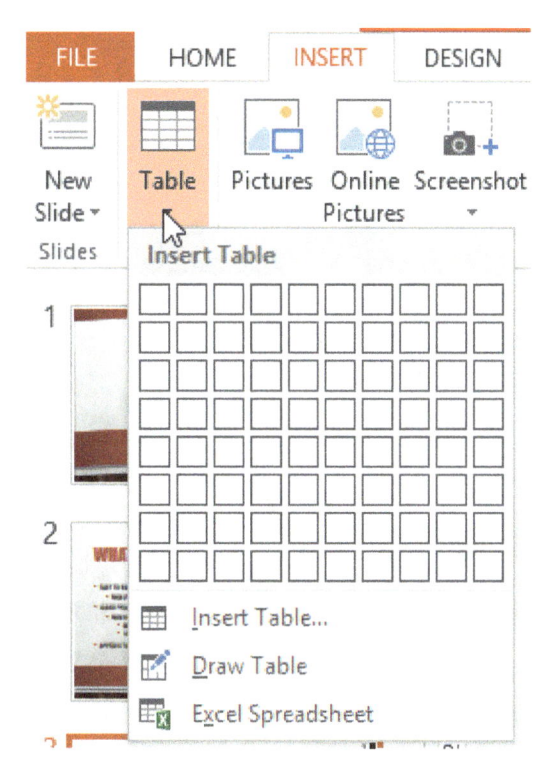

When choosing to include a table in your presentation, it is a good idea to have in your mind what information you would like to convey using the table. For example, you may want to show the administration in your firm that you or the staff members are meeting your monthly goal of hours worked.

Let's say that your goal is to docket 100 hours per month on client files and that you know that a few of the timekeepers are consistently working more than that each month. Perhaps you would present this information to the owners as evidence that they need to hire another paralegal or staff member. If you want to give a three-month sampling of docketable time, you would have three months of data plus perhaps four time keepers, including you. By knowing that your data has three months and four timekeepers, you know where to start when creating your table.

You will want your table to have headings so let's add one to each of your sets of data. So, instead of having a three (months) by four (staff) table, you will create a four by five table. The extra numbers will allow for labels and headings. Here is what it will look like:

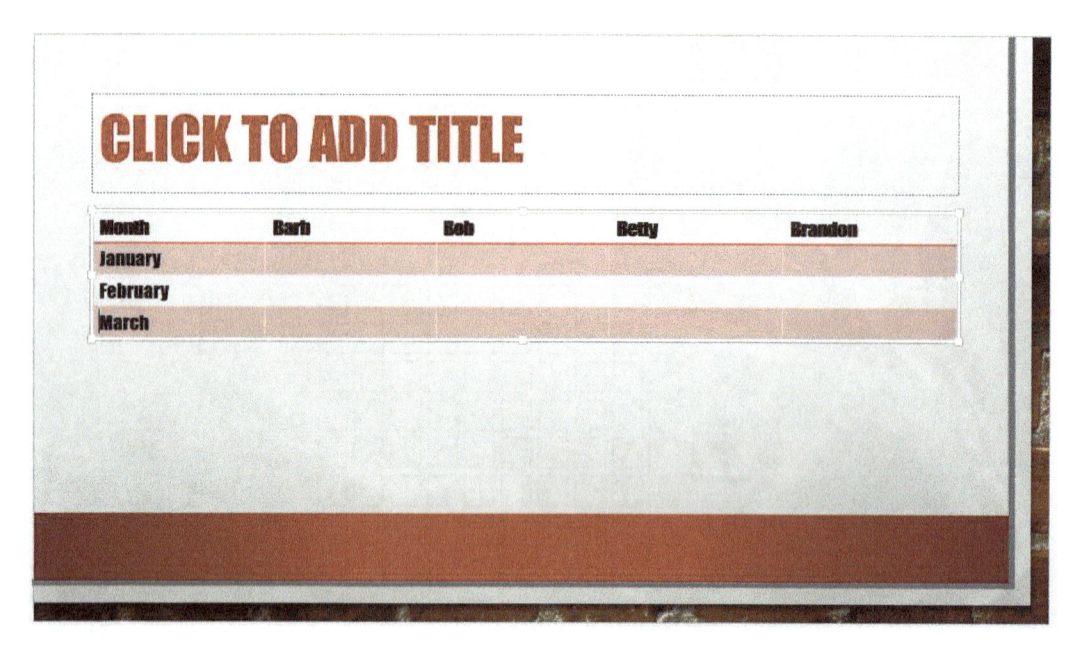

This is a five by four table and I have added the labels/headings. All that is left is to fill in the number of hours to complete the table.

Notice how PowerPoint chose a table that automatically matches the theme I chose. That is one of the main benefits of choosing a theme at the beginning of your presentation.

Every slide should have a title, so you will definitely want to click in the title box and add a title for this slide.

Additional changes made be made as well. If your mouse is in one of the cells of the table you just created, you will notice that there are two new tabs at the top of your ribbon. They are the Table Tools tabs.

The Design tab is shown here. You can use theme options to customize your table in a variety of different ways. By dropping down the arrow at the bottom right of the Table Styles grouping, you can choose from a number of preset table styles. Experiment with some of these options to get a feel for what they can do.

Computer Applications for Paralegals

This next graphic is the Layout tab:

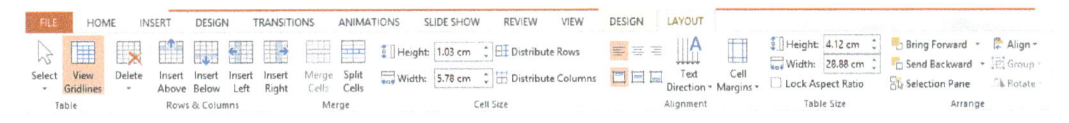

Among other things, the Layout tab allows you to:

- Delete a row, a column, or your entire table
- Insert a new row above your point of insertion
- Insert a new row below your point of insertion
- Insert a new column either to the right or the left of your point of insertion
- Merge cells together (notice how the merge function is currently grayed out – you will need to select more than one cell by clicking and dragging your mouse across your selected cells in order to activate this feature)
- Split cells apart
- Change the height of a row or the width of a column, and
- Change the direction of your text within a particular cell.

## Charts

There is an instructional video for students on this topic at:
Webpage:    http://www.asselingroup.com/paralegals
Password:   paralegals

Charts are another way to add meaningful graphics to a presentation that represent a set of data. To access Charts, do one of the following:

- Create a new slide and click on the middle symbol on the top row of symbols at the center of your new slide, or
- Go to the Insert tab and click on Chart.

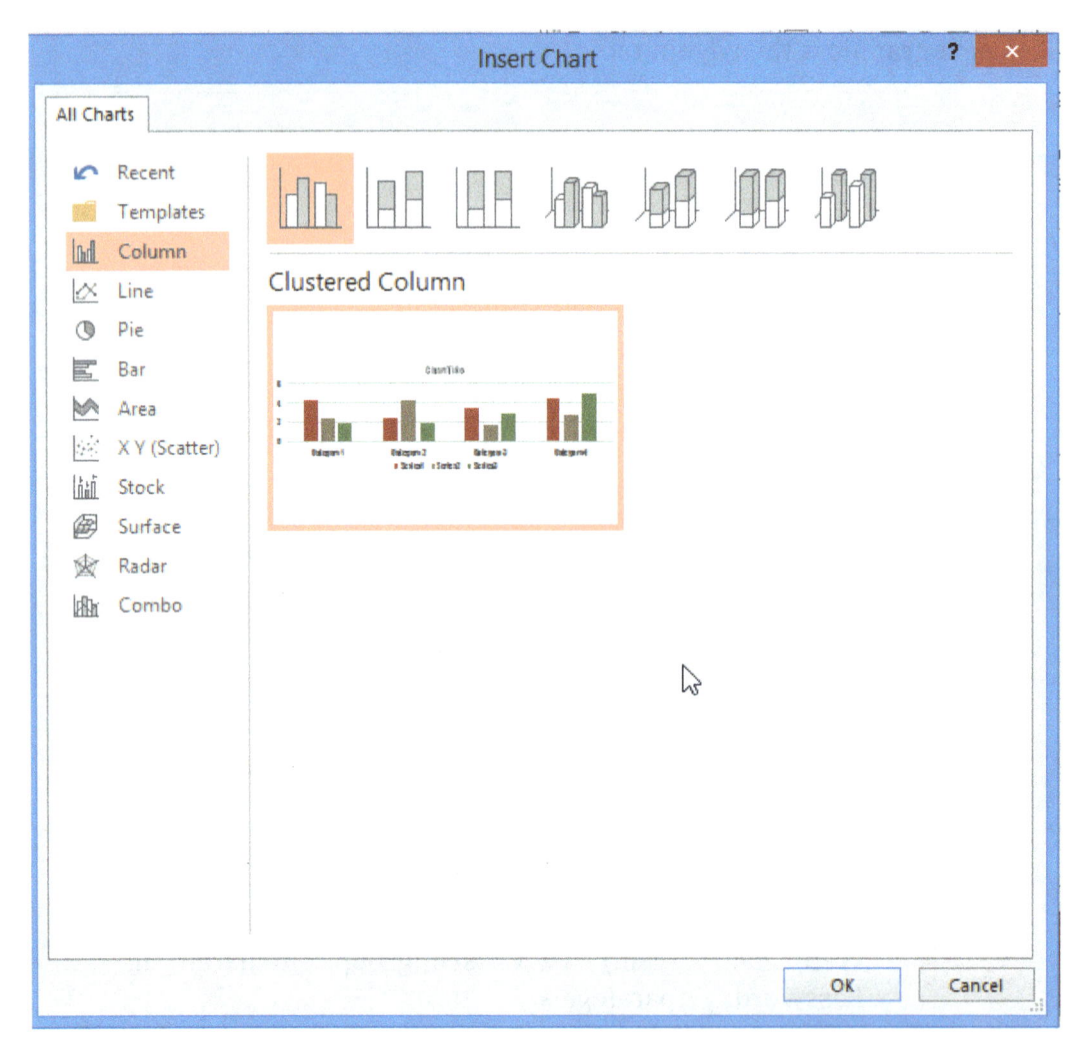

You will see a variety of types of charts to choose from listed on the left side of the dialogue box. Clicking on any of the options will show you what type of chart that is.

Let's say I want to create a pie chart to illustrate the types of clients we have in our firm. Some of them are legal aid clients, some of them are family members, some are referred by other clients, and some just found us in the phone book or online. Let's click on Pie and then choose the first pie chart in the options. Then, click OK.

Computer Applications for Paralegals                                          85

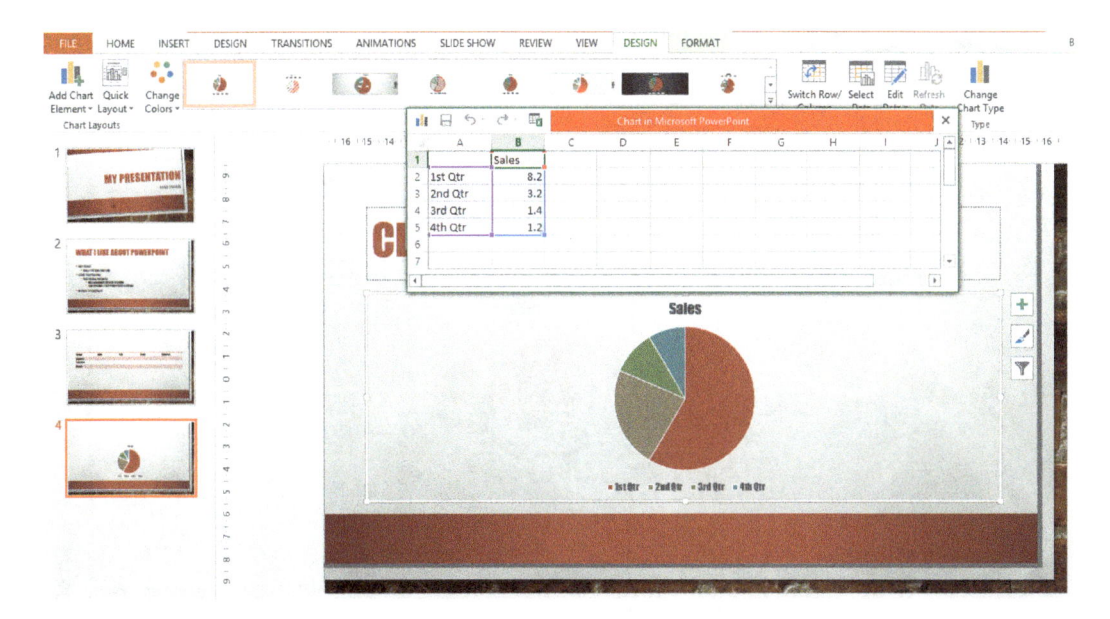

You will notice a few things:

- There are two new Chart Tool tabs at the top of the ribbon: Design and Format
- The Design tab allows you to change the chart to a different type, in case you don't like the one you've chose, as well as change the color scheme and style of chart
- The Format tab allows you to have a greater say in the design of the chart with outlines, fill color, and more
- A chart has appeared in our slide, and
- A mini Excel spreadsheet has appeared on our screen.

The chart shown has nothing to do with the types of clients at my firm, which is what I wanted it to show. What it does show, is a sample of how data is used to create a chart. Now, I have to amend the Excel spreadsheet to make the necessary changes to the chart, as follows:

- If you change the word Sales in the Excel portion, it will change the title of the chart
- If you change the 1st-4th quarters in the Excel portion, it will change the items in the legend on the chart, and
- If you change the numbers in the Excel portion, it will change the configuration of the pie in the chart.

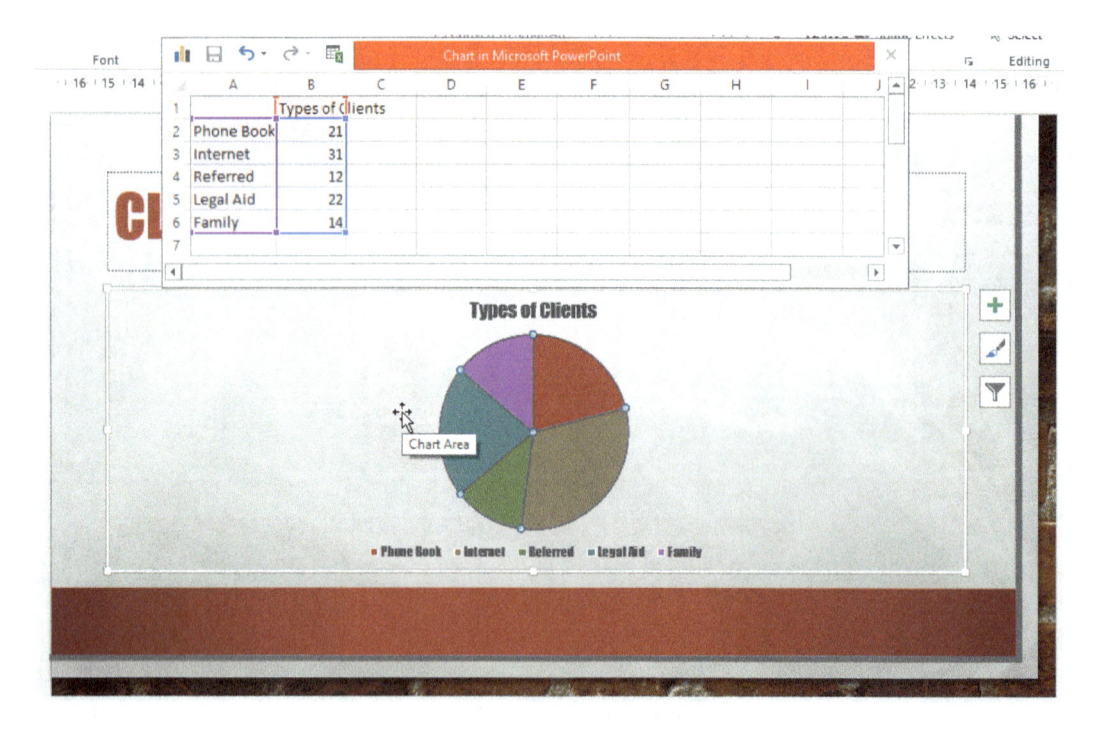

Different styles of the same graphic will show different items on the chart. Some will show the title and some won't. Some will show the legend on the top, left, right, or bottom. Others will show the labels of the data on the pieces of the pie chart, in either numbers, currency, or percentages. You can customize these options by clicking on the green "+" sign to the right of your chart (when your chart is selected).

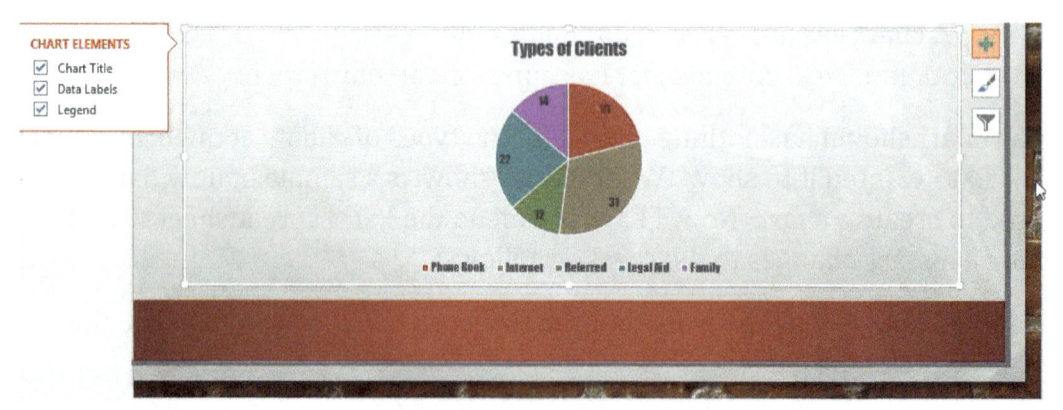

You can customize how the data labels are shown by taking the following steps:

- Right-click on one of the data labels inside your chart

Computer Applications for Paralegals 87

- Choose Format Data Labels near the bottom of the resulting list
- Either select or deselect options that you want or don't want to show on the chart

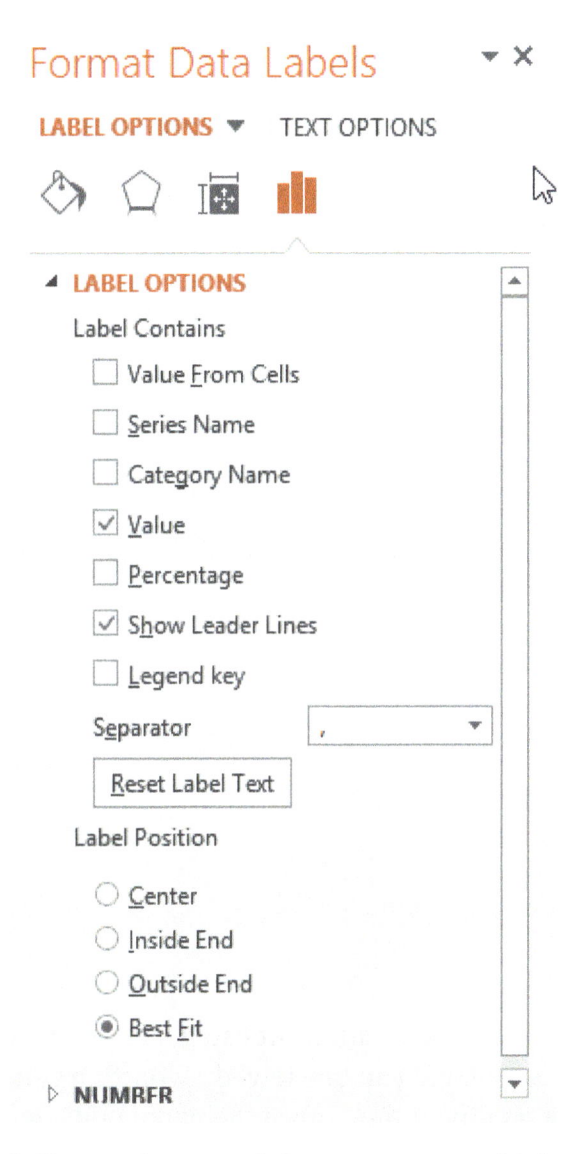

**Format Data Labels**

LABEL OPTIONS ▼ TEXT OPTIONS

▲ LABEL OPTIONS

Label Contains
- ☐ Value From Cells
- ☐ Series Name
- ☐ Category Name
- ☑ Value
- ☐ Percentage
- ☑ Show Leader Lines
- ☐ Legend key

Separator: ,

[Reset Label Text]

Label Position
- ○ Center
- ○ Inside End
- ○ Outside End
- ● Best Fit

▷ NUMBER

Play around with different charts and datasets to see which ones you like best and which would best display the information you want to include in your presentation.

## Smart Art Graphics

> There is an instructional video for students on this topic at:
> Webpage: http://www.asselingroup.com/paralegals
> Password: paralegals

SmartArt graphics are a great way to add something visual to your presentations, but also include text. To add a SmartArt graphic to a slide in your presentation, do one of the following:

- Create a new slide and click on the right symbol on the top row of symbols at the center of your new slide, or
- Go to the Insert tab and click on SmartArt.

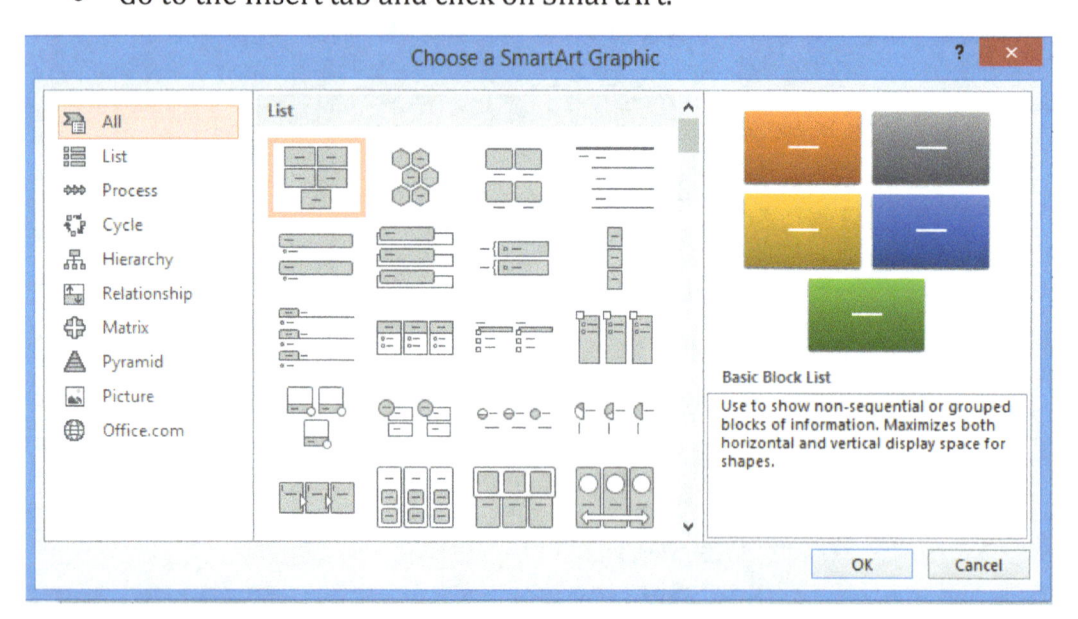

As you can see, there are lots of different categories of SmartArt graphics. Each graphic has a name that can be viewed by putting your curser over one of the graphics and holding it there until the name pops up as a tool tip.

Try creating a process graphic to show how to benefit the most from this textbook. I will choose the Step Up Process graphic.

Notice the following:

- Again, there are new tabs on the ribbon: SmartArt tabs for Design and Format

Computer Applications for Paralegals 89

- The Design tab allows you to choose a different graphic if you like, or change the design and color scheme of the one chosen
- The Format tab gives you more control over the design of the current graphic, such as outline and fill color
- The graphic has been inserted into your presentation with a text box in each shape so that you can add text to your graphic
- A side bar has opened up, allowing you to type the contents of the graphic there, instead of typing directly on the graphic
- The side bar can be closed by clicking the "x" at the top right corner, and
- The side bar can be re-opened and closed by clicking on the chevron (arrow) in the middle of the left side of the text box that contains the SmartArt graphic.

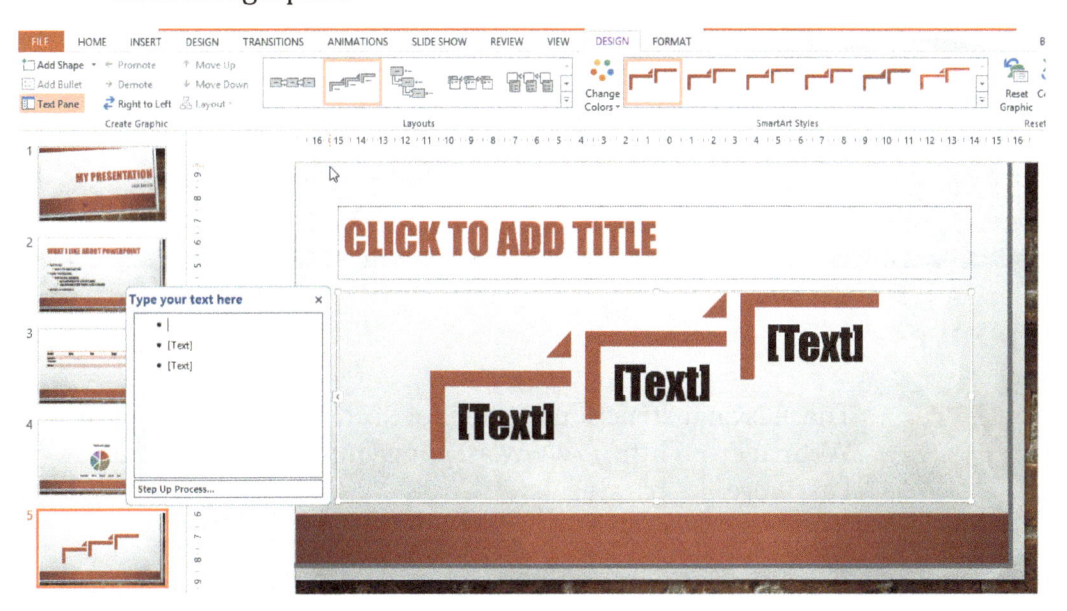

The example shows a graphic with three shapes. Most graphics can accommodate more than three shapes, but occasionally, you will choose a graphic that cannot accommodate all of the shapes that you need to show. In that case, simply choose a different graphic on the SmartArt Design tab and your content will be transferred to the new graphic.

To add or subtract shapes, do one of the following:

- Add or subtract bullet points in the side bar

- Right-click on a shape in the slide and chose Add Shape, or
- Click on Add Shape on the far left of the SmartArt Design tab.

Take some time to play around with different graphics and how they look. Some even have places where you can click to add a graphic as a bullet point.

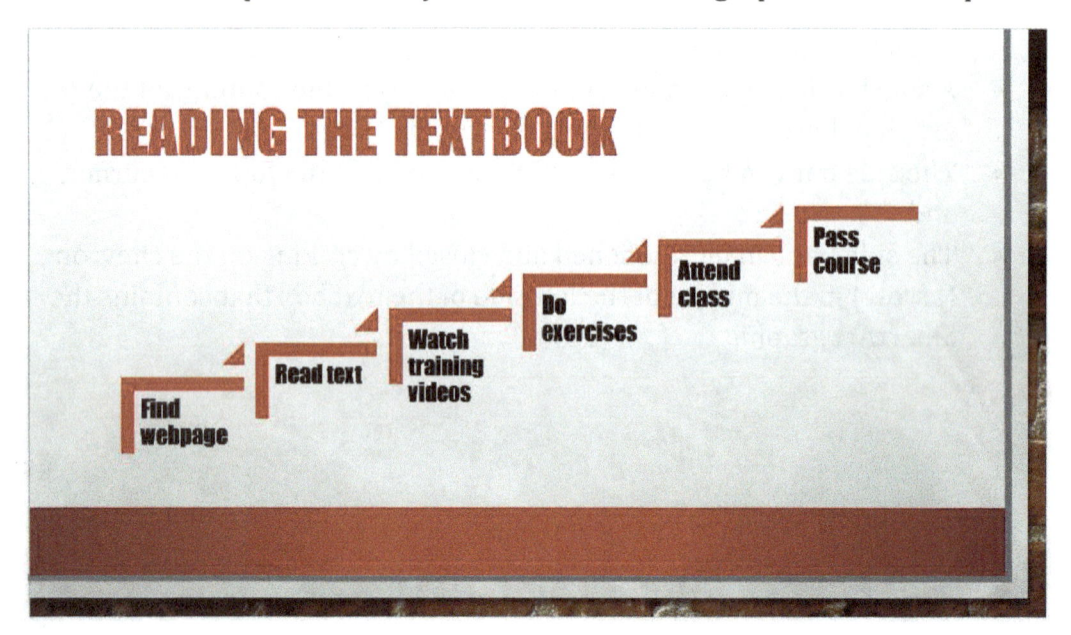

## Pictures

There is an instructional video for students on this topic at:
Webpage: http://www.asselingroup.com/paralegals
Password: paralegals

Adding pictures to a slide show is pretty easy. Here are a couple of ways:

- On a new slide, click on the bottom left symbol in the middle of your slide to select a picture from your computer
- On a new slide, click on the bottom middle symbol in the middle of your slide to search for a picture on the Internet,
- Click on Insert > Pictures to select a picture from your computer, or
- Click on Insert > Online Pictures to select a picture from the Internet.

Computer Applications for Paralegals 91

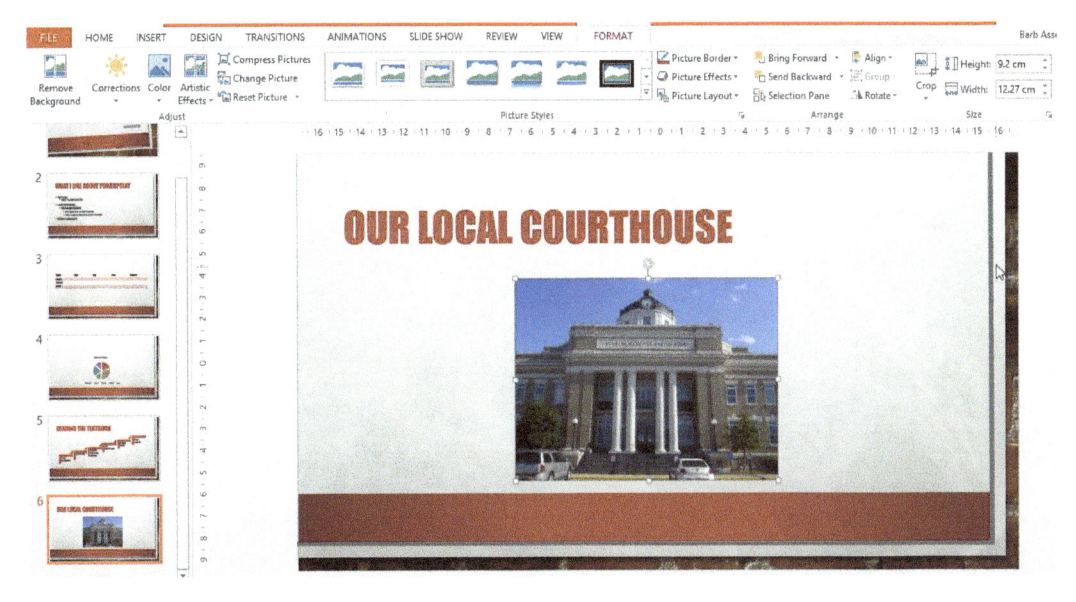

The picture shown in the example was found by searching the word "courthouse".

Notice the following about this example:

- When the picture is selected (clicked on), a new tab appears on the ribbon: Picture Format, and
- The Picture Format tab allows you to add various types of frames to the picture, edit the brightness and background, align it, and more.

## Videos

There is an instructional video for students on this topic at:
Webpage:    http://www.asselingroup.com/paralegals
Password:   paralegals

To add a video to a slide, do one of the following:

- Add a new slide and click on the bottom right symbol in the center of the slide, or
- Add a new slide and go to Insert > Video.

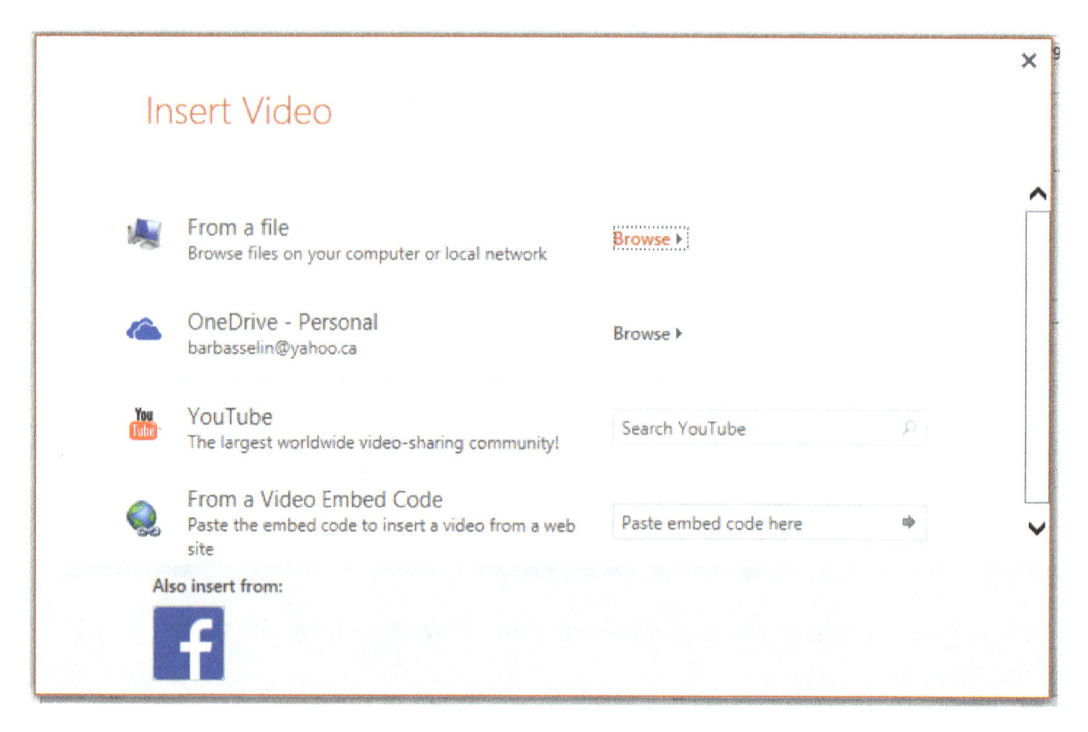

You can upload a video from your computer or personal OneDrive, search for a video on YouTube, or enter a video embed code.

To find one on YouTube, search for your topic in the search bar. I will search "adding video to PowerPoint" and select a video.

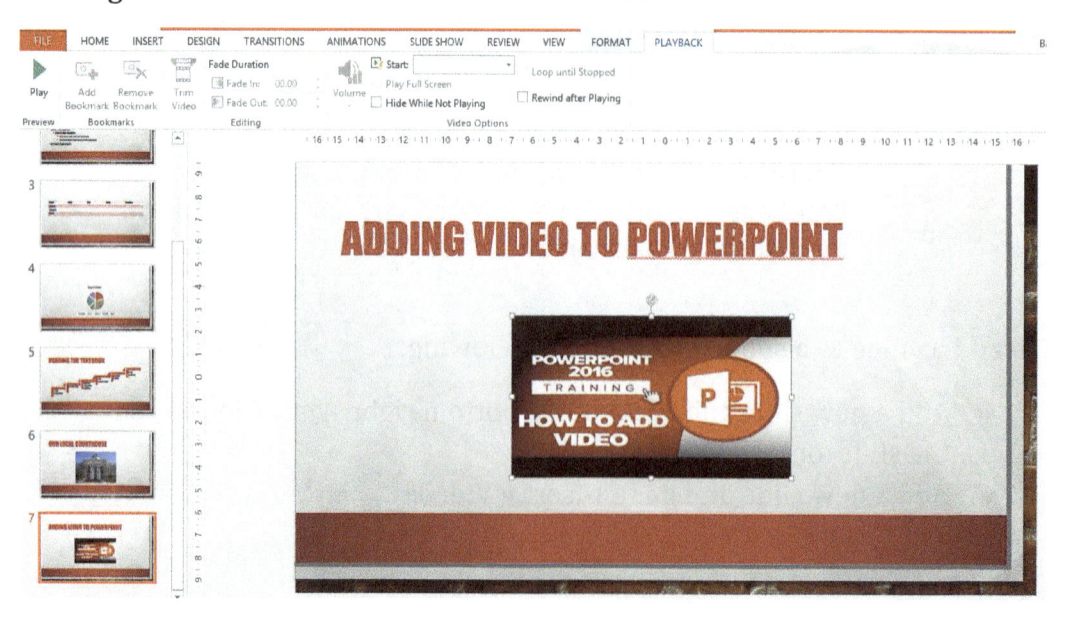

You will notice the following items on the example:

- There are two new Video tabs at the right of your ribbon: Format and Playback
- The Video Format tab allows you to add borders and other items similar to the Format tab for a picture, and
- The Video Playback tab allows you to select different playback options such as playing on click, or automatically.

## More Content

There is an instructional video for students on this topic at:
Webpage:     http://www.asselingroup.com/paralegals
Password:    paralegals

There are other visual items you can add to your presentations. They are all found on the Insert tab. If you go to the Insert tab, you will see all six of the options we have looked at already, plus the following others:

**Screen Shot**

This option allows you to add a screen shot to your slide as a graphic. Simply click on the Screen Shot option and click and drag your mouse to select what you want to be added to your slide.

**Photo Album**

This option is similar to adding a picture to your presentation. The difference is that you select a folder of pictures and the software adds one picture to each slide.

**Shapes**

Go to Insert > Shapes to see the wide variety of shapes that can be added to your presentation. Adding shapes is a bit different than adding the other content items we have discussed so far. To add a shape, follow these steps:

- Go to the slide where you would like to add a shape
- Go to insert > Shapes and choose the shape you would like
- Once you have selected a shape, a "bulls-eye" will appear on your screen, and

- Click in the upper left corner of where you would like the shape and, **holding the mouse down**, drag the mouse to the lower right corner of where you want the shape to go.

You can re-size the shape after you have created it by clicking on one of the eight control handles around the shape. Notice there is a Format tab on your ribbon that allows you to add color, outline, and special effects to your shape. You can even layer shapes together to create logos and other graphics by moving shapes to the front and back of one another.

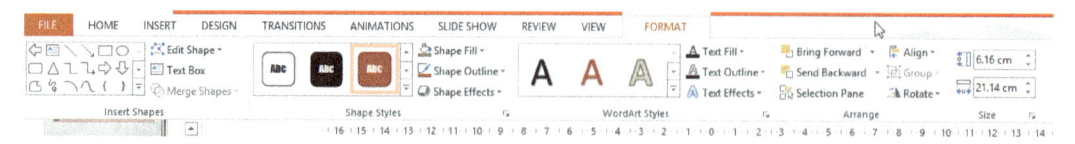

### Hyperlink

To add a hyperlink to your presentation, follow these steps:

- Click on the item or text that you would like to hyperlink
- Go to Insert > Hyperlink, and
- Enter the URL that you would like the user to go to when they click the link.

### Comment

If you are collaborating with someone else on a group presentation, you may be reviewing the work each other has done. Adding comments allows you to suggest changes without actually making them.

To add a comment, go to Insert > Comment. The Comment task pane will open up on the right side of your screen. Add your comment and close the screen. A speech bubble will show up on the slide to indicate that there is a comment. To see the comment, just double-click on the speech bubble.

Computer Applications for Paralegals    95

## Textbox

If you choose a slide layout that is blank, you can add your own textboxes.

To add a textbox, go to Insert > Textbox.  Textboxes are added in the same way that shapes are added.  A bullseye will appear on the screen.  Click and drag the bullseye to the size of textbox you would like and start typing.

## WordArt

PowerPoint has a number of pre-set text designs available to you, depending on the theme you have chosen for your presentation.  To access WordArt, go to Insert > WordArt and choose one of the options available to you.

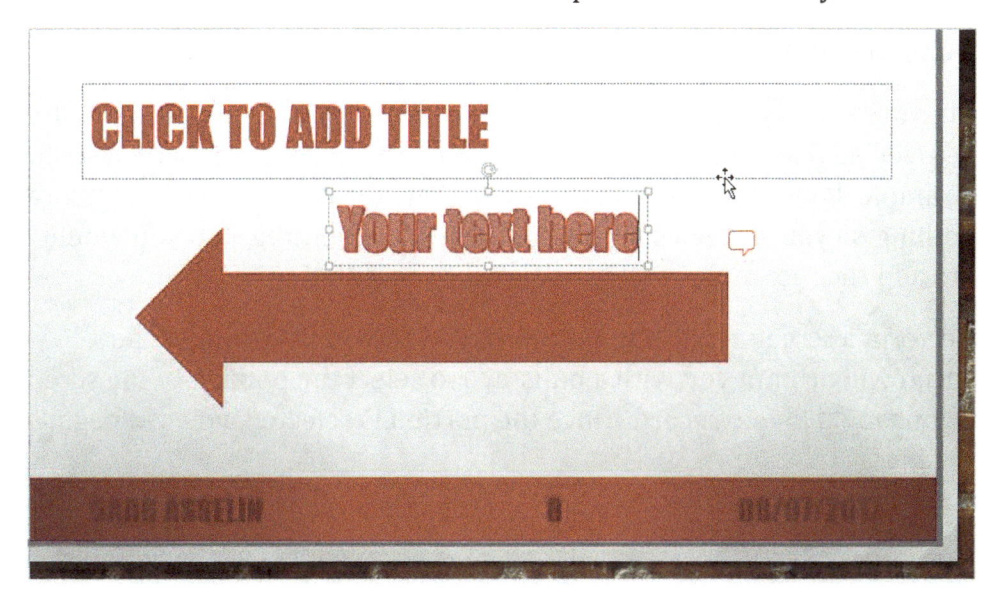

Once you have chosen, a textbox appears on your screen in the design you chose, with the words "Your text here". Simply change that text to whatever you want.

Note that, while in your WordArt selection, you have a Format tab available to you so that you can change the WordArt, if you like, or add a border, fill, and more.

**Audio**

If you want to add audio to your presentation, go to Insert > Audio and you will see two options:

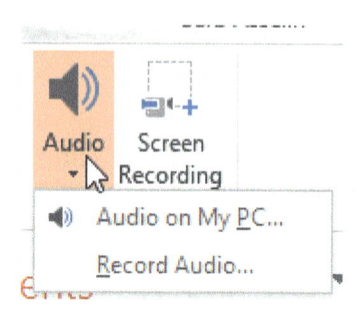

If you have music already on your computer that you would like to add to your presentation (if it's going to be playing automatically at a reception, for example), you can choose Audio on My PC and browse to find your music. If you would like to record a voice-over for your presentation and have it play that automatically, select Record Audio and begin your voice-over.

**Screen Recording**

If you would like to perform a screen recording of your presentation with a voice-over, so that the recording can be uploaded to your company website, for example, PowerPoint allows you to do that. Or, you may wish to record something on your screen such as a tutorial on something, and you would like to add the recording as a video on your presentation.

To perform a screen recording, go to Insert > Screen Recording. The program will prompt you with a bulls-eye to select the portion of the screen that you would like to record. Once the portion is selected, you can begin recording.

Computer Applications for Paralegals 97

## Notes

▶ There is an instructional video for students on this topic at:
Webpage: http://www.asselingroup.com/paralegals
Password: paralegals

At the bottom of your screen you will see an options to add Notes to each slide.

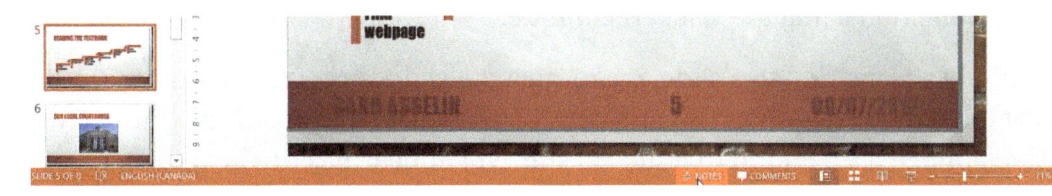

By clicking on the Notes option, you will activate this section and can type notes relating to the content of each slide.

The notes are only visible to you, the presenter, when you print them out (see printing section that follows).

You can expand the size of the notes section temporarily by placing your curser on the line between the notes section and your slide and, when you see the two-way arrow, you can click to expand the notes section.

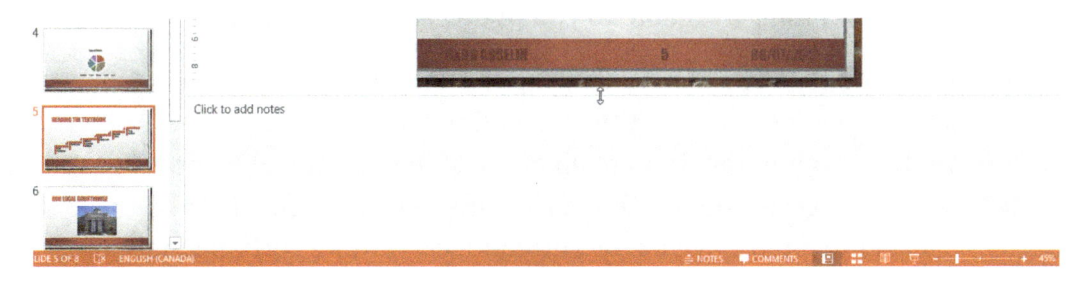

## Transitions

▶ There is an instructional video for students on this topic at:
Webpage: http://www.asselingroup.com/paralegals
Password: paralegals

Transitions allow you to control how each slide appears on the screen during a live presentation. You can add transitions to each slide by clicking on the Transitions tab at the top of your ribbon.

As you can see, there are many different styles of transitions. If you place your mouse on one of the options, you should be able to see your current slide transition using the select technique.

To apply a transition to a slide, make sure the slide is showing on the main part of your computer screen and click on the selected transition. Once you have applied a transition to a slide, a star will appear beside the mini version of that slide on your preview task pane on the left of your screen.

There are other options available to you in the Transitions tab:

- Add a sound that will occur during transition
- Set the length of time that the transition will take
- Apply the same transition to all of the slides in your presentation, and
- Set your presentation so that each slide will advance either on the click of the mouse by you, or automatically after a certain length of time, such as one or two seconds.

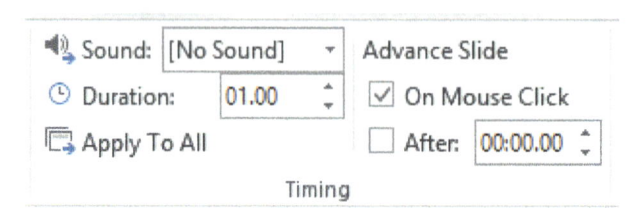

Computer Applications for Paralegals 99

# Animations

There is an instructional video for students on this topic at:
Webpage: http://www.asselingroup.com/paralegals
Password: paralegals

Transitions allow you to control how your slides move from one to the other, but you can also add animations to items within a slide. Animations can be found by clicking on the Animations tab on the ribbon.

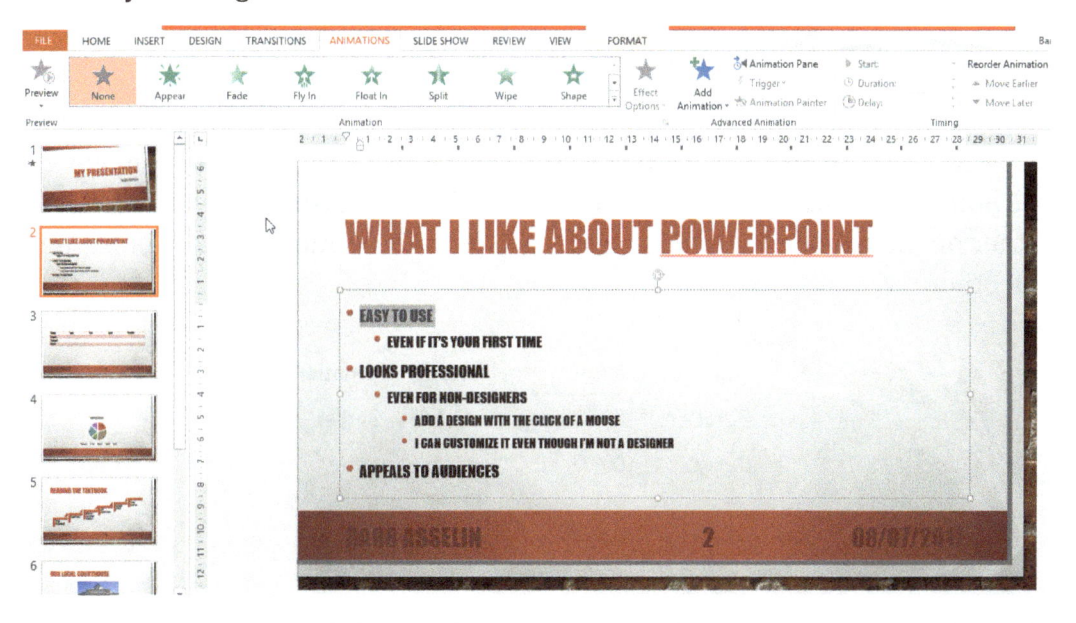

The example shows a slide with bullets on it. In the example, I have selected the text of one bullet. By selecting some text, I have activated the items on the Animations tab.

To add an animation to some selected text, simply click on the animation you would like. Notice that the order of the animated items will show on the slide.

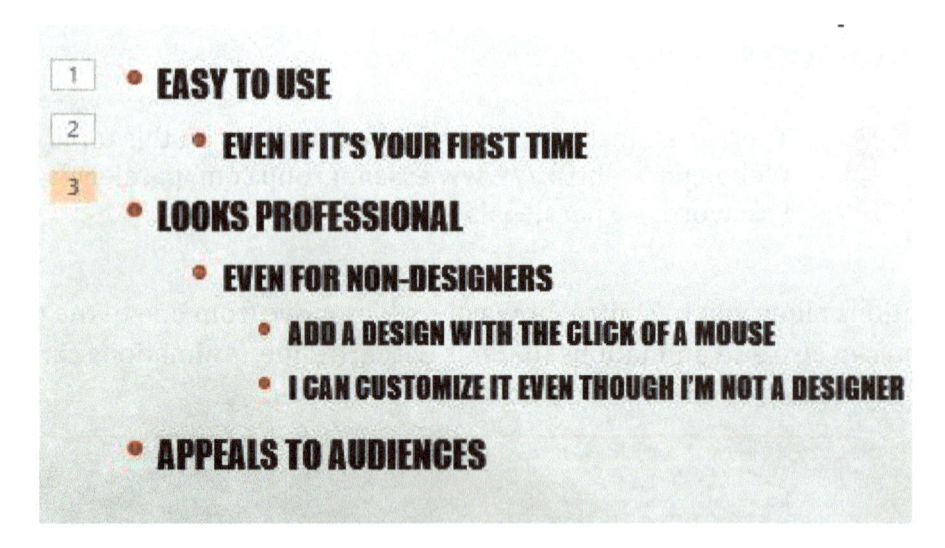

- **EASY TO USE**
  - **EVEN IF IT'S YOUR FIRST TIME**
- **LOOKS PROFESSIONAL**
  - **EVEN FOR NON-DESIGNERS**
    - **ADD A DESIGN WITH THE CLICK OF A MOUSE**
    - **I CAN CUSTOMIZE IT EVEN THOUGH I'M NOT A DESIGNER**
- **APPEALS TO AUDIENCES**

Once set, you can always use the options on the Animations tab to remove the animation (click none) or reorder them. You can also set them to occur either on mouse-click, or after a set length of time, or automatically one after the other.

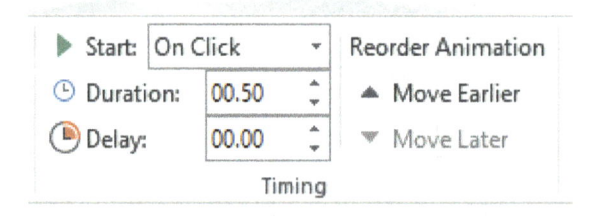

## Saving Different Formats

To save your presentation, go to the File tab and slick Save or Save As. This will bring up the Save As dialogue box where you can name your presentation and save it on your computer or USB, whichever you prefer.

By dropping down the options in the Save As Type field, you will find a variety of different options.

Computer Applications for Paralegals                                           101

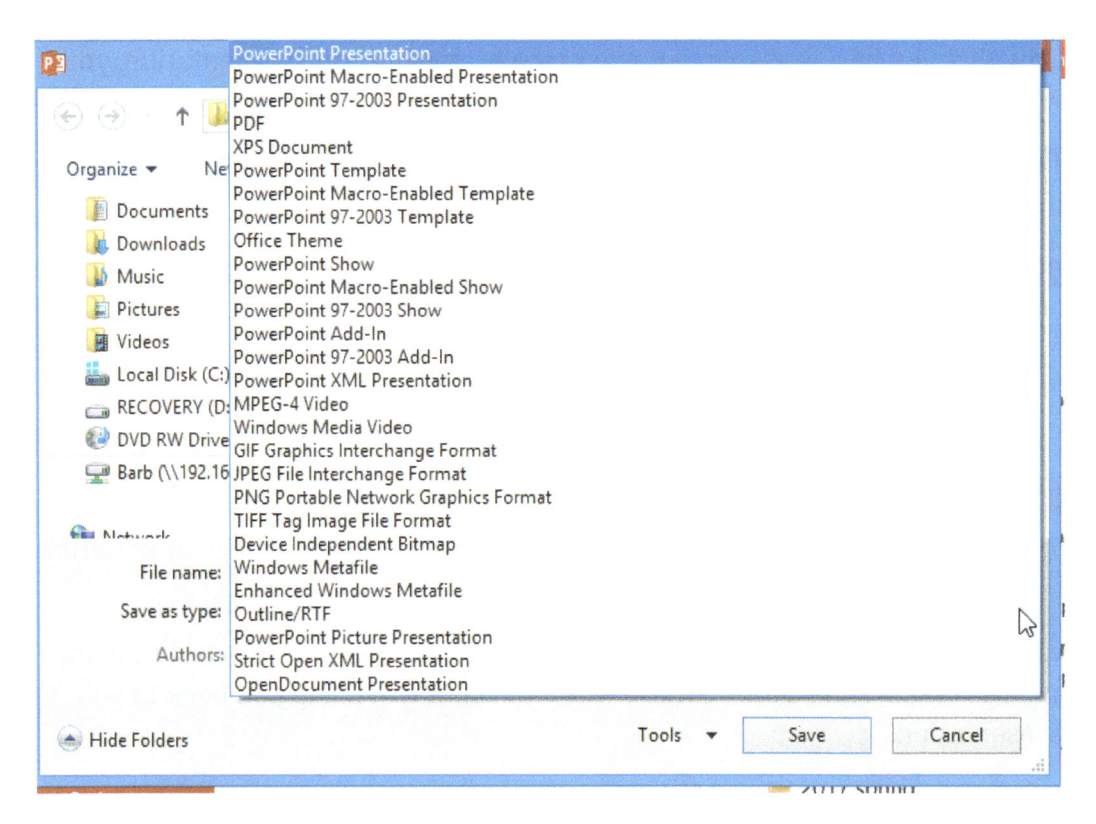

Options that may be of interest to you are:

- PowerPoint presentation (top option), which is the most common, and default option – it will save as a .pptx file
- PDF, which will save your presentation as a PDF so that it can be printed or provided to someone without giving them the options of making changes to it, and
- PowerPoint Show (.ppsx file), which creates a video-like show that, when opened, operates as a presentation only and cannot be edited. NOTE: save your presentation as a presentation first (.pptx file), otherwise, you will lose the opportunity to edit your presentation.

## Viewing Your Presentation

There is an instructional video for students on this topic at:
Webpage:   http://www.asselingroup.com/paralegals
Password:   paralegals

Now that you have put so much work into preparing your presentation, you will want to practice viewing it before you present it to an audience.

To view your presentation, go to the Slide Show tab and click on From Beginning.

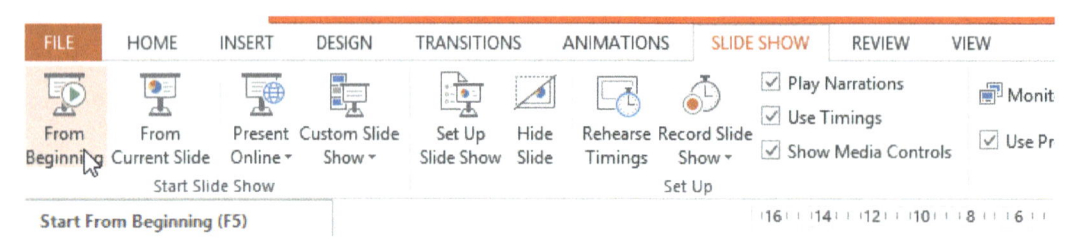

Your title slide will appear on your screen in full screen mode. By clicking your mouse, you will advance to the next slide. Continue in this manner until your presentation is complete.

When you click a final time, you will see a black screen with words at the top saying "End of slide show, click to exit". Clicking will bring you back to your presentation.

## Printing Your Presentation

There is an instructional video for students on this topic at:
Webpage: http://www.asselingroup.com/paralegals
Password: paralegals

There are many ways to print your presentation. If you click on File > Print, you will see the following options if you drop down the Full Page Slide option:

- Full Page Slides, which prints one slide per page
- Notes Pages, which shows one slide per page on the top and any notes you have added on the bottom portion of each page
- Outline, which shows your text only without the large graphics you may have included – note that this option will show your customized bullets
- 1 Slide, which gives you one slide per page in a handout style where you can see the footers on your slides as well as the header and footer on your handouts

- 2 Slides, which prints two slides per page as a handout
- 3 Slides, which prints three slides per page with lines beside each slide for your audience to take notes
- 4 Slides horizontal or vertical, which prints four slides per page as a handout
- 6 Slides horizontal or vertical, which prints six slides per page as a handout, and
- 9 Slides horizontal or vertical, which prints nine slides per page as a handout.

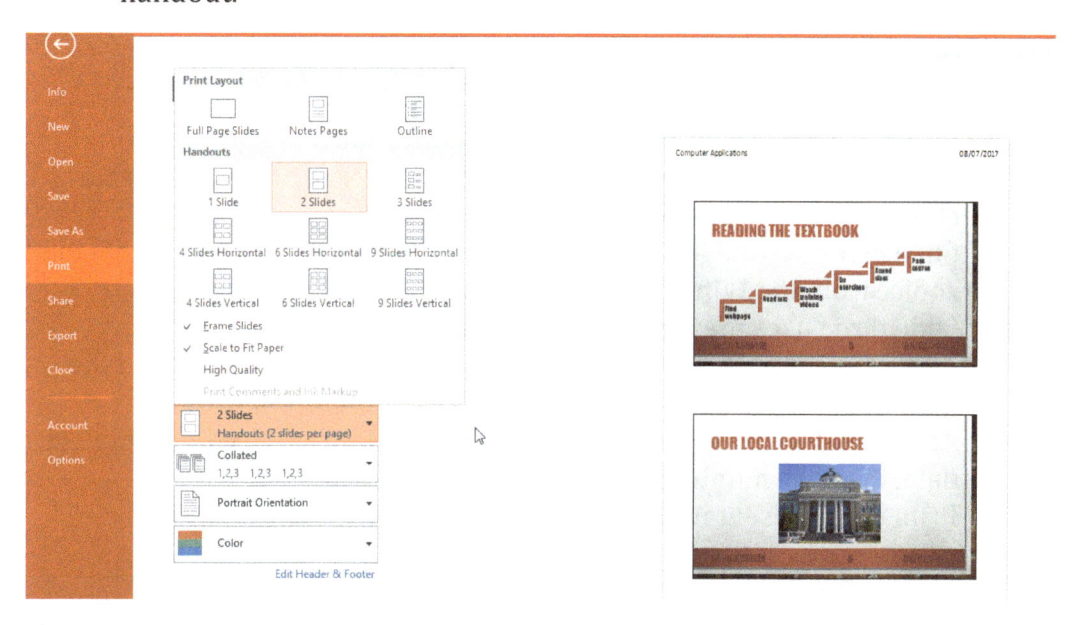

You can also choose to print your presentation either in full color, black and white, or grayscale.

# Chapter Summary

In this chapter, students learned how to effectively design, customize, print, and deliver a presentation. Students learned how to add various elements to a presentation that would increase its appeal and how to reach many different types of learners in an audience.

# Exercises

## Exercise 4.1

Your firm is hosting a seminar for recent paralegal graduates on their options when starting their own paralegal firm. Since you are one of the founding members of your firm, you have been asked to prepare the PowerPoint presentation that will be used in the seminar. Create the following presentation using these instructions:

1. The design used is Ion. If you do not have access to the Ion design, please select another design of your choice.
2. Please add your name as author on the title slide.
3. Change the first level bullet on the slide master to an image of your choice found by searching "business".
4. Change the second level bullet on the slide master to a symbol of your choice from the Wingdings font style.
5. Slide three uses the comparison format.
6. Add a footer to the slides that includes your name, the date, and the slide number. Do not show on title slide.
7. Add a header and footer to the handouts that includes your name, the date, the page number, and the name of the firm.
8. Print your presentation as a handout with two slides per page.

![Starting a New Paralegal Firm? — BARB ASSELIN]

## What Are Your Options?

- Sole Proprietorship
  - Operate a business on your own with low overhead – often from the comfort of your own home
- Partnership
  - Partner with one or more individuals to start a business
- Professional Corporation
  - Incorporate under the Ontario Business Corporations Act and obtain Certificate of Authorization from LSUC
- Multi-Discipline Organization
  - Join with other professionals who have compatible services so that you can share office space, resources, and clients

## Should You Incorporate?

**Professional Corporation**
- Limited liability
- Professional appearance to the public
- High cost to start the business
- Can choose any name that has not already been taken
- Requires annual resolutions and corporate bookkeeping
- Lower corporate income tax rate

**Sole Proprietor**
- Personal liability
- Less professional appearance to the public
- Less start-up costs
- Requires personal income tax
- Pay income tax at your personal rate

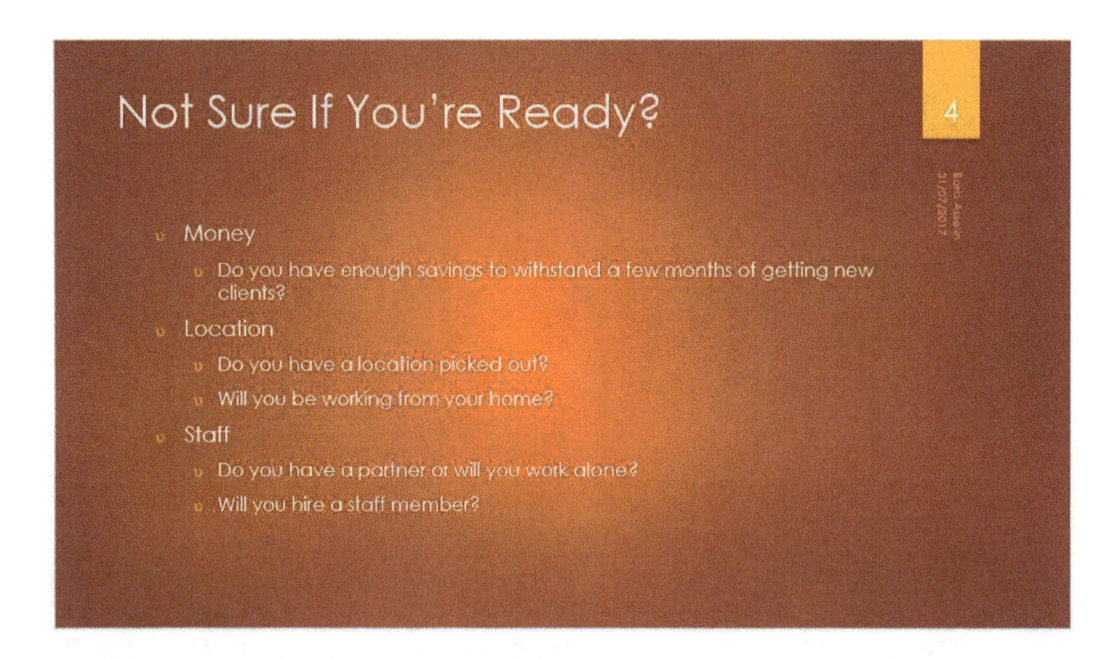

> **Not Sure If You're Ready?**
>
> - Money
>   - Do you have enough savings to withstand a few months of getting new clients?
> - Location
>   - Do you have a location picked out?
>   - Will you be working from your home?
> - Staff
>   - Do you have a partner or will you work alone?
>   - Will you hire a staff member?

## Exercise 4.2

Your firm is hosting a seminar for the paralegal students at your local college. They are trying to entice the top students to choose to apply for work at your firm. Since you are a PowerPoint whiz, you have been asked to prepare the presentation that will be used in the seminar. Create the following presentation using these instructions:

1. The design used is Main Event. If you do not have access to the Main Event design, please select another design of your choice.
2. Please add your name as author on the title slide.
3. Change the first level bullet on the slide master to a symbol of your choice.
4. Add a graphic of your choice to slide two after searching the word "choice".
5. Add a graphic of your choice to slide three after searching the word "courthouse".
6. Slide four uses the Continuous Picture List SmartArt graphic. Be sure to add a picture in each circle that represents each area of law.
7. Add a footer to the slides that includes your name, the date, and the slide number. Do not show on title slide.
8. Add a header and footer to the handouts that includes your name, the date, the page number, and the name of the firm.

Computer Applications for Paralegals

9. Print your presentation as a handout with two slides per page.

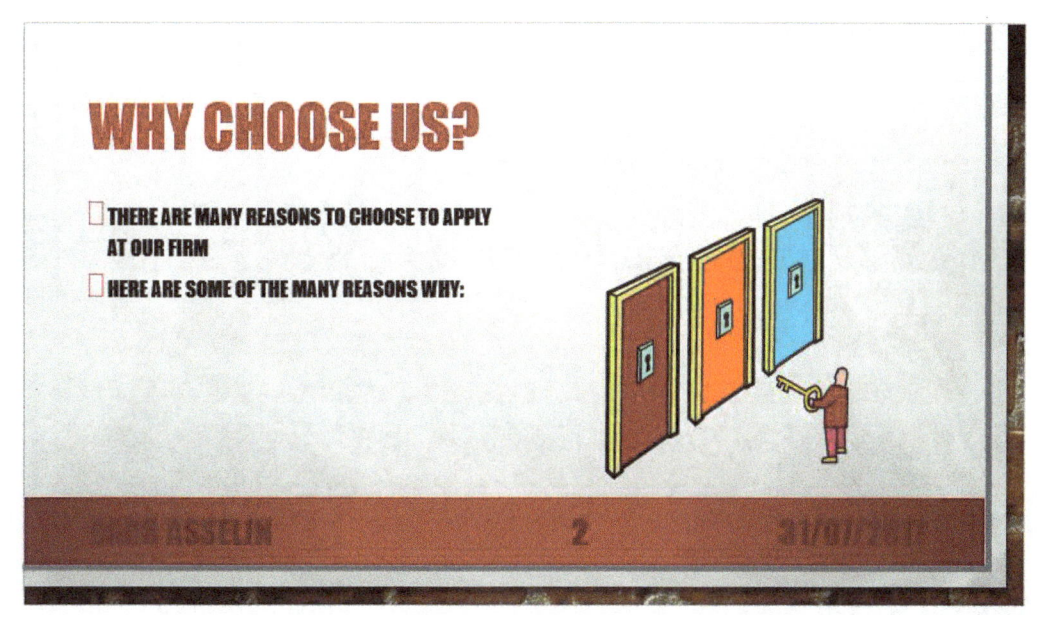

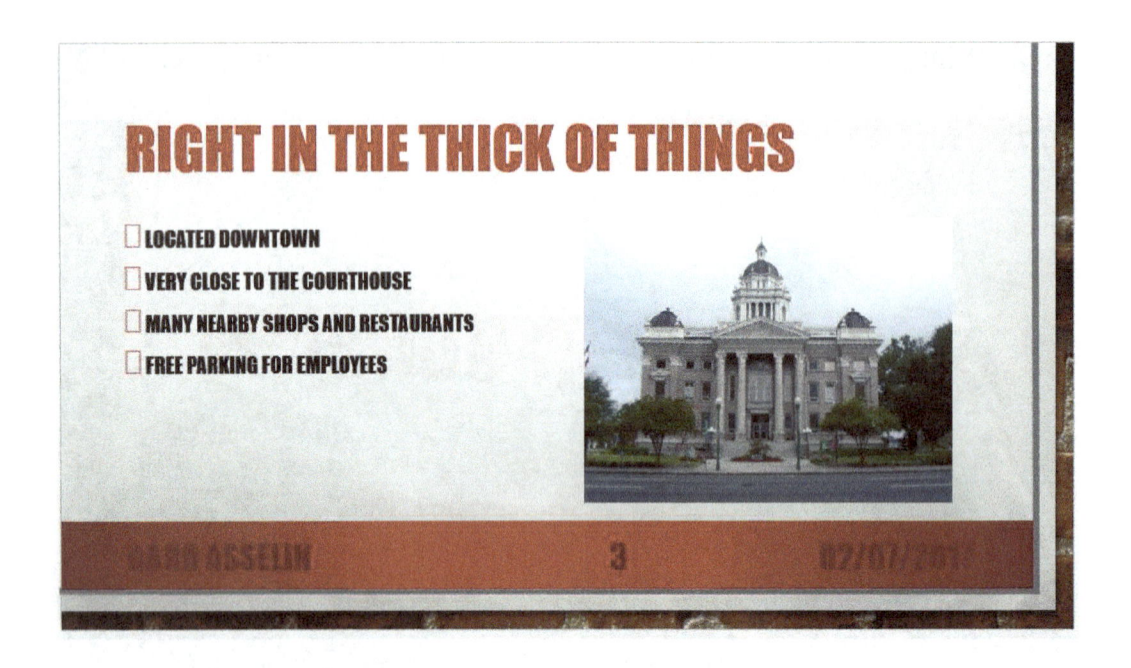

## Exercise 4.3

Your firm wants to deliver a presentation to high school students who are interested in becoming Paralegals. Since you are a PowerPoint expert, you have been asked to prepare the presentation that will be used. Create the following presentation using these instructions:

1. The design used is Parcel. If you do not have access to the Parcel design, please select another design of your choice.
2. Please add your name as author on the title slide.
3. Change the first level bullet to a picture of a law firm logo using the slide master and searching for an online picture using the term "law firm logo".
4. Add a graphic to slide three that you find by searching the phrase "law firm".
5. Slide four uses the Vertical Curved List SmartArt graphic.
6. Add a footer to the slides that includes your name, the date, and the slide number. Do not show on title slide.
7. Add a header and footer to the handouts that includes your name, the date, the page number, and the name of your presentation.
8. Save your presentation as a pptx file.
9. Upload your file in the format required by your professor so that your professor can mark your assignment.

## AREAS OF LAW

**YOU CAN PRACTICE**
- Small Claims
- Landlord and Tenant
- Immigration
- Employment
- Traffic
- Criminal (limited)

**YOU CANNOT PRACTICE**
- Real Estate
- Litigation
- Wills and Estates
- Family
- Criminal (some)
- Labour

## WHERE CAN YOU WORK?

- Law firm
- Paralegal firm
- Government offices
- Corporations with in-house legal departments
- Legal aid clinics
- Research firms
- Educational institutions
- Banks and financial institutions

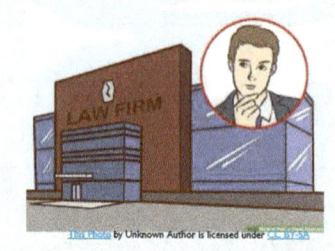

# Computer Applications for Paralegals

### PARALEGAL LICENSING PROCESS

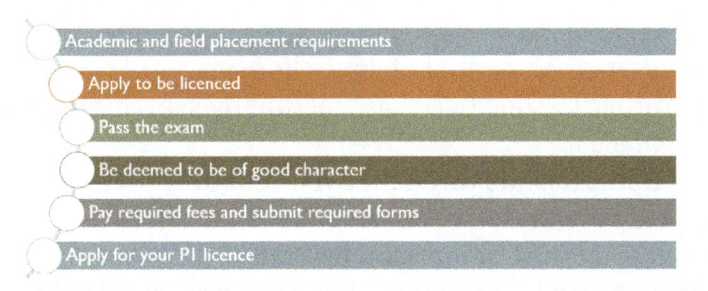

- Academic and field placement requirements
- Apply to be licenced
- Pass the exam
- Be deemed to be of good character
- Pay required fees and submit required forms
- Apply for your P1 licence

Barb Asselin  2020-11-17

### COME WORK WITH US

- Benefits of working with our firm:
  - Combined experience of 50 years between our Paralegals
  - Work in all Law Society approved areas of law
  - Excellent holiday and benefits package
  - Monthly training and team building
- Apply using our online application and let's get started!

This Photo by Unknown Author is licensed under CC BY-SA-NC

Barb Asselin  2020-11-17

## Exercise 4.4

Your firm has recently hired six new legal assistants. They would like to provide information to the new employees on various systems within the firm. Since you are a PowerPoint expert, you have been asked to prepare the presentation that will be used. Create the following presentation using these instructions:

1. The design used is Gallery. If you do not have access to the Gallery design, please select another design of your choice.
2. Please add your name as author on the title slide.
3. Change the first level bullet using the slide master. Choose "customize" and go to the Wingdings font grouping and choose a symbol that fits the workplace such as a computer, or a computer mouse, or another symbol of your choosing.
4. Add a graphic to slide two that you find by searching the word "workspace".
5. Add a graphic to slide three that you find by searching the phrase "computer network".
6. Slide four uses the Comparison Layout.
7. Slide five uses the Continuous Block Process SmartArt graphic.
8. Add a different transition to each slide in your presentation and set each slide to advance automatically after one second.
9. Add a footer to the slides that includes your name, the date, and the slide number. Do not show on title slide.
10. Add a header and footer to the handouts that includes your name, the date, the page number, and the name of the presentation.
11. Save your presentation as a pptx file.
12. Now save your presentation as a "show" (ppsx file).
13. Upload both your pptx and ppsx files so that your professor can check your transitions.

# Welcome to the Firm

BARB ASSELIN

# Computer Applications for Paralegals 113

## 2. Your Workspace

- Ensure that your workspace is suitable for your needs
  - Is the monitor at a good height?
  - Is the chair at a good height?
  - Advise us if you require an ergonomically-correct keyboard
  - Have the drawers in your desk been emptied?

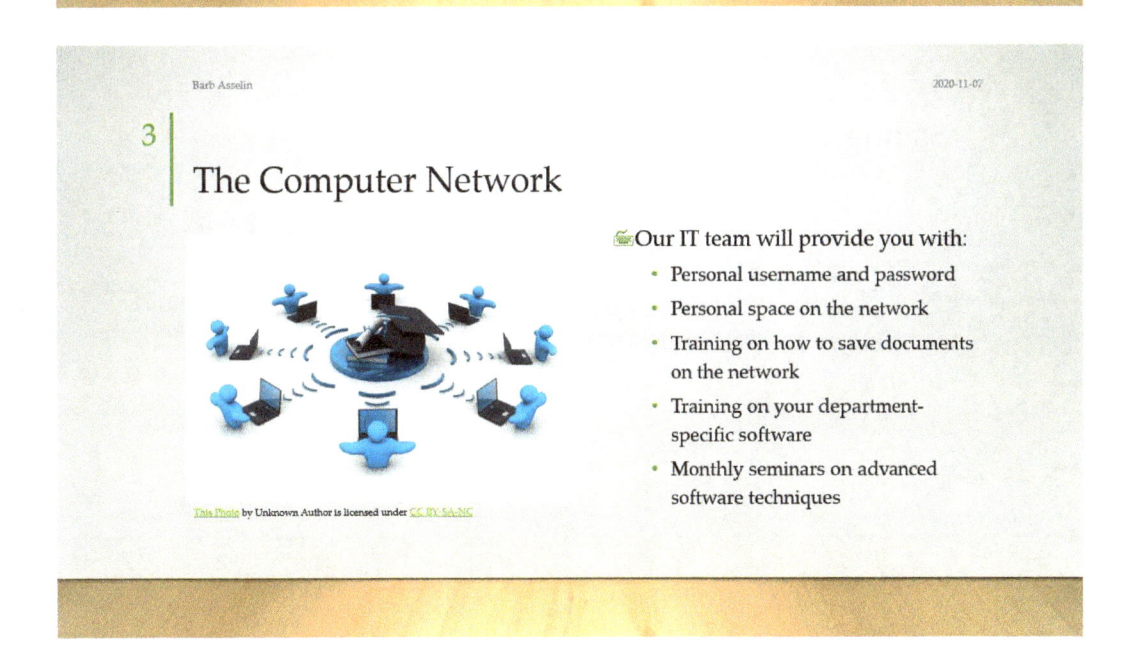

## 3. The Computer Network

- Our IT team will provide you with:
  - Personal username and password
  - Personal space on the network
  - Training on how to save documents on the network
  - Training on your department-specific software
  - Monthly seminars on advanced software techniques

This Photo by Unknown Author is licensed under CC BY-SA-NC

### Slide 4: What to Look Forward to

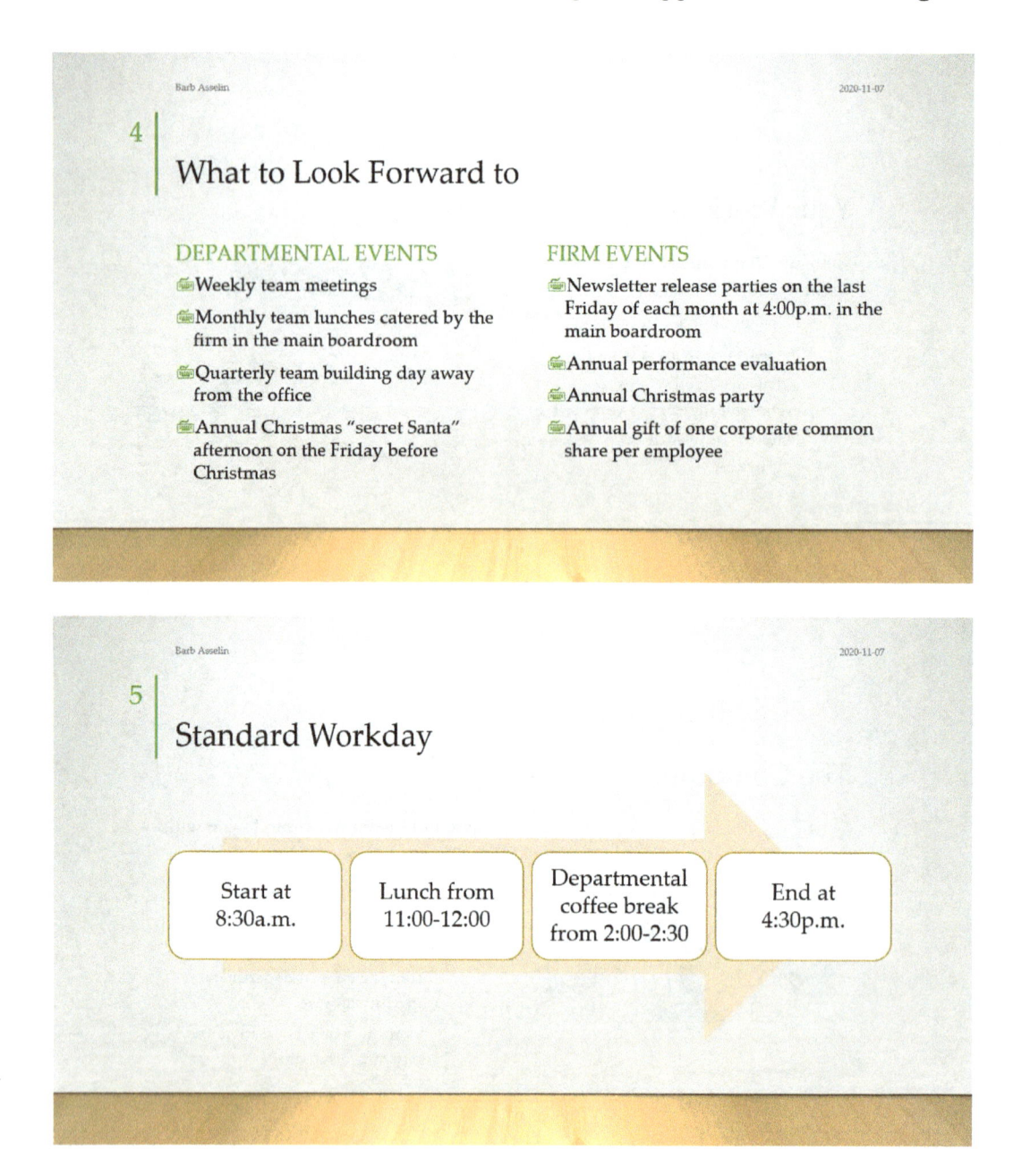

**DEPARTMENTAL EVENTS**
- Weekly team meetings
- Monthly team lunches catered by the firm in the main boardroom
- Quarterly team building day away from the office
- Annual Christmas "secret Santa" afternoon on the Friday before Christmas

**FIRM EVENTS**
- Newsletter release parties on the last Friday of each month at 4:00p.m. in the main boardroom
- Annual performance evaluation
- Annual Christmas party
- Annual gift of one corporate common share per employee

### Slide 5: Standard Workday

- Start at 8:30a.m.
- Lunch from 11:00-12:00
- Departmental coffee break from 2:00-2:30
- End at 4:30p.m.

## Exercise 4.5

Your firm would like to post a PowerPoint presentation on their website to attract new customers. They would like it to play like a video, but they don't have video software. Since you are a PowerPoint whiz, you have been asked to prepare the presentation that will be uploaded to the website. Create the following presentation using these instructions:

1. The design used is Crop. If you do not have access to the Crop design, please select another design of your choice.
2. Please add your name as author on the title slide.
3. Slide two uses the Step Up Process SmartArt graphic.
4. Add a video to slide three of a court case of your choice (the example uses Erin Brokovich). Increase the size of the video to fill the slide and set the video to play automatically.
5. Slide four uses the Lined List SmartArt graphic.
6. Add a different transition to each slide in your presentation and set each slide to advance automatically after one second.
7. Add a footer to the slides that includes your name, the date, and the slide number. Do not show on title slide.
8. Add a header and footer to the handouts that includes your name, the date, the page number, and the name of the firm.
9. Print your presentation as a handout with two slides per page.
10. Save your presentation as a pptx file.
11. Now save your presentation as a "show" (ppsx file).
12. Upload your ppsx file so that your professor can check your transitions and automation.

## We Work in the Following Areas of Law

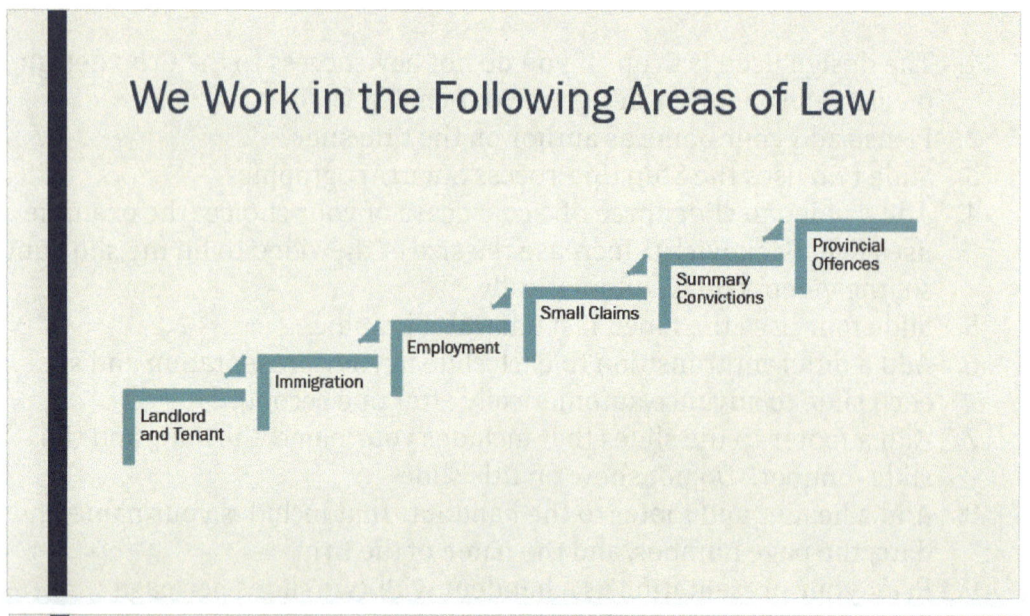

- Landlord and Tenant
- Immigration
- Employment
- Small Claims
- Summary Convictions
- Provincial Offences

## We Win Our Court Battles

## Our Team of Professionals

| | |
|---|---|
| Marc Bourque | 15 years of landlord and tenant experience |
| Margaret Childs | 10 years of small claims experience |
| Anna Bengali | 12 years of immigration law experience |
| Huili Chan | 8 years of employment law experience |
| Hassan Ahmad | 7 years of provincial offences experience |
| Victor Stanislov | 14 years of summary conviction experience |

31/07/2017   Barb Asselin

# Exercise 4.6

Your firm is hosting a seminar for the public in order to recruit some new landlord and tenant clients. They would like to provide information to potential clients interested in your services as either a landlord or a tenant. Since you are a PowerPoint expert, you have been asked to prepare the presentation that will be used in the seminar. Create the following presentation using these instructions:

1. The design used is Berlin. If you do not have access to the Berlin design, please select another design of your choice.
2. Please add your name as author on the title slide.
3. Change the first level bullet to a picture of a house using the slide master.
4. Add a graphic to slide two that you find by searching the word "team".
5. Add a different animation to each bullet point in slide two and set them to start after previous so that they happen automatically.
6. Slide three uses the Square Accent List SmartArt graphic.
7. Add a video to slide four that you find by searching YouTube for "landlord". Increase the size of the video to maximize it on the slide. Format the video so that it starts automatically.
8. Add a different transition to each slide in your presentation and set each slide to advance automatically after one second.

9. Add a footer to the slides that includes your name, the date, and the slide number. Do not show on title slide.
10. Add a header and footer to the handouts that includes your name, the date, the page number, and the name of the firm.
11. Print your presentation as a handout with two slides per page.
12. Save your presentation as a pptx file.
13. Now save your presentation as a "show" (ppsx file).
14. Upload your ppsx file so that your professor can check your transitions and automation.

## Things to Consider

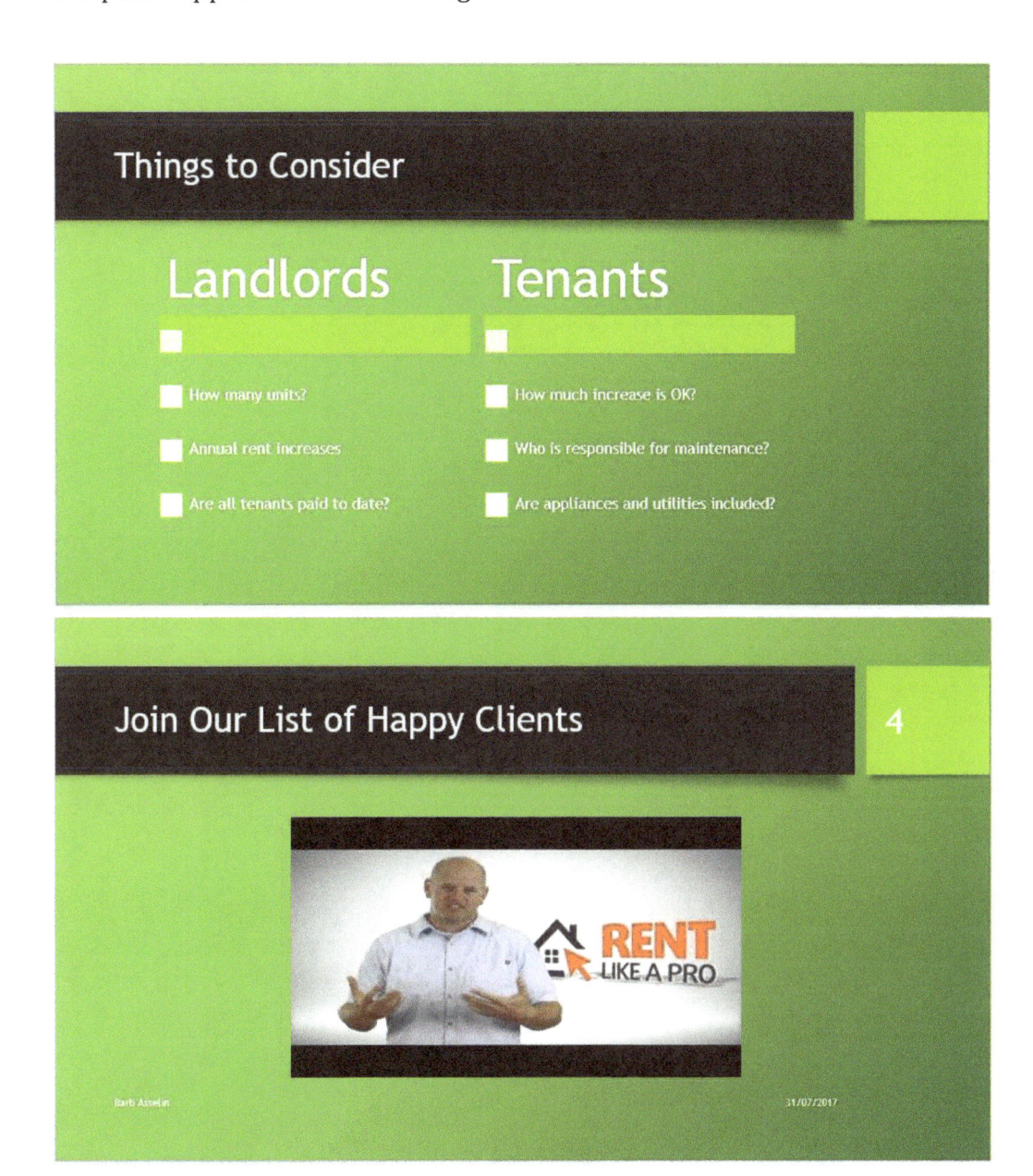

### Landlords
- How many units?
- Annual rent increases
- Are all tenants paid to date?

### Tenants
- How much increase is OK?
- Who is responsible for maintenance?
- Are appliances and utilities included?

## Join Our List of Happy Clients

Barb Asselin  31/07/2017

# Chapter 5: Excel

## Learning Outcomes

In this chapter, students will:

- Learn how to create a spreadsheet of data
- Manipulate their data through formulas
- Format their data for the workplace
- Use their data to create graphs and charts
- Perform a statistical analysis of their data
- Learn how functions work
- Answer questions about their data using pivot tables

## Overview

Excel is a powerful spreadsheet software that allows you to perform complex calculations, data analysis, and projections on large data sets with multiple variables. Spreadsheets can be linked to one another so that changes to the calculations on one spreadsheet will automatically affect the calculations in the linked spreadsheet.

## Creating a Spreadsheet

There is an instructional video for students on this topic at:
Webpage: http://www.asselingroup.com/paralegals
Password: paralegals

When you open up the program, you will see a blank spreadsheet that looks like a large table.

The software is set up similar to the other MS Office products we have covered so far. There is a ribbon at the top of the screen that changes as you click on different tabs at the top of the ribbon.

The grid in the main portion of the screen is divided up into cells. Each cell has a "name" based on letter and numbering systems. You will see that there are letters across the top of the grid and numbers along the left side of the grid. In the example, the cell A1 is selected. You can tell it is selected since it is outlined in green. The name or label A1 is shown in the address field above the A column. As you click on different cells, that cell's name or label will be shown in that same location.

At the bottom of the spreadsheet, you will see a tab with the name Sheet1. Beside that is a plus sign. One file can have many spreadsheets in it. To rename a sheet, right-click on the Sheet1 label and choose Rename. Then, type in the new name. Once you press ENTER, it will take effect.

If you click on the plus sign, you can open up a new spreadsheet, which you can then rename by right-clicking and renaming.

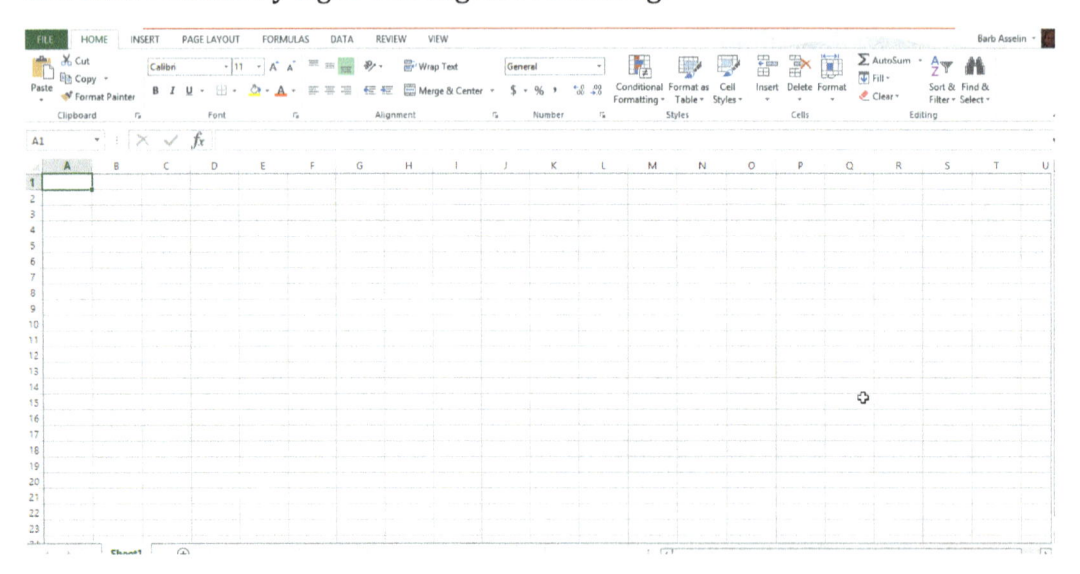

## Data

A cell can contain different types of data, such as:

- Names, addresses, postal codes, or other text combinations
- Numbers in the form of phone numbers, or fax numbers
- Numbers in the form of data such as total sales, legal fees, or disbursements, or
- Formulas that use data (numbers) in other fields to calculate solutions.

Computer Applications for Paralegals

The following example shows how you might keep track of clients and their contact information. This is an example of a data-only spreadsheet with no calculations.

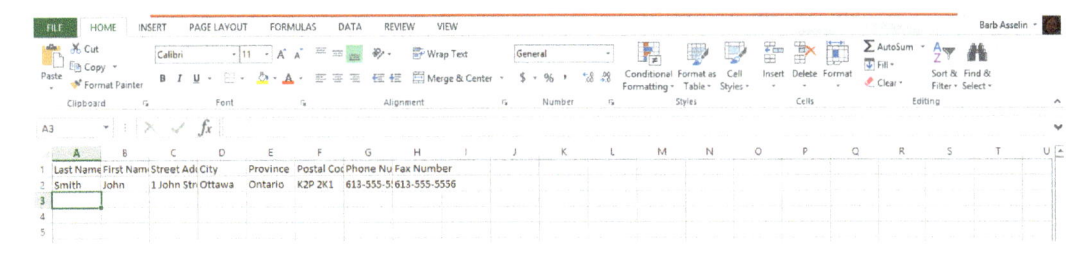

Notice how the cells are not wide enough for the information within them. Widen the columns using one of the following techniques:

- Widen each column individually by clicking on the line between the A and the B and dragging it to the correct width to widen the A column, or
- Click on the A to select the A column, then go to Home > Format > AutoFit Column Width.

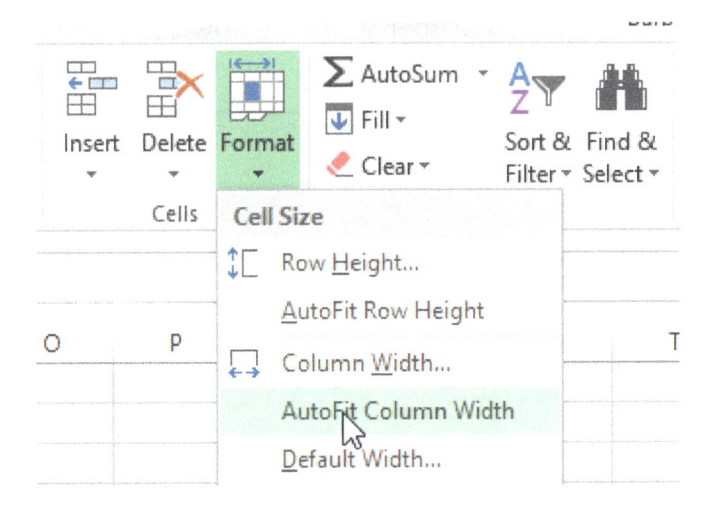

Continue with the rest of the columns until the data fits within each column. Now, your sample should look like this:

|   | A | B | C | D | E | F | G | H |
|---|---|---|---|---|---|---|---|---|
| 1 | Last Name | First Name | Street Address | City | Province | Postal Code | Phone Number | Fax Number |
| 2 | Smith | John | 1 John Street | Ottawa | Ontario | K2P 2K1 | 613-555-5555 | 613-555-5556 |
| 3 | | | | | | | | |
| 4 | | | | | | | | |

Next, let's create a spreadsheet with numbers and calculations. This example shows clients and the amount of their legal fees and disbursements.

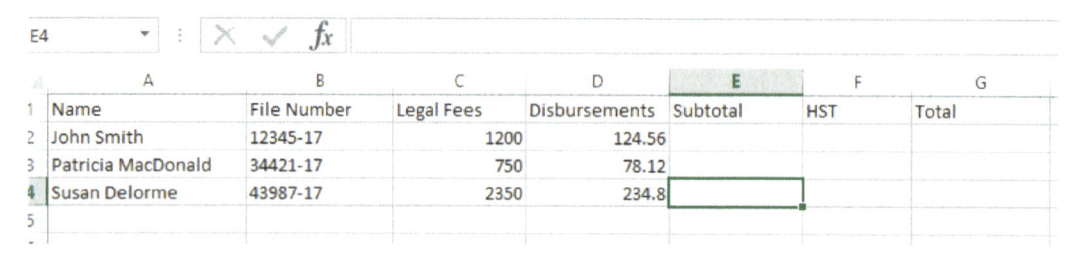

|   | A | B | C | D | E | F | G |
|---|---|---|---|---|---|---|---|
| 1 | Name | File Number | Legal Fees | Disbursements | Subtotal | HST | Total |
| 2 | John Smith | 12345-17 | 1200 | 124.56 | | | |
| 3 | Patricia MacDonald | 34421-17 | 750 | 78.12 | | | |
| 4 | Susan Delorme | 43987-17 | 2350 | 234.8 | | | |
| 5 | | | | | | | |

The numbers are not formatted properly as figures with a dollar sign and a decimal and two decimal points, so let's do that. First, select all of the fields that you would like to format properly. Notice how the following selection extends below the clients. That is because I will eventually total the columns.

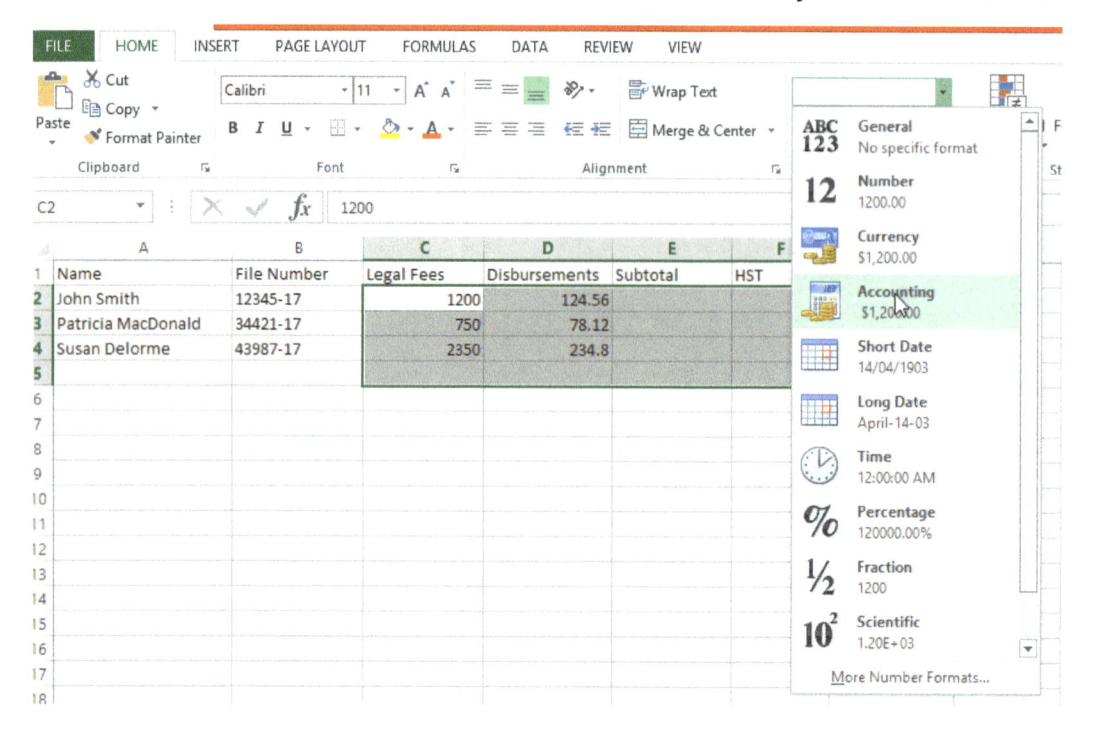

Computer Applications for Paralegals                                         125

Next, go to the Home tab and click on the drop-down box with General selected.  The drop-down menu will offer you additional options.  I have selected Accounting.

Now that our numbers are formatted properly, we will add some formulas.

# Formulas

There is an instructional video for students on this topic at:
Webpage:     http://www.asselingroup.com/paralegals
Password:    paralegals

## Basics

There are a few basics to know before creating a formula:

- Every formula starts with an equal sign
- Excel formulas follow the same order of operations as manual math or math with a calculator
- Basic math functions use the following symbols:

| Function | Excel Symbol |
|---|---|
| Add | + |
| Subtract | - |
| Multiply | * |
| Divide | / |

## Auto-Sum and Adding

The first formula we will look at is the sum of the Legal Fees and Disbursements in the example.  Take the following steps:

- Click in the John Smith Subtotal cell since that is where you want the answer to go
- Click on the AutoSum option in the Editing grouping of the Home tab

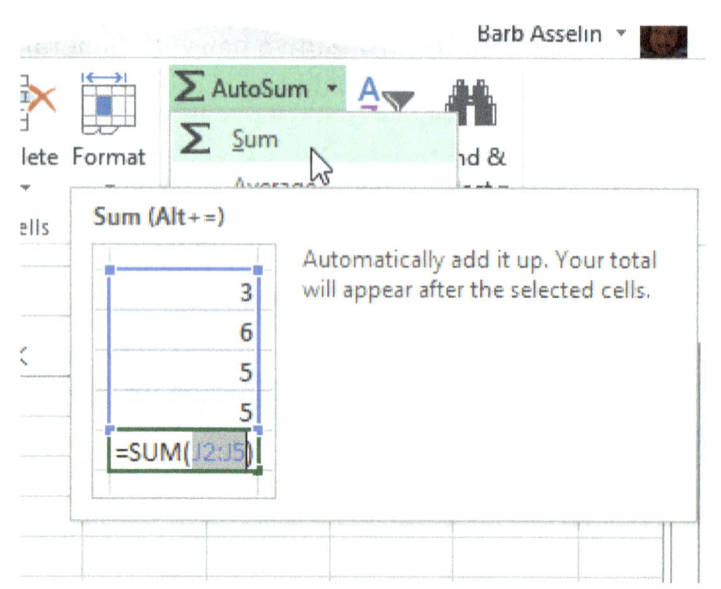

- Click on Sum and you will see the following happen on your spreadsheet:

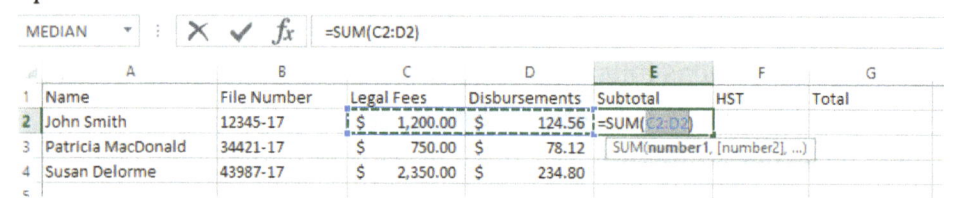

- The computer has anticipated your selection and it is correct so you can press ENTER and the answer will appear in the Subtotal field.

If the SUM function did not anticipate the correct selection of cells for you, simply click on the first cell of your selection and drag the mouse to the end of the correct selection.

## Anatomy of a Formula

If you look at the formula bar, which is signified by the "fx" above the columns B and C, you will see how Excel created a formula for this calculation:

- The formula starts with an equal sign
- The SUM is the name of the function used in this case
- The brackets indicate that a range of cells is going to be displayed for the SUM function to be applied to
- The C2 is the location of the first cell in the range to be added together

- The D2 is the location of the last cell in the range to be added together, and
- There is a colon between the first and the last cells in the range of cells that will be added together.

Where possible, it is a good idea to refer to cell locations instead of actual numbers. For example, the sample uses C2 instead of $1,200.00. That way, if the $1,200.00 in legal fees ever changes to another amount, the subtotal will automatically recalculate based on the new amount because you selected the cell itself instead of the number.

This example used the function SUM to add up the two amounts. There is another way to add two cells together. We could have used the following formula:

$$=C2+D2$$

That would have given us the same answer as the SUM function we used.

## Copying a Formula

There is an instructional video for students on this topic at:
Webpage: http://www.asselingroup.com/paralegals
Password: paralegals

Next, we need to do the same calculation for the other clients' subtotals. We only have three clients in our spreadsheet, however, there could be hundreds. Let's learn a "trick" for copying a formula to other cells. This will allow you to do the same calculation for all of the other entries in one action instead of doing them one at a time.

First, you should know the difference between Selecting and Copying. If you put your curser in the middle of a cell, you will see a wide, white plus sign. You can click and drag your curser to expand your selection of cells using this wide, white plus sign.

Alternatively, if you take your curser and place it at the bottom right of a cell where there is a small green square, then your curser will change to a small, black plus sign. If you click on the small, green square and drag the small, black plus sign to all of the other cells that you want to apply the same formatting or formula to, it will copy the formula to the other cells.

| E2 | ▼ | : | × | ✓ | fx | =SUM(C2:D2) |

|   | A | B | C | D | E | |
|---|---|---|---|---|---|---|
| 1 | Name | File Number | Legal Fees | Disbursements | Subtotal | HST |
| 2 | John Smith | 12345-17 | $ 1,200.00 | $ 124.56 | $ 1,324.56 | |
| 3 | Patricia MacDonald | 34421-17 | $ 750.00 | $ 78.12 | $ 828.12 | |
| 4 | Susan Delorme | 43987-17 | $ 2,350.00 | $ 234.80 | $ 2,584.80 | |
| 5 | | | | | | |

You can double-check to see if the formula was copied correctly by checking the formula in one of the new subtotal fields.

| E4 | ▼ | : | × | ✓ | fx | =SUM(C4:D4) |

|   | A | B | C | D | E |
|---|---|---|---|---|---|
| 1 | Name | File Number | Legal Fees | Disbursements | Subtotal |
| 2 | John Smith | 12345-17 | $ 1,200.00 | $ 124.56 | $ 1,324.56 |
| 3 | Patricia MacDonald | 34421-17 | $ 750.00 | $ 78.12 | $ 828.12 |
| 4 | Susan Delorme | 43987-17 | $ 2,350.00 | $ 234.80 | $ 2,584.80 |

This example shows that Susan Delorme's Subtotal is taken from the sum of the range of cells between C4 and D4. So, the copying function worked. It copied the formula down from John Smith to the other clients and it also changed the cell references to accommodate the new line of information for each client.

## Calculating Tax

The next step is to calculate HST on the subtotal. In Ontario, HST is 13%. Note that HST is charged on disbursements such as photocopies and faxes, however, it is usually already included in disbursements such as filing fees. For this exercise, we will assume that all of the disbursements require HST to be added. To calculate HST, follow these steps:

- Click in the cell where you want the answer to go
- Start with an equal sign
- Click in the cell of the amount that you want to apply tax to

Computer Applications for Paralegals                                              129

- Add a multiply symbol, which is the asterisks
- Add the amount of tax, and
- Press ENTER.

| | A | B | C | D | E | F | G |
|---|---|---|---|---|---|---|---|
| | | | | | | F2  fx =E2*0.13 | |
| 1 | Name | File Number | Legal Fees | Disbursements | Subtotal | HST | Total |
| 2 | John Smith | 12345-17 | $ 1,200.00 | $ 124.56 | $ 1,324.56 | $ 172.19 | |
| 3 | Patricia MacDonald | 34421-17 | $ 750.00 | $ 78.12 | $ 828.12 | | |
| 4 | Susan Delorme | 43987-17 | $ 2,350.00 | $ 234.80 | $ 2,584.80 | | |

You can check your formula against mine as it is shown in the formula bar above. Now, you can copy the formula to the other clients' subtotals by using your copying "trick".

The next step is to calculate the total of what each client owes us. To do that, we will have to add the Subtotal with the HST. You can do this calculation one of two ways:

- =E2+F2, or
- =SUM(E2:F2).

Finally, you can copy your formula to the other clients.

| | A | B | C | D | E | F | G |
|---|---|---|---|---|---|---|---|
| 1 | Name | File Number | Legal Fees | Disbursements | Subtotal | HST | Total |
| 2 | John Smith | 12345-17 | $ 1,200.00 | $ 124.56 | $ 1,324.56 | $ 172.19 | $ 1,496.75 |
| 3 | Patricia MacDonald | 34421-17 | $ 750.00 | $ 78.12 | $ 828.12 | $ 107.66 | $ 935.78 |
| 4 | Susan Delorme | 43987-17 | $ 2,350.00 | $ 234.80 | $ 2,584.80 | $ 336.02 | $ 2,920.82 |

## Totaling Columns and Rows

When creating a spreadsheet, it is usually useful to total the columns and the rows. We have already totaled the end of each row. Now, we should total the columns. Let's add a total row under the Susan Delorme row and use the SUM function to total each column.

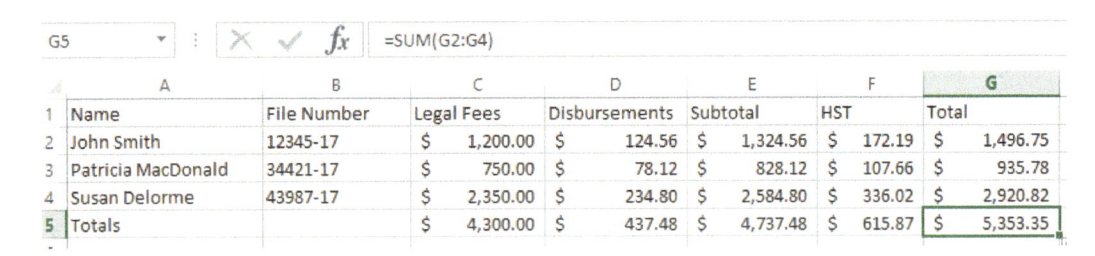

| | A | B | C | D | E | F | G |
|---|---|---|---|---|---|---|---|
| | | | | | | G5  fx =SUM(G2:G4) | |
| 1 | Name | File Number | Legal Fees | Disbursements | Subtotal | HST | Total |
| 2 | John Smith | 12345-17 | $ 1,200.00 | $ 124.56 | $ 1,324.56 | $ 172.19 | $ 1,496.75 |
| 3 | Patricia MacDonald | 34421-17 | $ 750.00 | $ 78.12 | $ 828.12 | $ 107.66 | $ 935.78 |
| 4 | Susan Delorme | 43987-17 | $ 2,350.00 | $ 234.80 | $ 2,584.80 | $ 336.02 | $ 2,920.82 |
| 5 | Totals | | $ 4,300.00 | $ 437.48 | $ 4,737.48 | $ 615.87 | $ 5,353.35 |

# Formatting

There is an instructional video for students on this topic at:
Webpage:   http://www.asselingroup.com/paralegals
Password:   paralegals

Now that we have a small spreadsheet, we can pretty it up with some formatting.

## Adding Rows and Columns

Let's add a title row to this spreadsheet. Click in the first row of information and go to Home > Insert > Sheet Row.

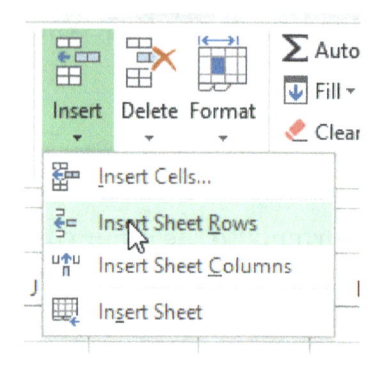

Now, we can add a title. I have added the title **Monthly Client Totals**.

It's nice for the title to be centered on the spreadsheet. To center your title, click in the title cell, then go to Home > Merge & Center.

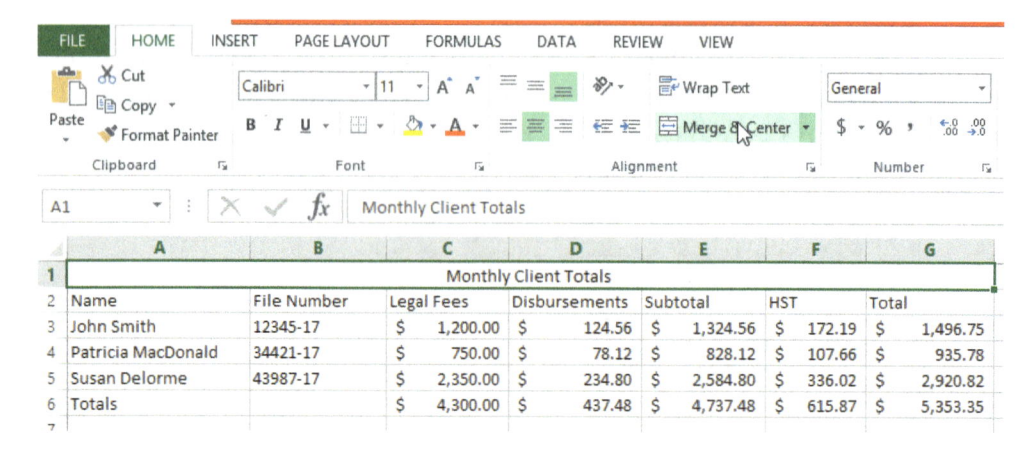

# Computer Applications for Paralegals 131

## Borders

To add borders to your spreadsheet, take the following steps:

- Select the portion of cells you want to add borders to
- Go to Home > Font Grouping and click on the arrow beside the border icon, and
- Select All Borders.

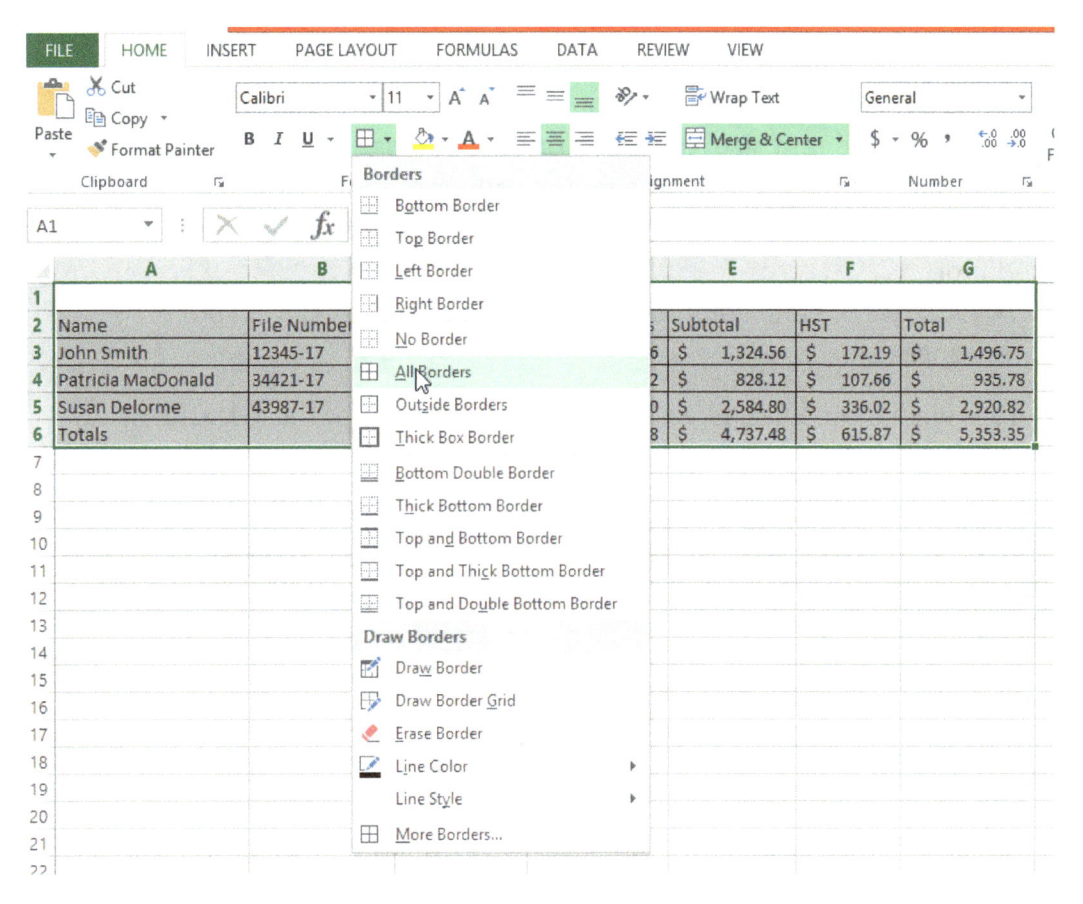

As you can see, there are all types of borders that you can add. One I often use is the Thick Box Border. Try it and see how it looks.

## Shading and Fonts

The font grouping on the Home tab gives you a number of options for formatting the data in your spreadsheet.

You can dress your spreadsheet up further by adding some of the following features:

- Bold and/or italics to the title or the headings
- Increased font size to the title or the headings
- Change the font type for some of your spreadsheet
- Change the background color of some of the cells of your spreadsheet, or
- Change the font color of the text in some of the cells of your spreadsheet.

Here is what mine looks like after I have added some of these features. Experiment with some of the features on the Home tab to see what you like.

| Name | File Number | Legal Fees | Disbursements | Subtotal | HST | Total |
|---|---|---|---|---|---|---|
| \multicolumn{7}{c}{Monthly Client Totals} |
| John Smith | 12345-17 | $ 1,200.00 | $ 124.56 | $ 1,324.56 | $ 172.19 | $ 1,496.75 |
| Patricia MacDonald | 34421-17 | $ 750.00 | $ 78.12 | $ 828.12 | $ 107.66 | $ 935.78 |
| Susan Delorme | 43987-17 | $ 2,350.00 | $ 234.80 | $ 2,584.80 | $ 336.02 | $ 2,920.82 |
| Totals | | $ 4,300.00 | $ 437.48 | $ 4,737.48 | $ 615.87 | $ 5,353.35 |

# Tables

There is an instructional video for students on this topic at:
Webpage:    http://www.asselingroup.com/paralegals
Password:   paralegals

Alternatively, you can use Excel's pre-set designs to add structure and color to your data by formatting your data as a table.

To start, we will need to remove the existing formatting elements from our data by going to the Editing grouping on the Home tab and clicking on the Clear chevron and then choosing Clear Formats.

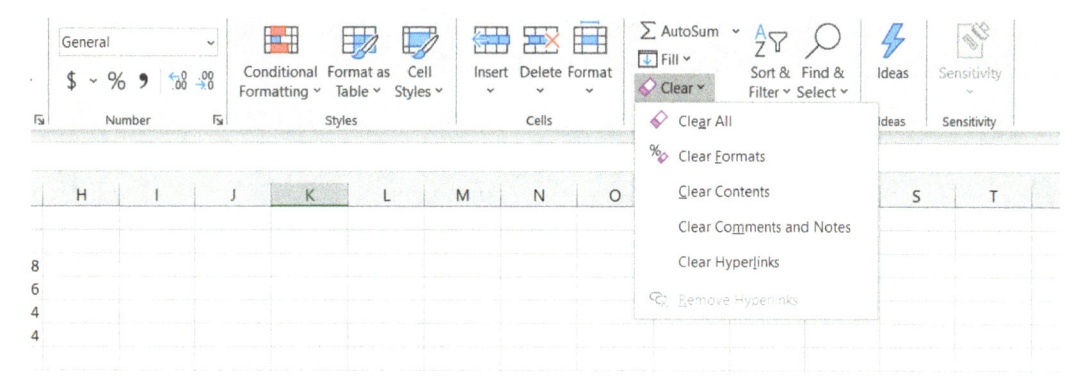

# Computer Applications for Paralegals                                               133

This will remove the borders and shading that were previously added.

Note that it will also remove the number formatting, so be sure to apply the Accounting formatting to those numbers that represent dollar amounts, if you wish.

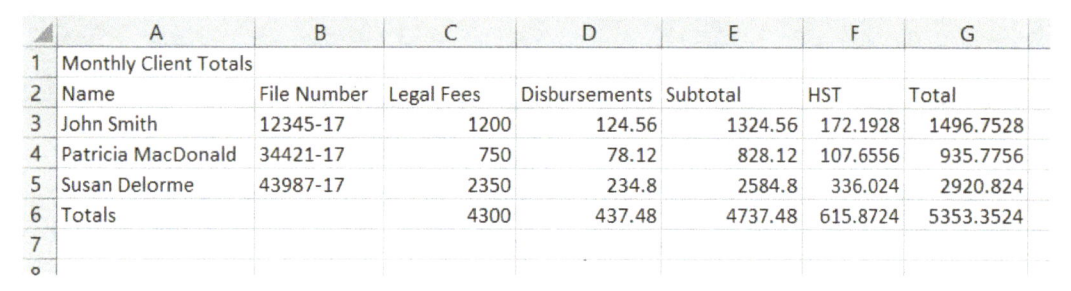

|   | A | B | C | D | E | F | G |
|---|---|---|---|---|---|---|---|
| 1 | Monthly Client Totals | | | | | | |
| 2 | Name | File Number | Legal Fees | Disbursements | Subtotal | HST | Total |
| 3 | John Smith | 12345-17 | 1200 | 124.56 | 1324.56 | 172.1928 | 1496.7528 |
| 4 | Patricia MacDonald | 34421-17 | 750 | 78.12 | 828.12 | 107.6556 | 935.7756 |
| 5 | Susan Delorme | 43987-17 | 2350 | 234.8 | 2584.8 | 336.024 | 2920.824 |
| 6 | Totals | | 4300 | 437.48 | 4737.48 | 615.8724 | 5353.3524 |
| 7 | | | | | | | |

Now, select the data that you would like to apply a table style, go to the Home tab, and click on the Format as Table option in the Styles grouping.

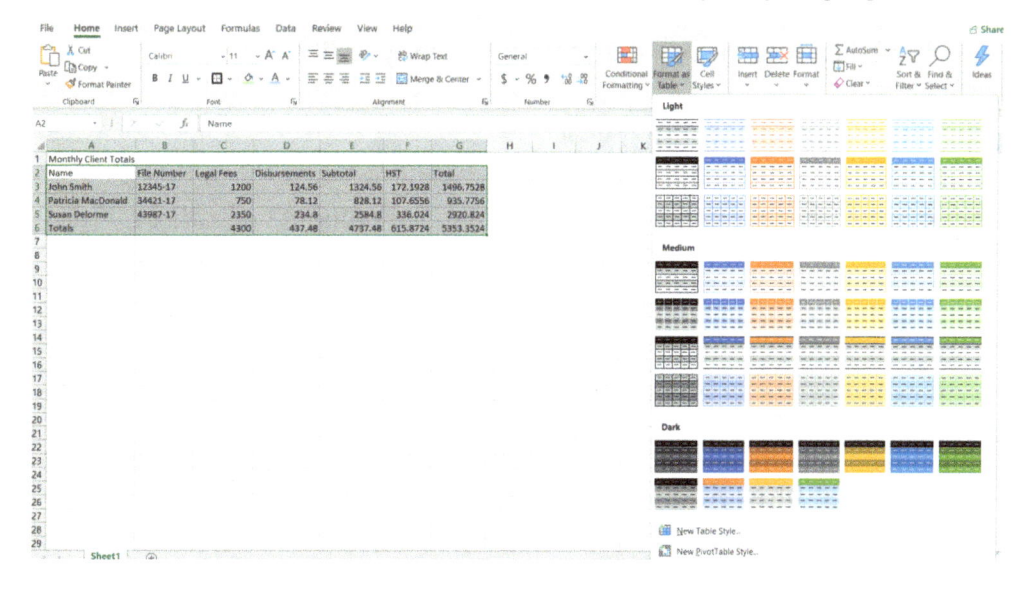

Choose an option that you like from the options available. I have chosen the second last option in the first row of the Dark section.

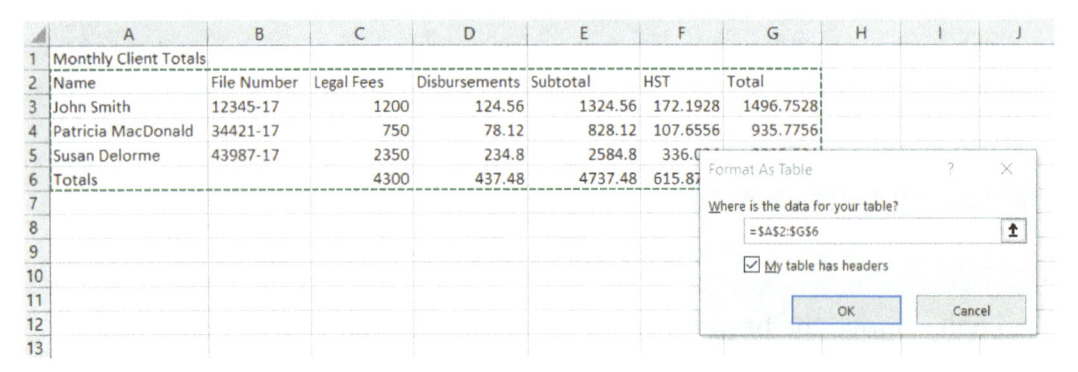

You will then see a dialogue box asking you to confirm the location of the data for your table. If your data has headers, make sure you check the "My data has headers" checkbox. Then, click OK.

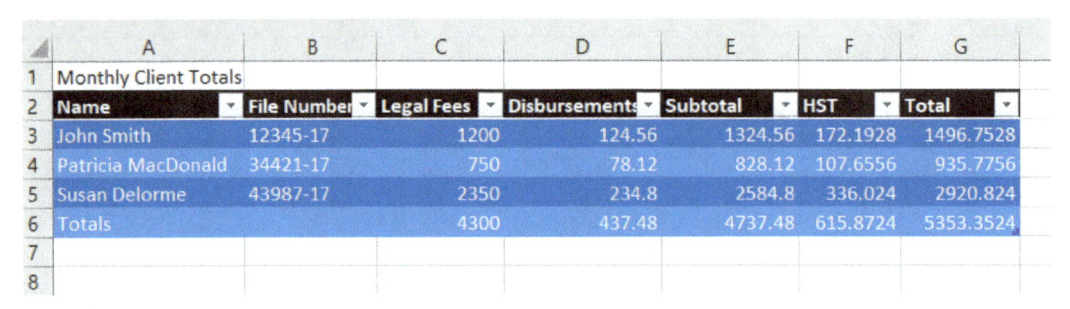

Now you can format the title as you see fit. By not choosing the title to be part of your table, you can now use the drop-down arrows to the right of each column heading to sort your data however you like.

## Sorting and Filtering

There is an instructional video for students on this topic at:
Webpage: http://www.asselingroup.com/paralegals
Password: paralegals

Excel allows you to sort and filter your data so that you can view it in more meaningful ways.

You can sort and filter your data in many ways. The first way is from the Home tab by clicking on the Sort & Filter option in the Editing grouping.

# Computer Applications for Paralegals

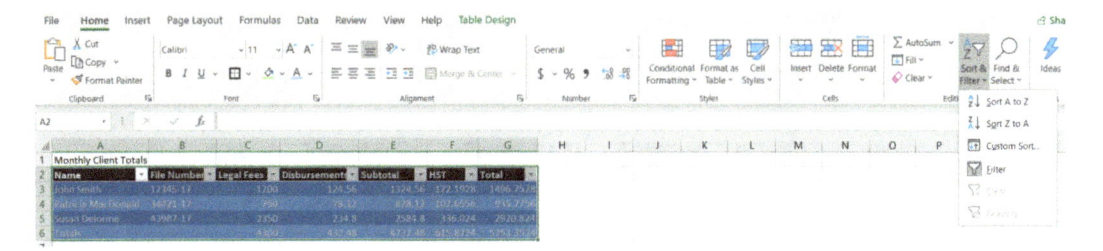

The second way is from the Data tab by clicking on either Sort or Filter in the Sort & Filter grouping.

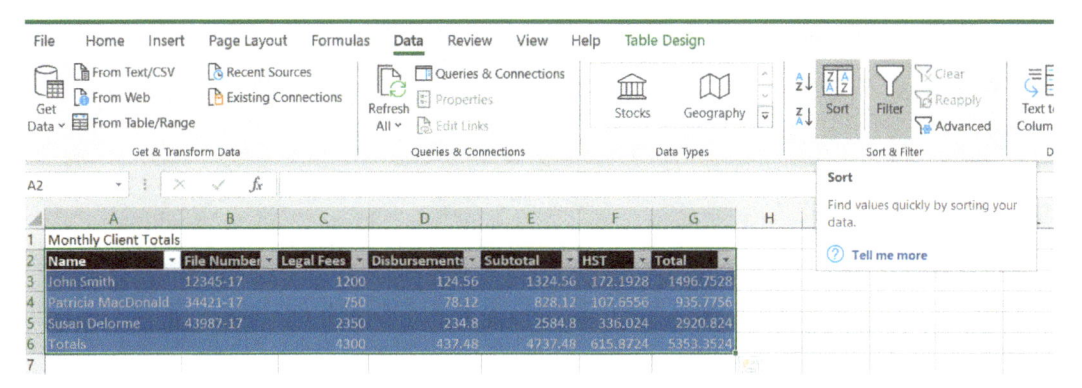

A third way to sort data is to use the drop-down arrows at the right edge of each item in the header row of a formatted table.

In this example, I might want to sort my data alphabetically by client's first name.

To do so, I would click on the drop-down arrow at the right edge of the Name header. You can see from the following image that I have some options to choose from. I can choose to sort alphabetically from A-Z, or in reverse from Z-A, or by color. I can choose A-Z to sort my client alphabetically, however, one of my rows of data is not the name of a client. It is the word "Totals".

Be sure to uncheck the box beside "Totals" so that row does not get alphabetized along with the others.

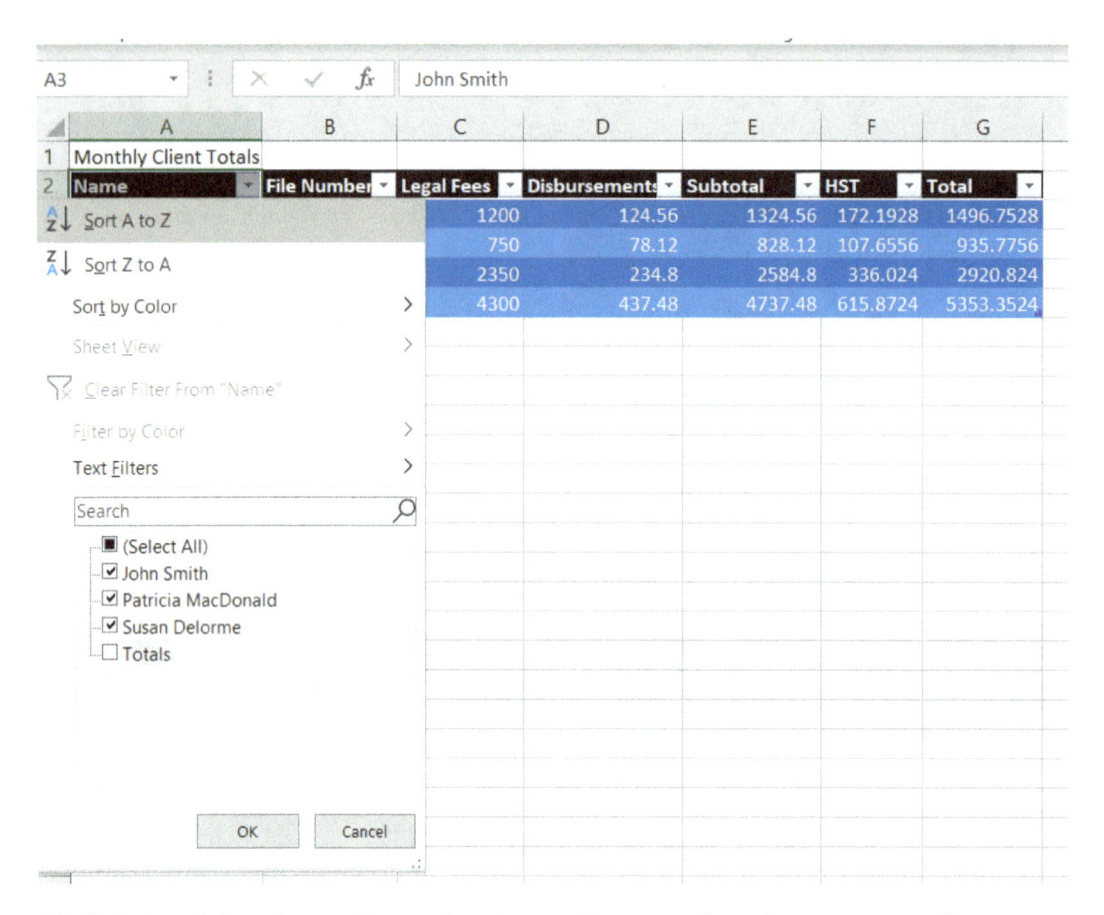

Click OK and the data will sort by client. You can also choose to sort by any other column heading. For example, try sorting by Legal Fees from smallest to largest.

Notice that all the data in each row associated with each client gets moved to the newly sorted order.

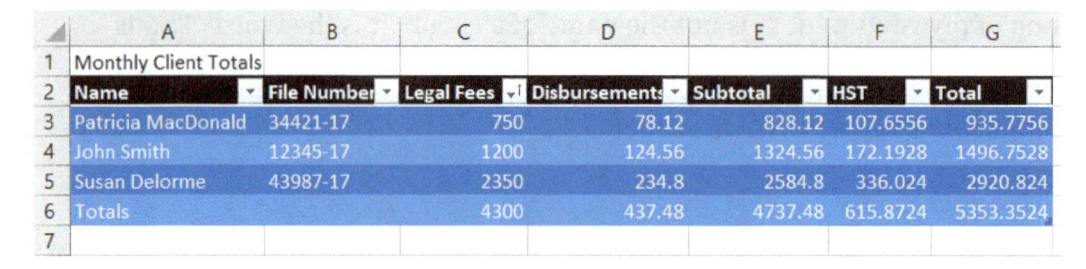

Now convert your table back to a normal range instead of a formatted table so that you can try sorting using the other options.

# Computer Applications for Paralegals 137

To convert your table back to a normal range, simply select the data of your formatted table, right-click in the selected cells, and choose Table > Convert to Range.

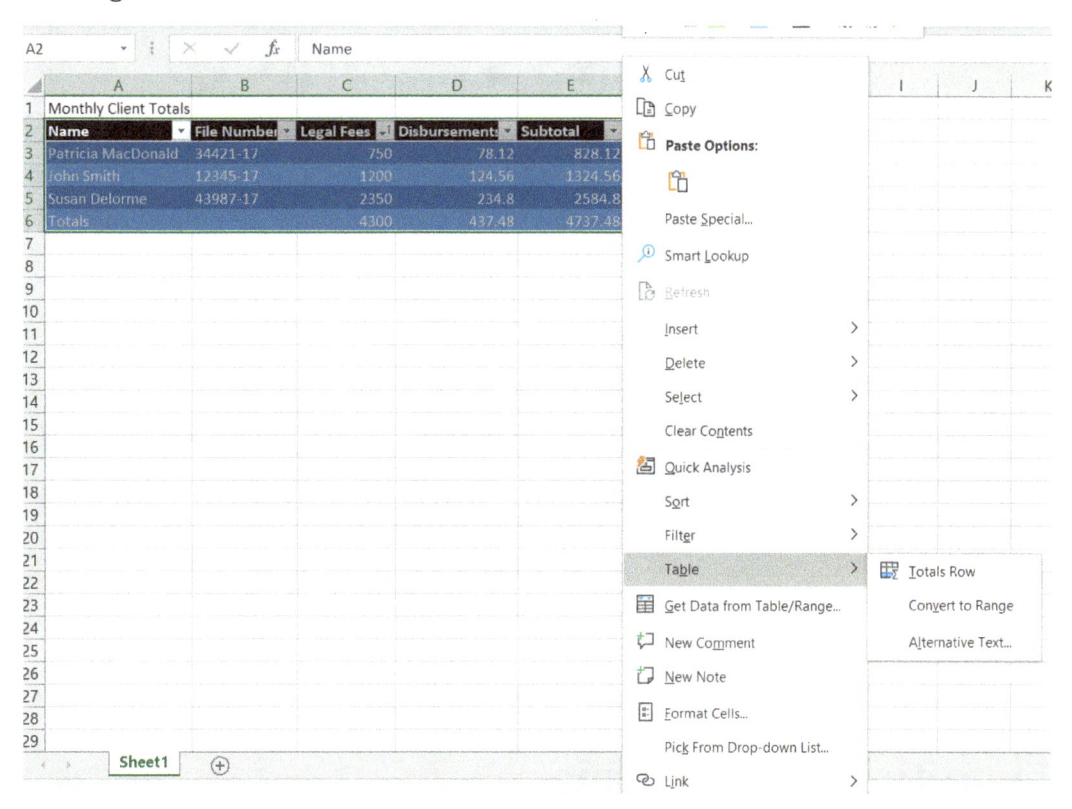

Choose Yes at the net dialogue box.

You will find that your data still has the table design you chose, but the drop-down arrows have disappeared.

Now try sorting using the Sort & Filter option on the Home tab.

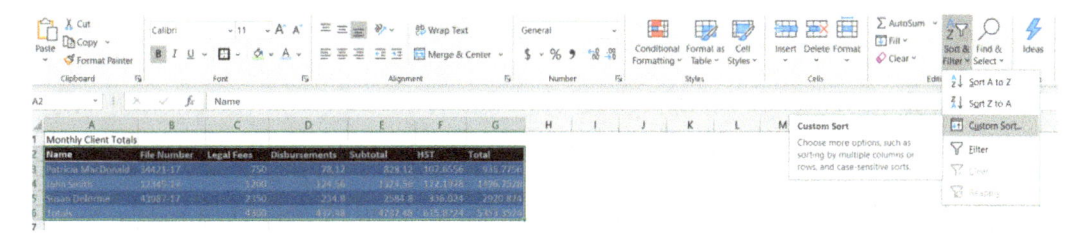

First, select the data in your table (not your title) and click on Sort & Filter. Then, click on Custom Sort.

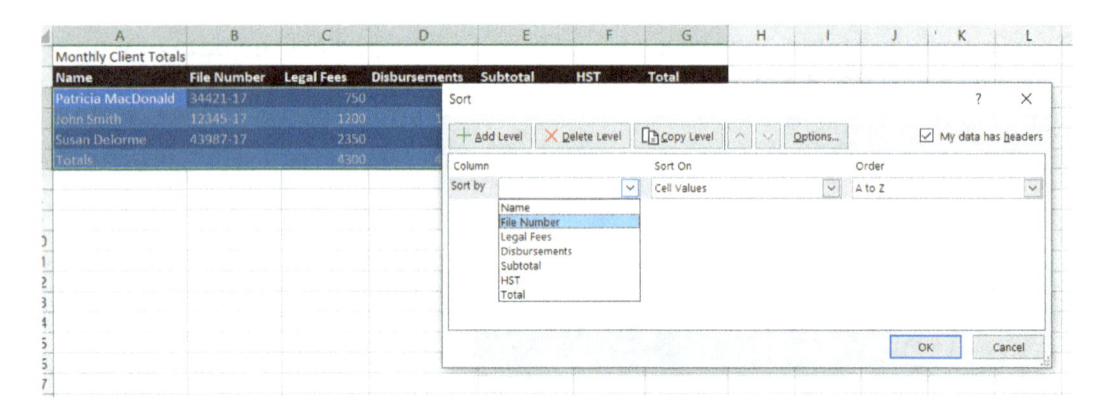

This time, sort by File Number in ascending order (A-Z). You will see that your data now has the numbers in numerical order.

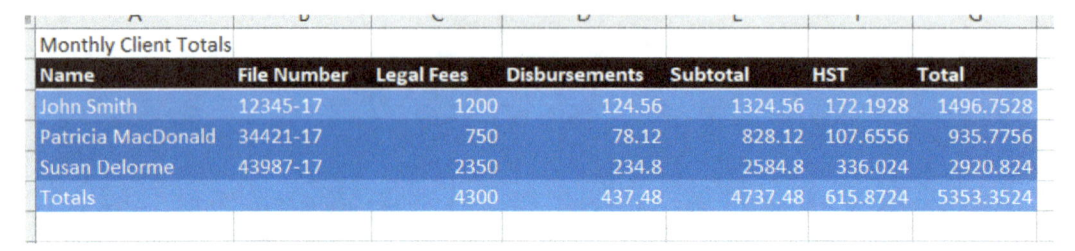

If you select your data and go to the Data tab and click on the Sort button, the same Sort dialogue box will pop up for you to choose File Number from A-Z.

# Conditional Formatting

There is an instructional video for students on this topic at:
Webpage: http://www.asselingroup.com/paralegals
Password: paralegals

Now, let's look at what conditional formatting is and why we would want to apply it to our data.

The example we have been using is a very small dataset of three clients. You could easily have hundreds or thousands of clients in a law firm.

Let's say that your law firm sends out bills every month to clients with outstanding legal fees of at least $1,000.00. We can use conditional formatting with our data to highlight any client with legal fees over $1,000.00. It will be much faster than scrolling through hundreds or thousands of entries and noting which ones are over $1,000.00.

Computer Applications for Paralegals 139

Start by selecting the Legal Fees column. Then, click on Conditional Formatting on the Home tab.

You'll see that there are a number of options of Conditional Formatting. You can choose:

- Highlight Cell Rules
- Top/Bottom Rules
- Data Bars
- Color Scales
- Icon Sets

There are also options at the bottom of the list for new rules, clearing rules, and managing rules.

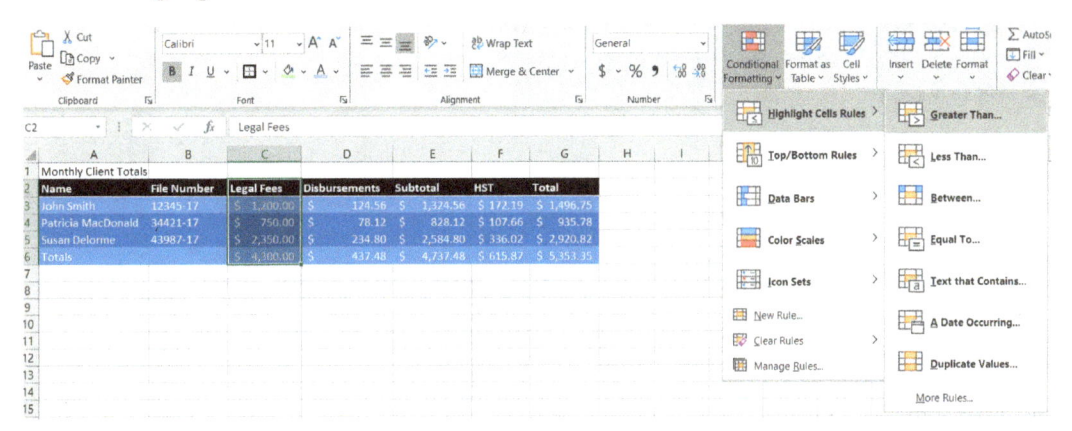

You are going to expand the Highlight Cell Rules and then click on the Greater Than option. Type $1,000.00 in the first field and select a color scheme from the drop-down menu. Then, click OK.

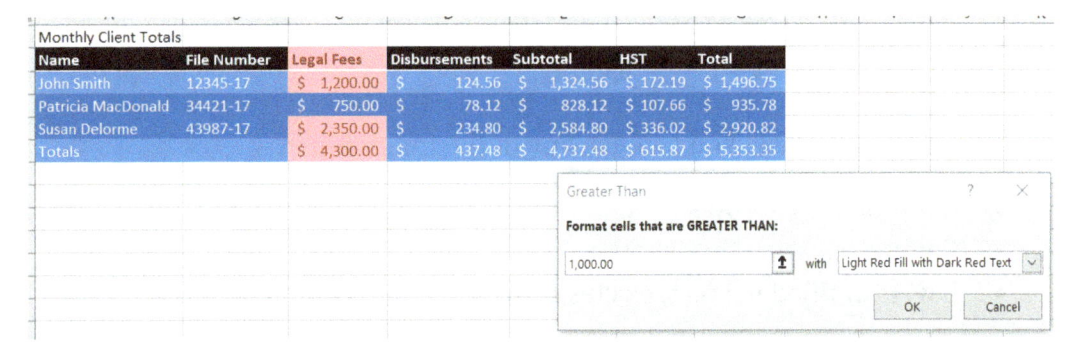

You will see that the Legal Fees column has now identified which clients have legal fees over $1,000.00. This could be used to generate a list of clients who will be billed this month by you or an assistant.

There are lots of choices available to you for conditional formatting, as noted above, which may seem overwhelming. Try playing around with your data and some of the other options to see how they are represented visually.

For example, try applying the Orange Data Bars to the Disbursements column.

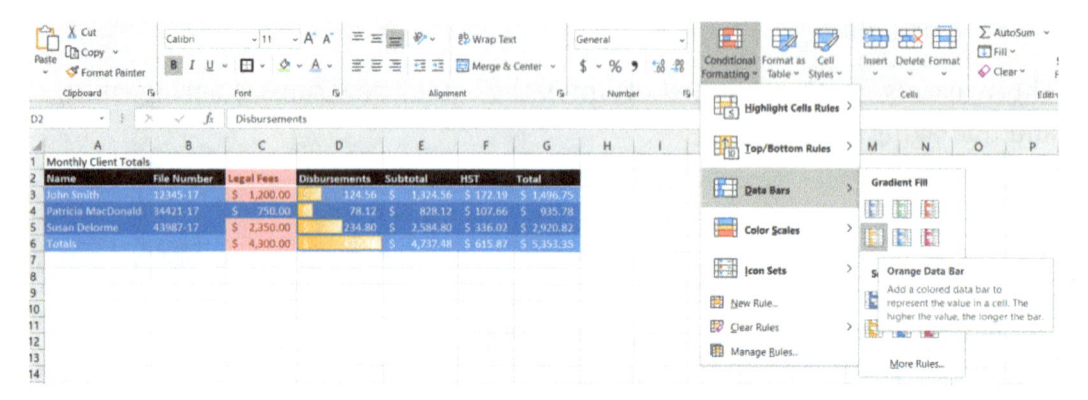

You will see that the cells in the Disbursements column now have gradient orange bars that visually indicate how much money has been spent in disbursements for each client.

Try a third one. This time select the Total column and apply one of the Icon Sets to your data. You will see that there are lots of options of icons. They generally mean:

- Low (red)
- Medium (yellow)
- High (green)

The choices are varied. You can use any of the following:

- Color or gray arrows
- Color circles or other shapes
- Levels of filled in stars, circles, squares, and column graph symbols

Computer Applications for Paralegals 141

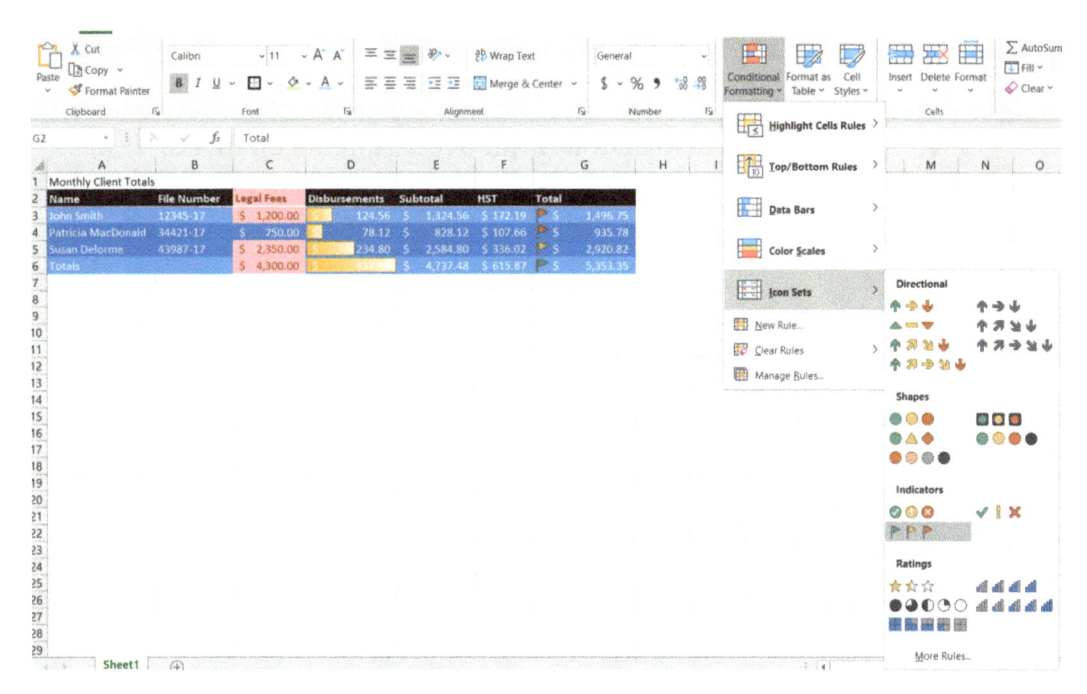

Now that you've had a chance to play around a bit with Conditional Formatting, use the Manage Rules options to delete the ones you no longer want. By selecting your entire table and choosing Manage Rules, you will see all three of the rules you just created. You can click on any one you like and then click Delete Rule.

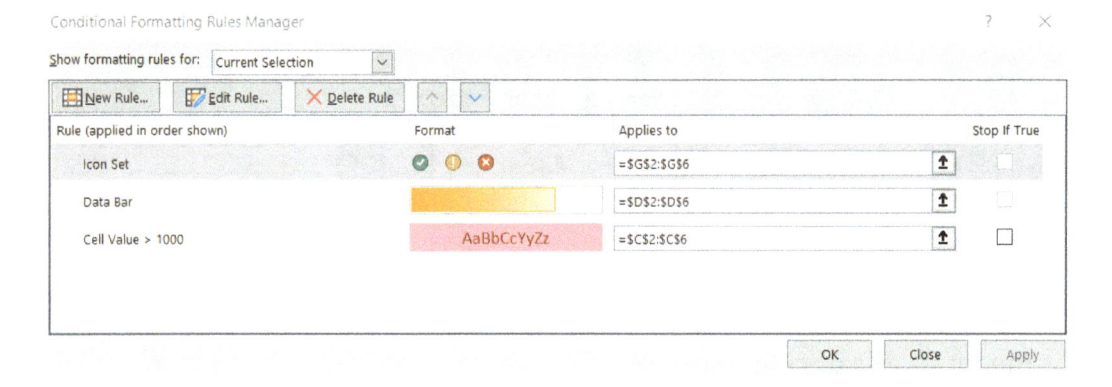

Alternatively, you can use the Clear Rules option to delete them all at once.

# Charts

There is an instructional video for students on this topic at:
Webpage: http://www.asselingroup.com/paralegals
Password: paralegals

Excel has a variety of charts that can be used to gain a better understanding of the data contained in a spreadsheet.

Charts are used to take numerical data and show relationships and trends that are only visible with either a deep analysis of the raw data, or using a visual representation such as a line chart, a bar chart, a scatter graph, or a pie chart, to name a few.

Until you have some experience creating charts, it can be overwhelming to decide which type of chart will give a meaningful representation of your data. Try experimenting with some of the charts available to you with different sets of data, to see which ones you like best. It may take some trial and error, but it will give you a good idea of where to start the next time you want to create a chart.

To create a chart from the data we have been using in this chapter so far, first select the data that you would like to create a chart with.

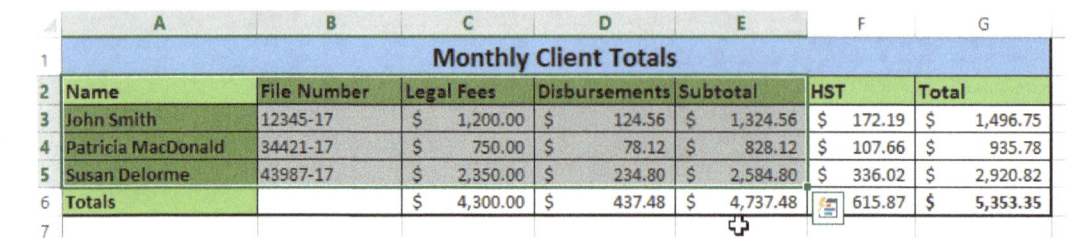

|   | A | B | C | D | E | F | G |
|---|---|---|---|---|---|---|---|
| 1 | Monthly Client Totals ||||||||
| 2 | Name | File Number | Legal Fees | Disbursements | Subtotal | HST | Total |
| 3 | John Smith | 12345-17 | $ 1,200.00 | $ 124.56 | $ 1,324.56 | $ 172.19 | $ 1,496.75 |
| 4 | Patricia MacDonald | 34421-17 | $ 750.00 | $ 78.12 | $ 828.12 | $ 107.66 | $ 935.78 |
| 5 | Susan Delorme | 43987-17 | $ 2,350.00 | $ 234.80 | $ 2,584.80 | $ 336.02 | $ 2,920.82 |
| 6 | Totals | | $ 4,300.00 | $ 437.48 | $ 4,737.48 | $ 615.87 | $ 5,353.35 |
| 7 | | | | | | | |

Notice that I have selected some of my data, but not the title and not the HST or the total rows or column.

Next, go to Insert > Charts and choose a chart from the Charts grouping.

Computer Applications for Paralegals                                           143

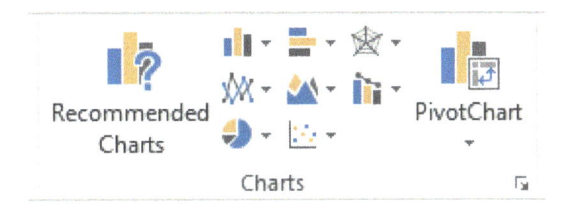

Often, you will get a good idea of what type of chart would best display your selected data by clicking on Recommended Charts. By clicking on Recommended Charts, you will get the dialogue box that follows.

It will show you the best options. Scroll through the options and click on each one to see how your information is displayed.

Pick the one you like best, click on it, and then click OK.

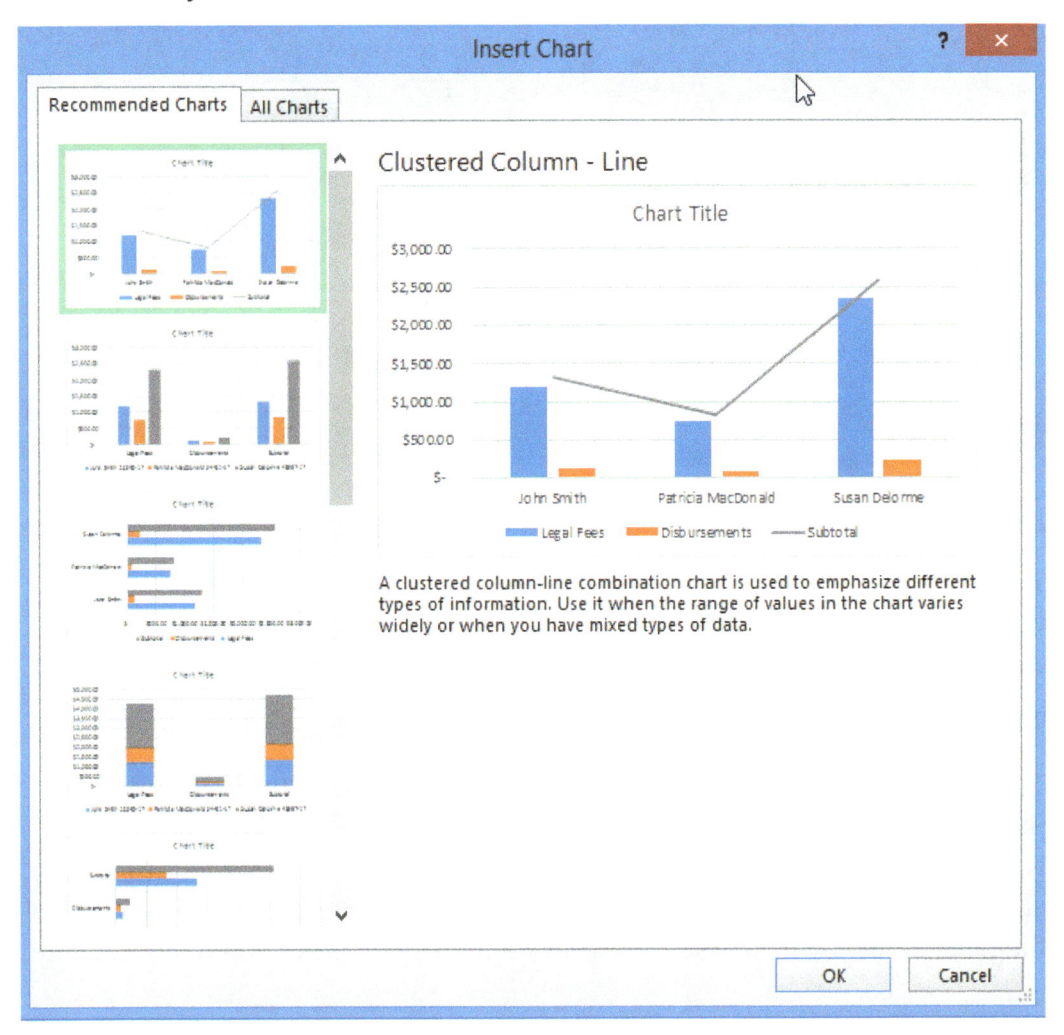

I chose the Stacked Bar chart.  Note the following:

- The chart appeared on my screen right in the middle, even though it is on top of some of my data
- The chart has no title, even though there is a spot for a title
- My dataset has different sections outlined in different colors:
    - The legend items are outlined in red
    - The Y axis labels are outlined in purple, and
    - The data itself is outlined in blue.

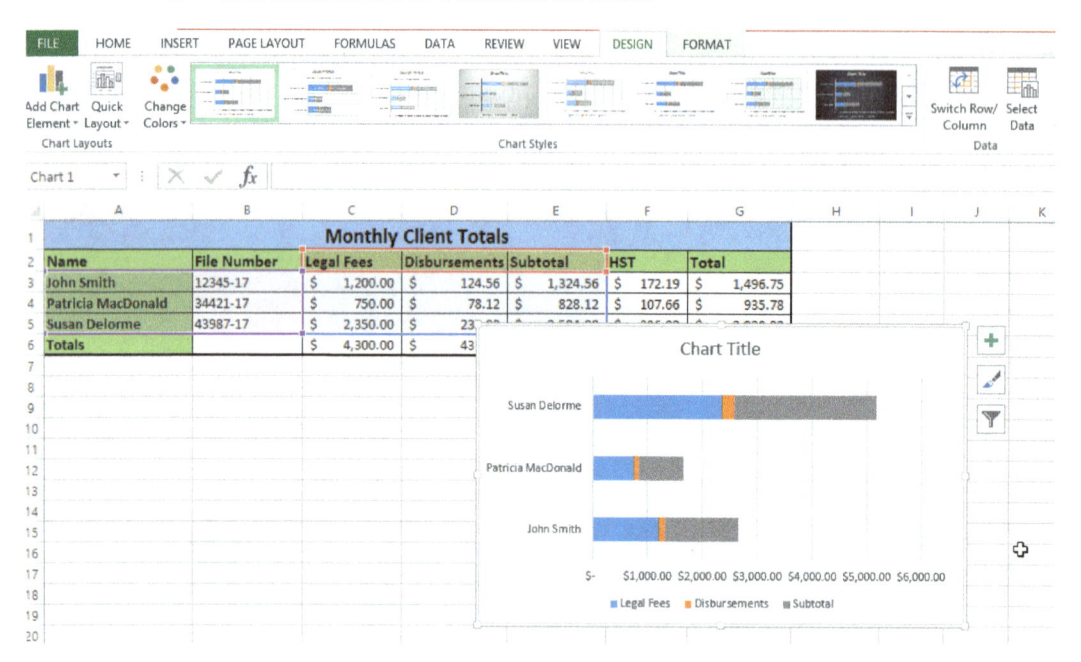

I like this chart, but there are a few things I'd like to change about it.

To move the chart out of the way of the data, click anywhere on the chart where you see a four-way arrow by your curser, and click and drag your chart to a spot that is not covering up your data.

To change the title, click in the chart title textbox and type a relevant title.

The Y axis on this chart only shows the names of my clients, however, the purple selection in my data covers both the names and the file numbers.  If I want to change that selection so that it only contains the client names, I can click on any of the four purple corner squares and, when I see a two-way diagonal arrow by my curser, I can click and drag the selection to not include

Computer Applications for Paralegals                                    145

the file numbers. Or I can hide the File Number column (see later on in this chapter for Show/Hide instructions).

The green + sign at the right of your chart allows you to add or subtract or control the location of different elements such as the title and the legend.

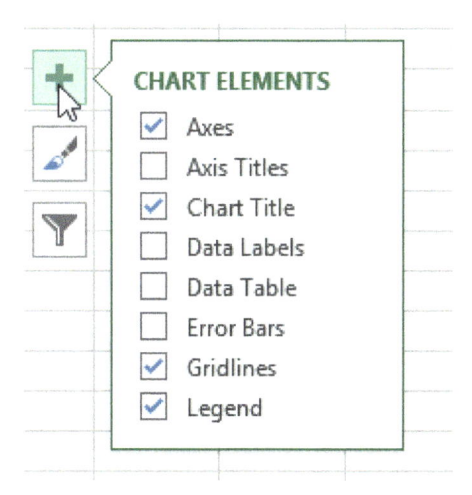

**CHART ELEMENTS**
- ☑ Axes
- ☐ Axis Titles
- ☑ Chart Title
- ☐ Data Labels
- ☐ Data Table
- ☐ Error Bars
- ☑ Gridlines
- ☑ Legend

The paint brush to the right of your chart allows you to choose different styles and color schemes for your chart.

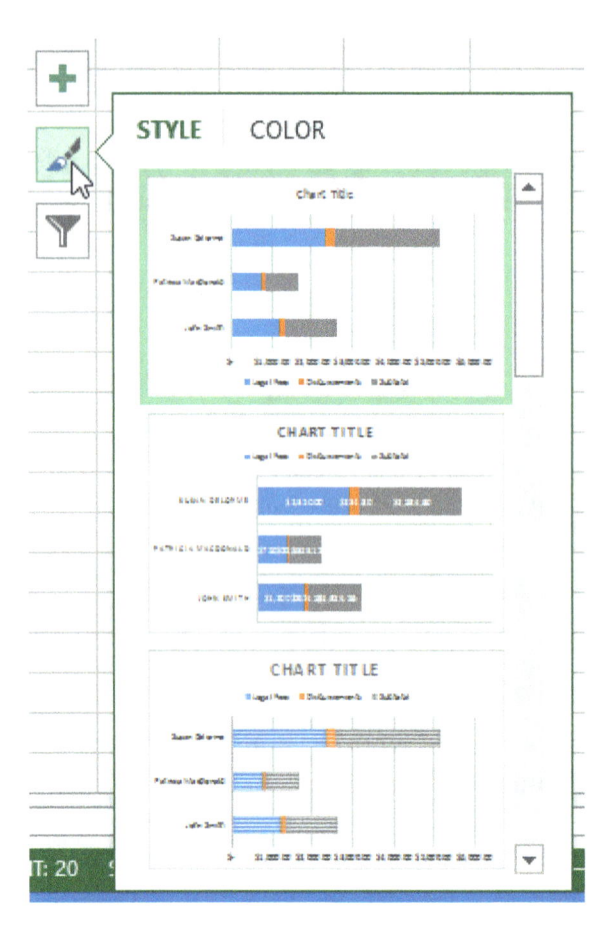

The filter icon to the right of your chart allows you to select or deselect or otherwise edit the data selection that is the basis for your chart.

Computer Applications for Paralegals 147

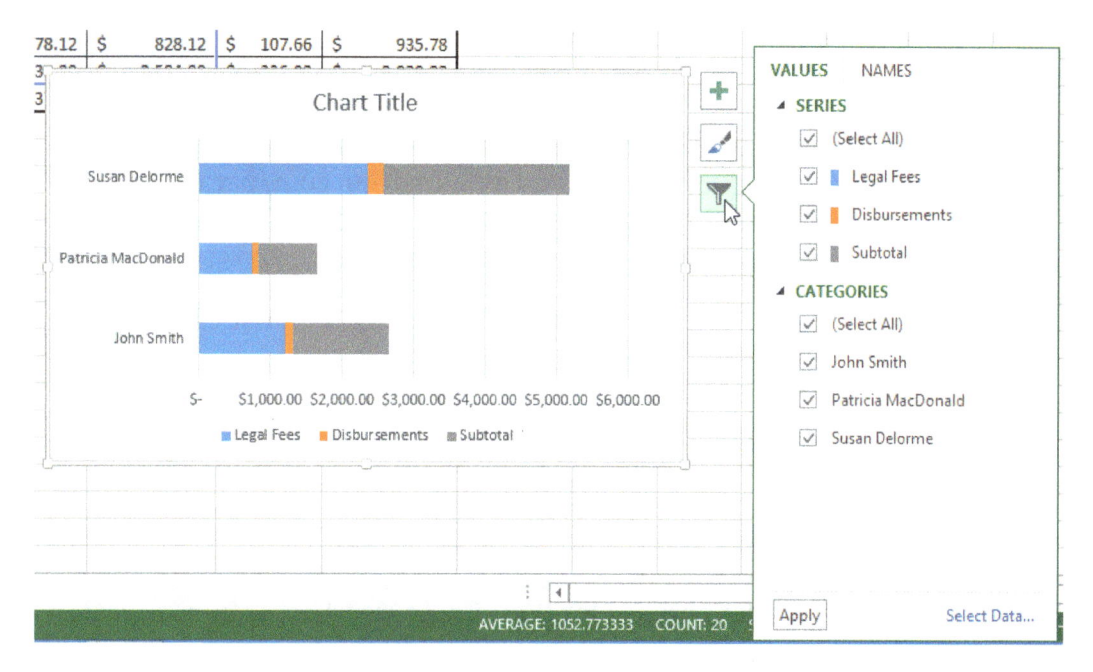

Finally, when your chart is active (you have clicked on it), you will notice that there are two new tabs on your ribbon. They are the Chart Tools Design tab and the Chart Tools Format tab.

The Design tab allows you to add chart elements, change the layout, design, or color scheme, or change the chart type. An interesting option on the Design tab is the Switch Row/Column option. Try this will some of your charts. It will change which source of data is the X axis verses the legend and can often give you a different perspective on your data.

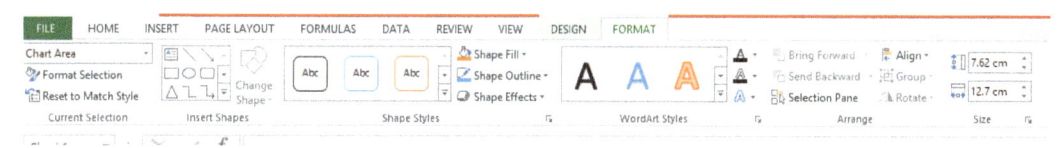

The Format tab allows you to control the look of your chart, including adding WordArt styles to your title, adding borders or fill, and aligning your table elements.

# Statistics

There is an instructional video for students on this topic at:
Webpage: http://www.asselingroup.com/paralegals
Password: paralegals

With large sets of data, it is often beneficial to perform a statistical analysis of the data, such as:

- The AVERAGE of a set of numbers
- The COUNT of a set of numbers (how many there are)
- The MINIMUM of a set of numbers, or
- The MAXIMUM of a set of numbers, to name a few.

Here is a dataset of student grades for their Computer Applications course:

|   | A | B | C | D | E | F | G | H |
|---|---|---|---|---|---|---|---|---|
| 1 | Student | Test 1 (15) | Test 2 (20) | Test 3 (20) | Portfolio (10) | Class Participation (15) | Attendance (10) | Total (100) |
| 2 | Allison | 12 | 20 | 19 | 10 | 14 | 2 | 77 |
| 3 | Barry | 15 | 20 | 18 | 10 | 13 | 8 | 84 |
| 4 | Charlie | 10 | 18 | 17 | 9 | 13 | 4 | 71 |
| 5 | Diana | 9 | 6 | 17 | 9 | 12 | 5 | 58 |
| 6 | Edward | 8 | 10 | 14 | 9 | 10 | 9 | 60 |
| 7 | Fiona | 10 | 8 | 13 | 0 | 15 | 1 | 47 |
| 8 | Greg | 11 | 8 | 15 | 0 | 9 | 10 | 53 |
| 9 | Harrison | 14 | 14 | 20 | 2 | 8 | 10 | 68 |
| 10 | Inez | 15 | 15 | 6 | 8 | 8 | 9 | 61 |
| 11 | Joaquim | 0 | 17 | 7 | 3 | 12 | 6 | 45 |
| 12 | Kelly | 13 | 20 | 18 | 7 | 13 | 5 | 76 |
| 13 | Larry | 5 | 3 | 14 | 0 | 4 | 8 | 34 |
| 14 | Margaret | 12 | 16 | 13 | 10 | 18 | 7 | 76 |

Let's create a statistics section below our spreadsheet for some calculations. We will find out the average, minimum, and maximum of each type of evaluation. Create a section below your data that looks like this:

|   | A | B | C | D | E | F | G | H |
|---|---|---|---|---|---|---|---|---|
| 12 | Kelly | 13 | 20 | 18 | 7 | 13 | 5 | 76 |
| 13 | Larry | 5 | 3 | 14 | 0 | 4 | 8 | 34 |
| 14 | Margaret | 12 | 16 | 13 | 10 | 18 | 7 | 76 |
| 15 |  |  |  |  |  |  |  |  |
| 16 | Average |  |  |  |  |  |  |  |
| 17 | Minimum |  |  |  |  |  |  |  |
| 18 | Maximum |  |  |  |  |  |  |  |

These statistical functions are easily found on the Home tab in the Editing grouping, by dropping down the arrow beside the Auto Sum function.

Computer Applications for Paralegals

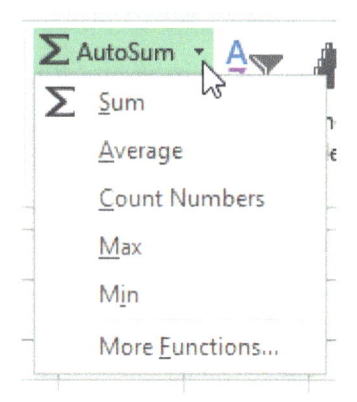

*[AutoSum dropdown menu showing: Sum, Average, Count Numbers, Max, Min, More Functions...]*

To calculate the Average function for Test 1, do the following:

- Place your curser in the Average cell for Test 1
- Click on the down arrow beside Auto Sum and choose Average, and
- Your computer will select the data either above or to the left of the cell your curser is in. If you are happy with the selection, press ENTER. If you are not happy with the selection, click and drag your mouse from the first cell in the proper selection to the last cell in the proper selection.

B16  fx  =AVERAGE(B2:B15)

| | A | B | C | D | E | F | G | H |
|---|---|---|---|---|---|---|---|---|
| 1 | Student | Test 1 (15) | Test 2 (20) | Test 3 (20) | Portfolio (10) | Class Participation (15) | Attendance (10) | Total (100) |
| 2 | Allison | 12 | 20 | 19 | 10 | 14 | 2 | 77 |
| 3 | Barry | 15 | 20 | 18 | 10 | 13 | 8 | 84 |
| 4 | Charlie | 10 | 18 | 17 | 9 | 13 | 4 | 71 |
| 5 | Diana | 9 | 6 | 17 | 9 | 12 | 5 | 58 |
| 6 | Edward | 8 | 10 | 14 | 9 | 10 | 9 | 60 |
| 7 | Fiona | 10 | 8 | 13 | 0 | 15 | 1 | 47 |
| 8 | Greg | 11 | 8 | 15 | 0 | 9 | 10 | 53 |
| 9 | Harrison | 14 | 14 | 20 | 2 | 8 | 10 | 68 |
| 10 | Inez | 15 | 15 | 6 | 8 | 8 | 9 | 61 |
| 11 | Joaquim | 0 | 17 | 7 | 3 | 12 | 6 | 45 |
| 12 | Kelly | 13 | 20 | 18 | 7 | 13 | 5 | 76 |
| 13 | Larry | 5 | 3 | 14 | 0 | 4 | 8 | 34 |
| 14 | Margaret | 12 | 16 | 13 | 10 | 18 | 7 | 76 |
| 15 | | | | | | | | |
| 16 | Average | 10.307692 | | | | | | |
| 17 | Minimum | | | | | | | |
| 18 | Maximum | | | | | | | |

The answer will display in the cell you chose to place your curser in at the beginning. Notice in the formula bar, that the formula is similar to the auto sum formula we created earlier:

- It starts with an equal sign
- The equal sign is followed by the name of the function in all caps (in this case AVERAGE)
- The name of the function is followed by parenthesis, and
- Inside the parenthesis are the range of cells that are included in the calculation, separated by a colon.

$$=AVERAGE(B2:B15)$$

Fill in the rest of the statistics section by:

- Repeating the steps for the Minimum Function by using the MIN option after dropping down the arrow beside Auto Sum on the Home tab
- Repeating the steps for the Maximum Function by using the MAX option after dropping down the arrow beside Auto Sum on the Home tab, and
- Using your copy formatting technique to copy the formulas to the other cells to complete the dataset.

| | | | | | | | |
|---|---|---|---|---|---|---|---|
| Average | 10.307692 | 13.4615385 | 14.69230769 | 5.923076923 | 11.46153846 | 6.461538462 | 62.3076923 |
| Minimum | 0 | 3 | 6 | 0 | 4 | 1 | 34 |
| Maximum | 15 | 20 | 20 | 10 | 18 | 10 | 84 |

# Functions

There is an instructional video for students on this topic at:
Webpage: http://www.asselingroup.com/paralegals
Password: paralegals

The statistics section above is an example of how to use functions to enhance your data. There are a great deal more functions in Excel that you can use.

Functions can be found in a few different places.

On the Home tab, click the down arrow beside AutoSum and choose More Functions.

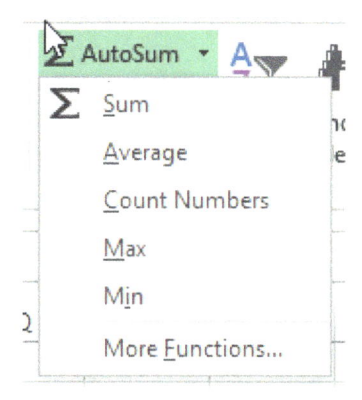

Alternatively, you can go to the Formulas tab and choose Insert Function. Either way, you will see this dialogue box:

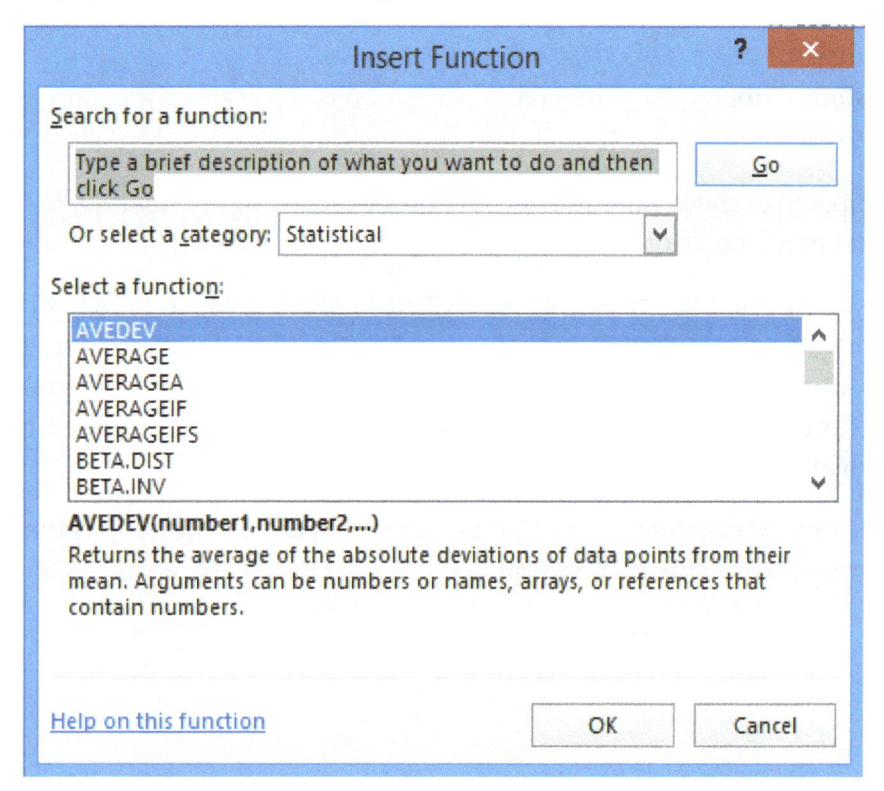

Functions are listed in alphabetical order. As you click on each function, a brief description of it appears at the bottom of the dialogue box. You can also find a function by using the search field at the top or dropping down the list of function categories. Categories include:

- Most Recently Used
- All
- Financial
- Date & Time
- Math & Trig
- Statistical
- Lookup & Reference
- Database
- Text
- Logical
- Information
- Engineering
- Cube
- Compatibility
- Web

Explaining all of these functions is beyond the scope of this textbook, however, many functions will be used in one of two ways.

The first way is similar to the SUM, AVERAGE, MINIMUM, and MAXIMUM functions we have looked at previously, where the equal sign is followed by the function name, then parenthesis, inside of which are a range of cells. This type of function will perform a specific calculation on the range of numbers inside the parenthesis.

Another type of function is one that calculates based on specific arguments. An example of this type of function is the IF function.

# Computer Applications for Paralegals

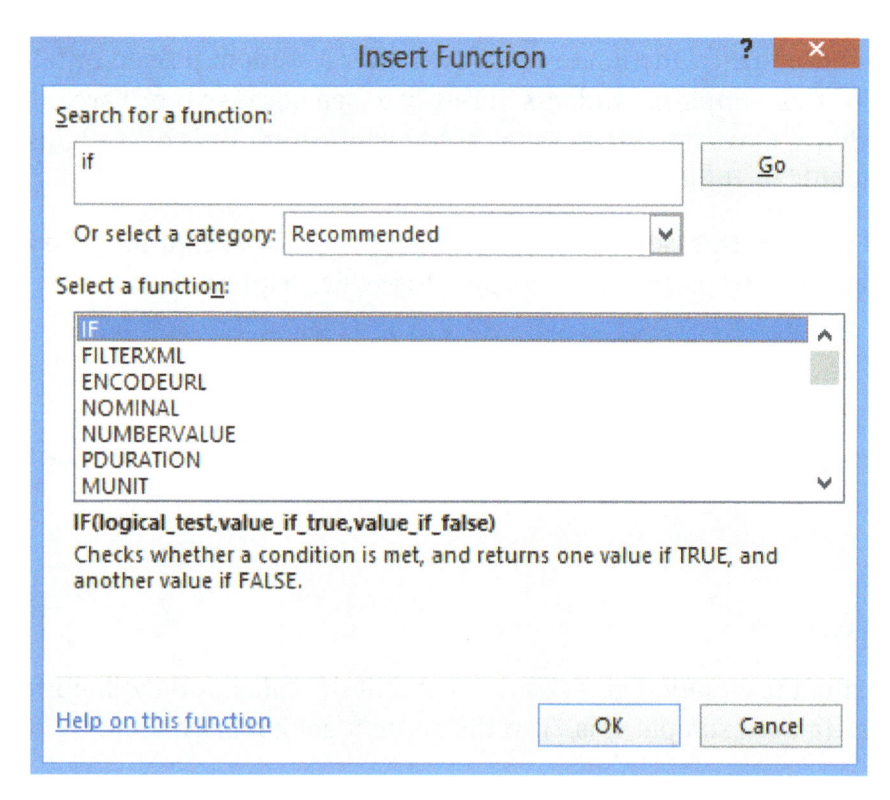

*[Screenshot of Excel Insert Function dialog box with "if" entered in search, IF function selected, showing description: "IF(logical_test,value_if_true,value_if_false) Checks whether a condition is met, and returns one value if TRUE, and another value if FALSE."]*

The IF function, according to the description, "checks whether a condition is met, and returns one value if TRUE, and another value if FALSE."

Here is the spreadsheet we worked on earlier with statistics:

| Student | Test 1 (15) | Test 2 (20) | Test 3 (20) | Portfolio (10) | Class Participation (15) | Attendance (10) | Total (100) |
|---|---|---|---|---|---|---|---|
| Allison | 12 | 20 | 19 | 10 | 14 | 2 | 77 |
| Barry | 15 | 20 | 18 | 10 | 13 | 8 | 84 |
| Charlie | 10 | 18 | 17 | 9 | 13 | 4 | 71 |
| Diana | 9 | 6 | 17 | 9 | 12 | 5 | 58 |
| Edward | 8 | 10 | 14 | 9 | 10 | 9 | 60 |
| Fiona | 10 | 8 | 13 | 0 | 15 | 1 | 47 |
| Greg | 11 | 8 | 15 | 0 | 9 | 10 | 53 |
| Harrison | 14 | 14 | 20 | 2 | 8 | 10 | 68 |
| Inez | 15 | 15 | 6 | 8 | 8 | 9 | 61 |
| Joaquim | 0 | 17 | 7 | 3 | 12 | 6 | 45 |
| Kelly | 13 | 20 | 18 | 7 | 13 | 5 | 76 |
| Larry | 5 | 3 | 14 | 0 | 4 | 8 | 34 |
| Margaret | 12 | 16 | 13 | 10 | 18 | 7 | 76 |
| | | | | | | | |
| Average | 10.307692 | 13.4615385 | 14.69230769 | 5.923076923 | 11.46153846 | 6.461538462 | 62.3076923 |
| Minimum | 0 | 3 | 6 | 0 | 4 | 1 | 34 |
| Maximum | 15 | 20 | 20 | 10 | 18 | 10 | 84 |

We could use the IF function to report whether a student passed or failed the class. For this sample of students, it's easy to see because there are only a few students, however, our sample could include hundreds of students, and then it would be difficult to see.

We will perform this calculation to the right of the Total column. The IF function has three parts to it, according to the description:

> IF(logical_test,value_if_true,value_if_false)
> Checks whether a condition is met, and returns one value if TRUE, and another value if FALSE.

The parts are contained in the brackets after the IF and are separated by commas.

**Part 1**

Logical_test

This part of the equation gives us the test that the calculation will perform on the data. In our example, it is, "Did the student get a mark of at least 50?"

So we need an equation that means, "Is the student's mark greater than or equal to 50?"

CELL>=50

**Part 2**

Value_if_true

This part of the equation tells us what will be displayed in the cell if the test is true. For our example, if the mark is 50 or more, we can display the word, "PASS."

**Part 3**

Value_if_false

This part of the equation tells us what will be displayed in the cell if the test is false. For our example, if the mark is less than 50, we can display the word, "FAIL."

One thing to note is if you do not want to display anything, you can choose " " (quotes with a space in the middle).

Computer Applications for Paralegals                                           155

Let's write an IF function that displays FAIL if the student failed and nothing if the student passed.

=IF(CELL>=50," ","FAIL")

Note that the word CELL is used to let you know that you should choose the cell where the student's total grade is. Also note that the word "FAIL" is in quotation marks. If you want Excel to display a word here, it must be in quotation marks.

If you click into the cell where you want the answer to go and start typing the following formula, once you type the =IF(, you will see the three sections of the formula appear and the first part will be bold. As you enter each part of the formula, the next part will be become bold, etc., until you have completed the formula.

| Total (100) | PASS/FAIL |
| --- | --- |
| 77 | =IF( |
| 84 | IF(**logical_test**, [value_if_true], [value_if_false]) |

Here is what my spreadsheet looks like once I have completed the formula. Remember to use your copying technique to copy the formula to the rest of the column, once you are sure that you know how to do it on your own.

| Student | Test 1 (15) | Test 2 (20) | Test 3 (20) | Portfolio (10) | Class Participation (15) | Attendance (10) | Total (100) | PASS/FAIL |
| --- | --- | --- | --- | --- | --- | --- | --- | --- |
| Allison | 12 | 20 | 19 | 10 | 14 | 2 | 77 | |
| Barry | 15 | 20 | 18 | 10 | 13 | 8 | 84 | |
| Charlie | 10 | 18 | 17 | 9 | 13 | 4 | 71 | |
| Diana | 9 | 6 | 17 | 9 | 12 | 5 | 58 | |
| Edward | 8 | 10 | 14 | 9 | 10 | 9 | 60 | |
| Fiona | 10 | 8 | 13 | 0 | 15 | 1 | 47 | FAIL |
| Greg | 11 | 8 | 15 | 0 | 9 | 10 | 53 | |
| Harrison | 14 | 14 | 20 | 2 | 8 | 10 | 68 | |
| Inez | 15 | 15 | 6 | 8 | 8 | 9 | 61 | |
| Joaquim | 0 | 17 | 7 | 3 | 12 | 6 | 45 | FAIL |
| Kelly | 13 | 20 | 18 | 7 | 13 | 5 | 76 | |
| Larry | 5 | 3 | 14 | 0 | 4 | 8 | 34 | FAIL |
| Margaret | 12 | 16 | 13 | 10 | 18 | 7 | 76 | |

My calculations show that three students failed the course. Try performing the IF function on your own data and see if you get the same results.

# Pivot Tables

There is an instructional video for students on this topic at:
Webpage:    http://www.asselingroup.com/paralegals
Password:   paralegals

Pivot tables are used when you have a large database of information with a lot of different variables and you want to ask some specific questions about the data. Here is a database that we can use to demonstrate pivot tables. Try typing it into your program as a starting point.

| | A | B | C | D | E | F |
|---|---|---|---|---|---|---|
| 1 | Client | Lawyer | Clerk | Paralegal | Office | Legal Fees |
| 2 | Abraham | David | Chelsea | Susan | Ottawa | $ 2,314.56 |
| 3 | Baker | Donna | Chris | Seth | Kingston | $ 5,487.99 |
| 4 | Charles | Darryl | Chelsea | Sam | Renfrew | $ 1,893.22 |
| 5 | Duchovney | David | Chris | Serena | Ottawa | $ 3,541.34 |
| 6 | Edwards | Donna | Chelsea | Susan | Kingston | $ 7,340.08 |
| 7 | Frank | Darryl | Chris | Seth | Renfrew | $ 4,532.68 |
| 8 | Georgetown | David | Chelsea | Sam | Ottawa | $ 6,208.34 |
| 9 | Harris | Donna | Chris | Serena | Kingston | $ 2,587.51 |
| 10 | Ignace | Darryl | Chelsea | Susan | Renfrew | $ 1,843.50 |
| 11 | Johnston | David | Chris | Seth | Ottawa | $ 4,536.76 |
| 12 | Khalid | Donna | Chelsea | Sam | Kingston | $ 5,905.34 |
| 13 | Lawrence | Darryl | Chris | Serena | Renfrew | $ 7,276.07 |
| 14 | Martin | David | Chelsea | Susan | Ottawa | $ 3,256.12 |

Notice the following things about this dataset:

- There are three different lawyers
- There are two different clerks
- There are four different paralegals, and
- There are three different satellite offices.

Now, we have a dataset with many different variables.

To create a pivot table, the first step is to select your data. Be sure that you don't include any totals in your data selection, otherwise, the totals in your pivot tables will be double what they should be.

| | A | B | C | D | E | F |
|---|---|---|---|---|---|---|
| 1 | Client | Lawyer | Clerk | Paralegal | Office | Legal Fees |
| 2 | Abraham | David | Chelsea | Susan | Ottawa | $ 2,314.56 |
| 3 | Baker | Donna | Chris | Seth | Kingston | $ 5,487.99 |
| 4 | Charles | Darryl | Chelsea | Sam | Renfrew | $ 1,893.22 |
| 5 | Duchovney | David | Chris | Serena | Ottawa | $ 3,541.34 |
| 6 | Edwards | Donna | Chelsea | Susan | Kingston | $ 7,340.08 |
| 7 | Frank | Darryl | Chris | Seth | Renfrew | $ 4,532.68 |
| 8 | Georgetown | David | Chelsea | Sam | Ottawa | $ 6,208.34 |
| 9 | Harris | Donna | Chris | Serena | Kingston | $ 2,587.51 |
| 10 | Ignace | Darryl | Chelsea | Susan | Renfrew | $ 1,843.50 |
| 11 | Johnston | David | Chris | Seth | Ottawa | $ 4,536.76 |
| 12 | Khalid | Donna | Chelsea | Sam | Kingston | $ 5,905.34 |
| 13 | Lawrence | Darryl | Chris | Serena | Renfrew | $ 7,276.07 |
| 14 | Martin | David | Chelsea | Susan | Ottawa | $ 3,256.12 |

The next step is to go to the Insert tab and choose Pivot Table, which is the first option on the left.

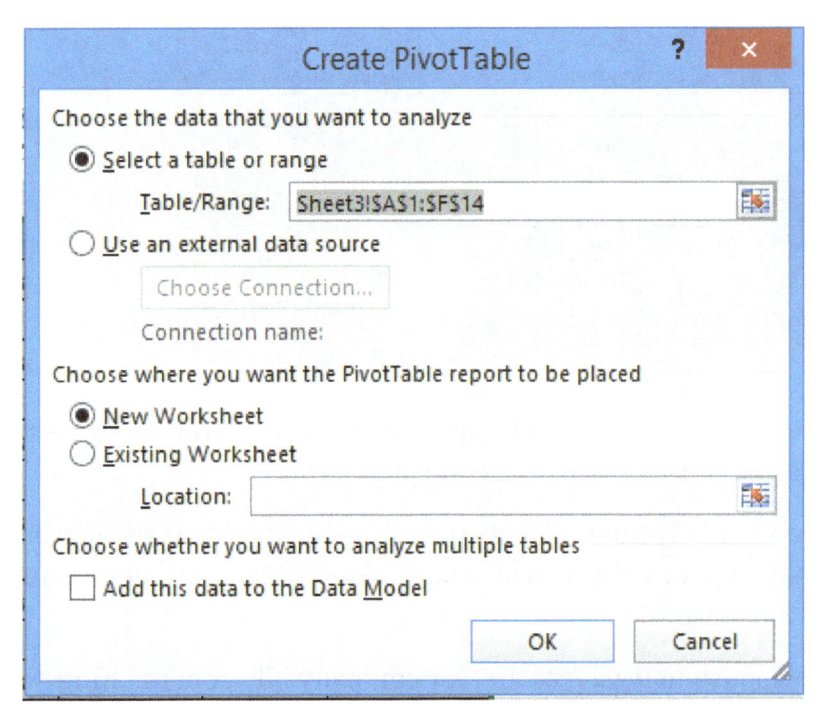

This dialogue box will pop up giving you some choice to make. In the top portion, you can see that the range of the data to be used in the pivot table is defined already since you made that selection before clicking on pivot table.

The bottom section allows you to choose where your pivot table will go. Your choices are to have it appear on a different sheet, or on the same sheet as your data. To make a choice, click on the red and blue sheet icon on the right side of this section. That will minimize the pivot table dialogue box and allow you to choose a cell. Either click one cell in the current sheet, or navigate to another sheet in your file by clicking on the tabs at the bottom of your sheet and then clicking one cell in the new sheet.

|    | A | B | C | D | E | F |
|----|---|---|---|---|---|---|
| 1  | Client | Lawyer | Clerk | Paralegal | Office | Legal Fees |
| 2  | Abraham | David | Chelsea | Susan | Ottawa | $ 2,314.56 |
| 3  | Baker | Donna | Chris | Seth | Kingston | $ 5,487.99 |
| 4  | Charles | Darryl | Chelsea | Sam | Renfrew | $ 1,893.22 |
| 5  | Duchovney | David | Chris | Serena | Ottawa | $ 3,541.34 |
| 6  | Edwards | Donna | Chelsea | Susan | Kingston | $ 7,340.08 |
| 7  | Frank | Darryl | Chris | Seth | Renfrew | $ 4,532.68 |
| 8  | Georgetown | David | Chelsea | Sam | Ottawa | $ 6,208.34 |
| 9  | Harris | Donna | Chris | Serena | Kingston | $ 2,587.51 |
| 10 | Ignace | Darryl | Chelsea | Susan | Renfrew | $ 1,843.50 |
| 11 | Johnston | David | Chris | Seth | Ottawa | $ 4,536.76 |
| 12 | Khalid | Donna | Chelsea | Sam | Kingston | $ 5,905.34 |
| 13 | Lawrence | Darryl | Chris | Serena | Renfrew | $ 7,276.07 |
| 14 | Martin | David | Chelsea | Susan | Ottawa | $ 3,256.12 |

Create PivotTable — Sheet3!$H$1

You can see that I have chosen to place my pivot table on the same sheet, and I have selected the cell H1 to place my pivot table.

Now, to select our options. The purpose of a pivot table is to answer a question about your data, usually a large set of data. Examples of questions I could ask about this data are:

- How much in legal fees did our company bill from the Kingston office?
- How much in legal fees did each lawyer bill?
- How much in legal fees did each clerk or paralegal bill by office?

Once you have selected where your pivot table will go, click again on the red and blue sheet icon. This will open up the pivot table task pane on the right of your screen.

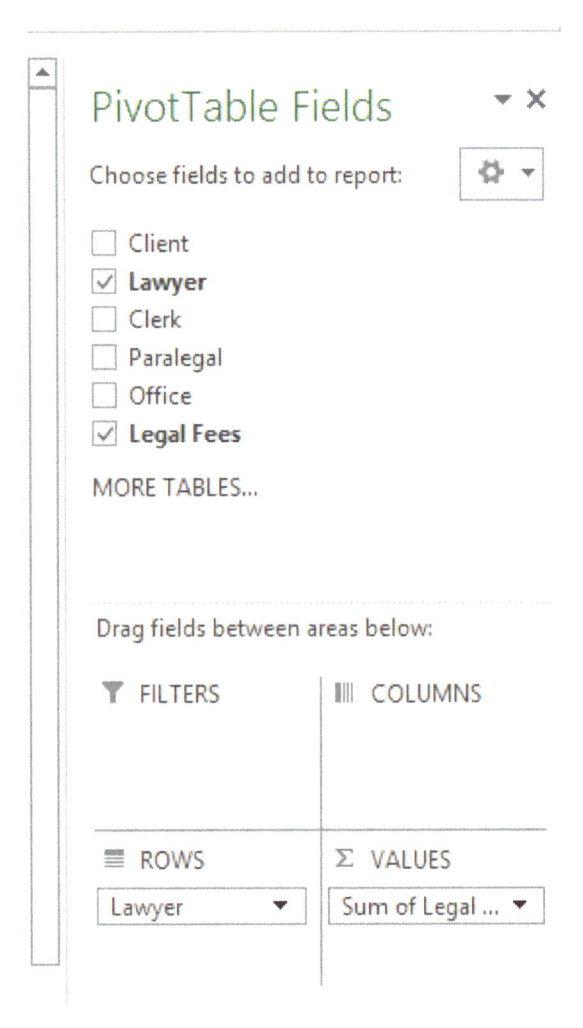

**PivotTable Fields**

Choose fields to add to report:

- [ ] Client
- [x] **Lawyer**
- [ ] Clerk
- [ ] Paralegal
- [ ] Office
- [x] **Legal Fees**

MORE TABLES...

Drag fields between areas below:

| ▼ FILTERS | ||| COLUMNS |
|---|---|
| ≡ ROWS | Σ VALUES |
| Lawyer ▼ | Sum of Legal ... ▼ |

You can see that each of our labeled columns are represented at the top portion of the task pane as Pivot Table Fields. I have chosen Lawyer and Legal Fees as my two categories.

A pivot table has now appeared where I had placed my curser.

| Row Labels | Sum of Legal Fees |
|---|---|
| Darryl | 15545.47 |
| David | 19857.12 |
| Donna | 21320.92 |
| **Grand Total** | **56723.51** |

The pivot table shows the sum of legal fees per lawyer with the total legal fees at the bottom. It would look more professional if my amounts were properly represented as dollar amounts. To change the format of the numbers, select all four numbers, right-click on the selection, and choose to apply the Accounting Number Format.

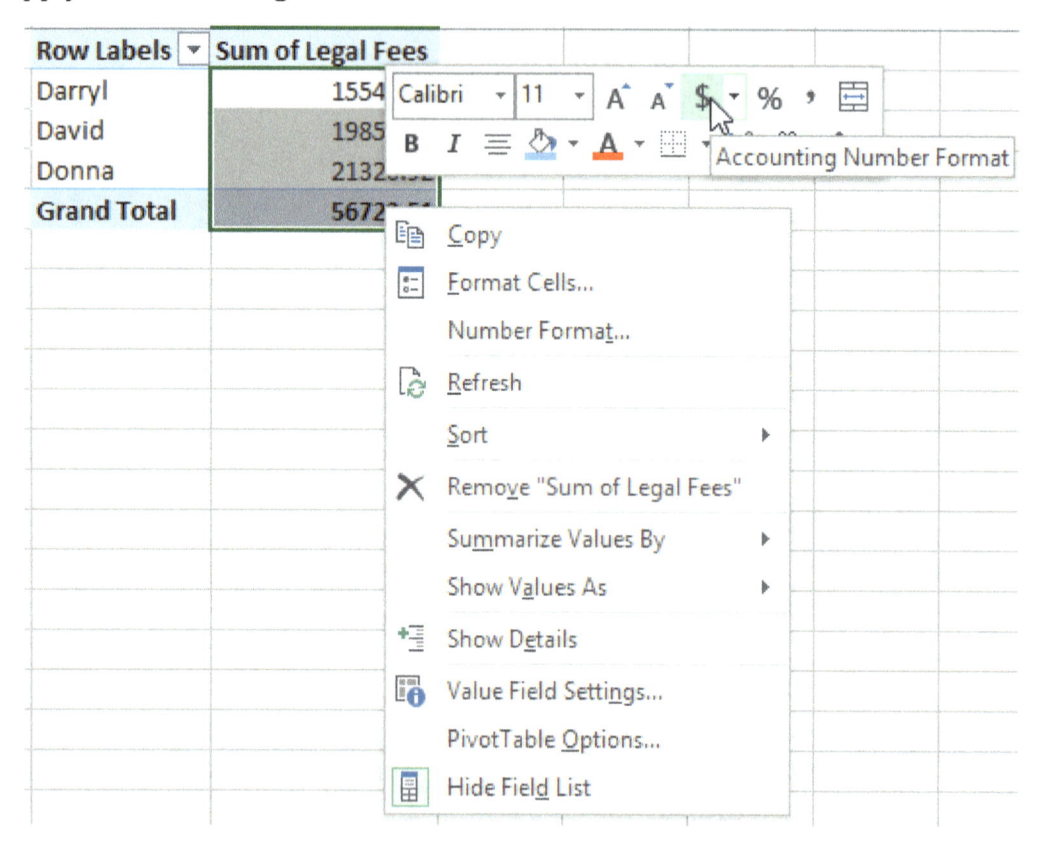

Now you know how to create a pivot table. Try experimenting with the data to create new pivot tables with different information.

A common mistake people make when creating pivot tables is to include the total of the data in their selection. Here is what my data looks like with the total selected.

|   | A | B | C | D | E | F |
|---|---|---|---|---|---|---|
| 1 | Client | Lawyer | Clerk | Paralegal | Office | Legal Fees |
| 2 | Abraham | David | Chelsea | Susan | Ottawa | $ 2,314.56 |
| 3 | Baker | Donna | Chris | Seth | Kingston | $ 5,487.99 |
| 4 | Charles | Darryl | Chelsea | Sam | Renfrew | $ 1,893.22 |
| 5 | Duchovney | David | Chris | Serena | Ottawa | $ 3,541.34 |
| 6 | Edwards | Donna | Chelsea | Susan | Kingston | $ 7,340.08 |
| 7 | Frank | Darryl | Chris | Seth | Renfrew | $ 4,532.68 |
| 8 | Georgetown | David | Chelsea | Sam | Ottawa | $ 6,208.34 |
| 9 | Harris | Donna | Chris | Serena | Kingston | $ 2,587.51 |
| 10 | Ignace | Darryl | Chelsea | Susan | Renfrew | $ 1,843.50 |
| 11 | Johnston | David | Chris | Seth | Ottawa | $ 4,536.76 |
| 12 | Khalid | Donna | Chelsea | Sam | Kingston | $ 5,905.34 |
| 13 | Lawrence | Darryl | Chris | Serena | Renfrew | $ 7,276.07 |
| 14 | Martin | David | Chelsea | Susan | Ottawa | $ 3,256.12 |
| 15 |  |  |  |  | TOTAL | $ 56,723.51 |

If I create the exact same pivot table as before, but with the total as part of my selection, here is what I will get:

| Row Labels | Sum of Legal Fees |
|---|---|
| Darryl | $ 15,545.47 |
| David | $ 19,857.12 |
| Donna | $ 21,320.92 |
| **Grand Total** | **$ 56,723.51** |

| Row Labels | Sum of Legal Fees |
|---|---|
| Darryl | $ 15,545.47 |
| David | $ 19,857.12 |
| Donna | $ 21,320.92 |
| (blank) | $ 56,723.51 |
| **Grand Total** | **$ 113,447.02** |

Notice how the second pivot table has a fourth entry at the bottom, named (blank) and that the total is double what it should be.

## Other Things to Note

There are a few other formatting and viewing techniques that I think will help you navigate through Excel.

### Freezing Rows or Columns

There is an instructional video for students on this topic at:
Webpage:    http://www.asselingroup.com/paralegals
Password:   paralegals

When creating a large database with many rows and columns, it can be difficult to remember which piece of data goes where. For example, the main screen of Excel shows 23 rows and up to column P. If the data you are entering goes past the 23rd row or column P, you may have to scroll either up to the top or back to the left to see the headings of your data.

Excel offers a freezing feature that allows you to freeze the rows or columns or both, so that as you scroll down or across past the main screen, you can see the headings no matter how far you go.

To access the freezing options, go to View > Freeze panes and click the down arrow.

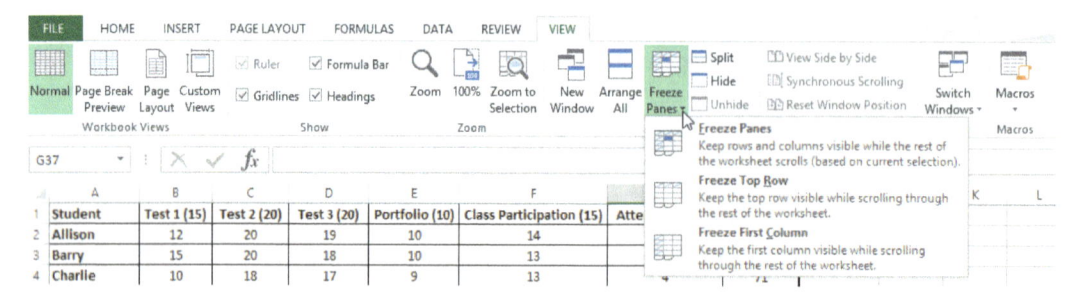

You will see that there are three options available to you.

- Freeze the top row, which allows you to scroll down but keep the first row visible
- Freeze the first column, which allows you to scroll to the right past the letter P, but keep the first column visible, and

# Computer Applications for Paralegals 163

- Freeze Panes. If your curser is in a cell, this selection will freeze the first 10 rows, which will stay visible as you scroll down. If you have your curser select the column A, this selection will freeze up to column G, which will stay visible if you scroll across.

To un-freeze a selection, simply drop down the options again the click Un-Freeze.

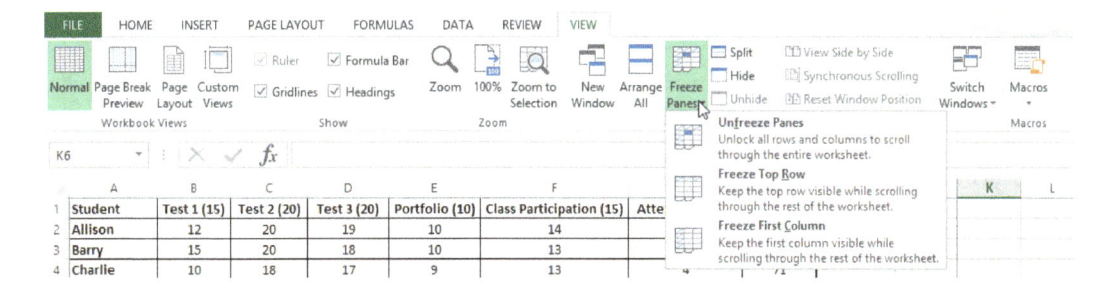

## Hiding and Un-hiding Data

There is an instructional video for students on this topic at:
Webpage:   http://www.asselingroup.com/paralegals
Password:   paralegals

If you are creating or working with a large set of data, you may wish to hide some rows or columns, as the case may be, so that you can see certain rows or columns instead of all of them all of the time.

Hiding certain rows or columns is easy, as is un-hiding them.

Here is an example of some data:

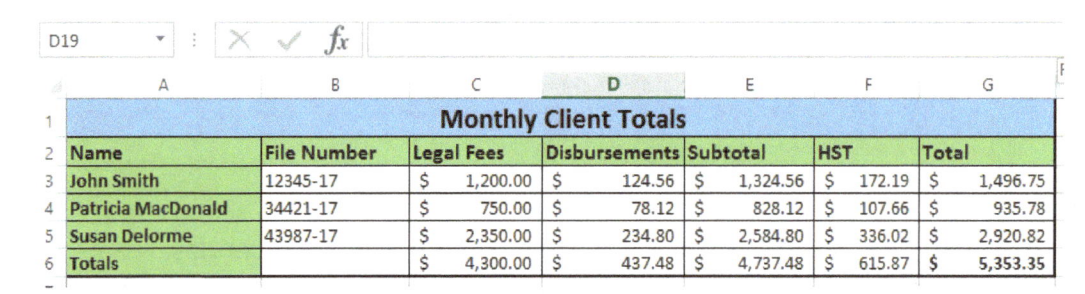

Let's say I want to hide the File Number column so that I can make some charts that won't use that column as header information. To hide the File Number column, right-click on the B column heading and choose Hide.

|   | A | C | D | E | F | G |
|---|---|---|---|---|---|---|
| 1 |   | Monthly Client Totals ||||||
| 2 | Name | Legal Fees | Disbursements | Subtotal | HST | Total |
| 3 | John Smith | $ 1,200.00 | $ 124.56 | $ 1,324.56 | $ 172.19 | $ 1,496.75 |
| 4 | Patricia MacDonald | $ 750.00 | $ 78.12 | $ 828.12 | $ 107.66 | $ 935.78 |
| 5 | Susan Delorme | $ 2,350.00 | $ 234.80 | $ 2,584.80 | $ 336.02 | $ 2,920.82 |
| 6 | Totals | $ 4,300.00 | $ 437.48 | $ 4,737.48 | $ 615.87 | $ 5,353.35 |

Now you can see that there is a faint double line between the A and C columns. If you right-click on that double line, you can choose Un-Hide. You can also select the A and C columns by clicking and dragging your mouse across them, and then right-click to choose Un-Hide.

To hide more than one column, simply click and drag your mouse across the desired columns (i.e., A, B, and C), right-click, and choose Hide.

## Show Formulas

There is an instructional video for students on this topic at:
Webpage:    http://www.asselingroup.com/paralegals
Password:   paralegals

Your instructor may want to see that you are able to create formulas properly. There is an easy way to allow your formulas to show, instead of the answers. Go to the Formulas tab and in the Formula Auditing grouping, click on Show Formulas.

Now, all of the cells with formulas in them will display the formulas themselves instead of the answers. You can then print this version of the spreadsheet or upload it to your online portal so that your instructor can mark your assignment.

Computer Applications for Paralegals                                                                                       165

| Average | =AVERAGE(B2:B15) | =AVERAGE(C2:C15) | =AVERAGE(D2:D15) | =AVERAGE(E2:E15) |
| Minimum | =MIN(B2:B14) | =MIN(C2:C14) | =MIN(D2:D14) | =MIN(E2:E14) |
| Maximum | =MAX(B2:B14) | =MAX(C2:C14) | =MAX(D2:D14) | =MAX(E2:E14) |

## Absolute Cell Reference

Throughout this chapter, we have used a copying technique to copy our formulas to other cells in the same column or row. When you do this, the program automatically assumes you are requesting it to make the same calculation but related to the new row or column.

For example, you can see in the sample below that the formula for cell E3 is:

=SUM(C3:D3)

It is calculating the sum of the legal fees and disbursements in row 3 and placing the answer in cell E3. If I use my copying technique to finish the calculations for the remainder of column E, you can see that the formulas are the same except the references automatically change for each row.

E3     fx   =SUM(C3:D3)

|   | A | B | C | D | E |
|---|---|---|---|---|---|
| 1 |   |   | Monthly Client Totals |   |   |
| 2 | Name | File Number | Legal Fees | Disbursements | Subtotal |
| 3 | John Smith | 12345-17 | $ 1,200.00 | $ 124.56 | $ 1,324.56 |
| 4 | Patricia MacDonald | 34421-17 | $ 750.00 | $ 78.12 | $ 828.12 |
| 5 | Susan Delorme | 43987-17 | $ 2,350.00 | $ 234.80 | $ 2,584.80 |
| 6 | Totals |   | $ 4,300.00 | $ 437.48 | $ 4,737.48 |

Here is the formula for cell E6:

E6     fx   =SUM(E3:E5)

|   | A | B | C | D | E |
|---|---|---|---|---|---|
| 1 |   |   | Monthly Client Totals |   |   |
| 2 | Name | File Number | Legal Fees | Disbursements | Subtotal |
| 3 | John Smith | 12345-17 | $ 1,200.00 | $ 124.56 | $ 1,324.56 |
| 4 | Patricia MacDonald | 34421-17 | $ 750.00 | $ 78.12 | $ 828.12 |
| 5 | Susan Delorme | 43987-17 | $ 2,350.00 | $ 234.80 | $ 2,584.80 |
| 6 | Totals |   | $ 4,300.00 | $ 437.48 | $ 4,737.48 |

An absolute cell reference will not automatically increase as in the above examples.

To create an absolute cell reference, you use a $ before both the row and the column reference in a formula. Let's try it. Here is a spreadsheet that you can start with.

|   | A | B | C | D | E | F |
|---|---|---|---|---|---|---|
| 1 | Monthly Client Totals |||||| 
| 2 | Name | File Number | Legal Fees | Disbursements | Subtotal | HST |
| 3 | John Smith | 12345-17 | $ 1,200.00 | $ 124.56 | $ 1,324.56 | |
| 4 | Patricia MacDonald | 34421-17 | $ 750.00 | $ 78.12 | $ 828.12 | |
| 5 | Susan Delorme | 43987-17 | $ 2,350.00 | $ 234.80 | $ 2,584.80 | |
| 6 | Totals | | $ 4,300.00 | $ 437.48 | $ 4,737.48 | |
| 7 | | | | | | |
| 8 | HST | | 13% | | | |

I have added an HST reference field at the bottom of my data. Now when calculating the HST amount, I will reference that 13% cell instead of typing in 13% in my formula. I will type the new formula with the absolute cell reference in cell F3.

E3  fx  =E3*$B$8

|   | A | B | C | D | E | F |
|---|---|---|---|---|---|---|
| 1 | Monthly Client Totals |||||| 
| 2 | Name | File Number | Legal Fees | Disbursements | Subtotal | HST |
| 3 | John Smith | 12345-17 | $ 1,200.00 | $ 124.56 | $ 1,324.56 | =E3*$B$8 |
| 4 | Patricia MacDonald | 34421-17 | $ 750.00 | $ 78.12 | $ 828.12 | |
| 5 | Susan Delorme | 43987-17 | $ 2,350.00 | $ 234.80 | $ 2,584.80 | |
| 6 | Totals | | $ 4,300.00 | $ 437.48 | $ 4,737.48 | |
| 7 | | | | | | |
| 8 | HST | | 13% | | | |

My formula tells the program to take the amount in cell E3 (subtotal) and multiple it by B8 (HST percentage).

Now, I will use the same copying technique I have used in the past to copy this formula to the other clients in the database. Notice how in cell F6, the formula still references cell B8 because I used the absolute cell reference of $B$8.

Computer Applications for Paralegals

| | A | B | C | D | E | F |
|---|---|---|---|---|---|---|
| 1 | | | Monthly Client Totals | | | |
| 2 | Name | File Number | Legal Fees | Disbursements | Subtotal | HST |
| 3 | John Smith | 12345-17 | $ 1,200.00 | $ 124.56 | $ 1,324.56 | $ 172.19 |
| 4 | Patricia MacDonald | 34421-17 | $ 750.00 | $ 78.12 | $ 828.12 | $ 107.66 |
| 5 | Susan Delorme | 43987-17 | $ 2,350.00 | $ 234.80 | $ 2,584.80 | $ 336.02 |
| 6 | Totals | | $ 4,300.00 | $ 437.48 | $ 4,737.48 | $ 615.87 |
| 7 | | | | | | |
| 8 | HST | | 13% | | | |

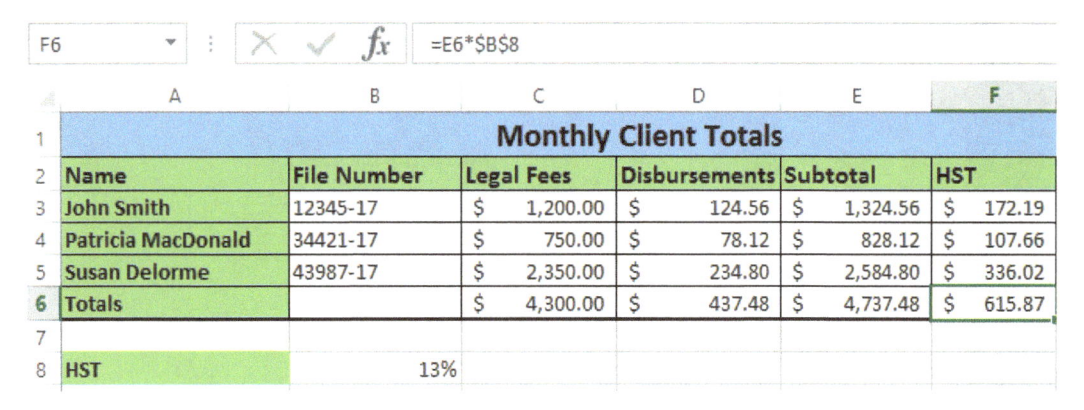

F6 fx =E6*$B$8

You can use absolute cell references to hold any cell in a formula, but you can also use it to:

- Hold the row only (in the above example, I would hold the row only by using the reference B$8), or to
- Hold the column only (in the above example, I would hold the column only by using the reference $B8).

## Printing

There is an instructional video for students on this topic at:
Webpage: http://www.asselingroup.com/paralegals
Password: paralegals

To print, go to the File tab and click on Print. You will see some print options on the left-hand side of the screen and a preview of your document on the right hand side of the screen. The preview will show you the current page based on where your curser was when you clicked print.

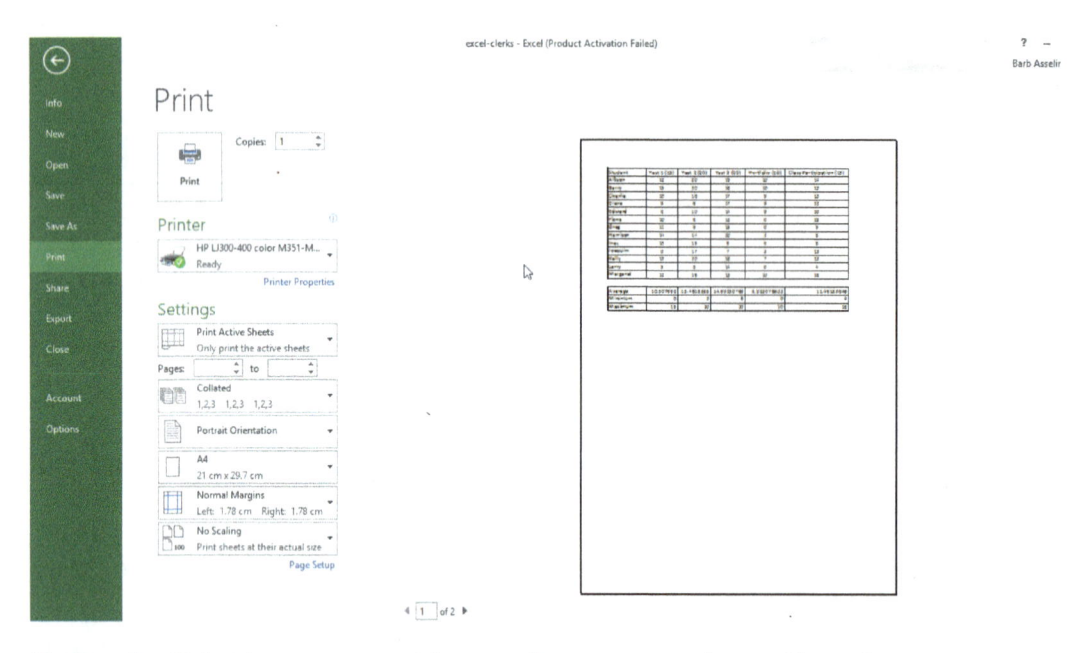

Under the Print icon, you can choose the correct printer, if you have access to more than one printer. Beside the Print icon, you can choose how many copies to print.

Below the options for choosing a printer, you can change your paper size, orientation, which pages you want to print, and the margins of your document.

In the example, you can see that the preview shows page 1 of 2, however the spreadsheet should be all on one page. There are a few options. The first is to landscape the spreadsheet. I can do this using the orientation option in the print settings. Simply drop down the arrow beside portrait orientation and choose landscape. I could also do this on the Page Layout tab.

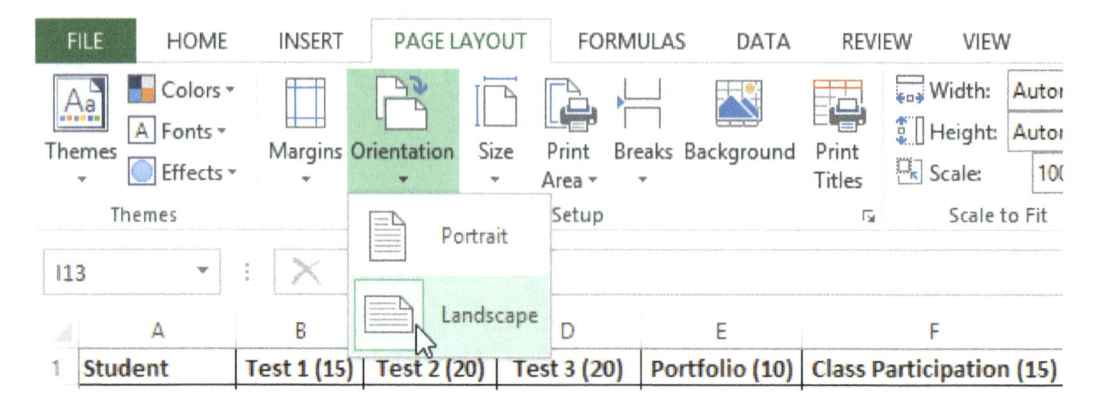

Computer Applications for Paralegals

I can also choose to scale my spreadsheet using the scaling option at the bottom of the printer settings. The scaling options are to:

- print all columns on one sheet
- print all rows on one sheet, or
- print the entire spreadsheet on one sheet.

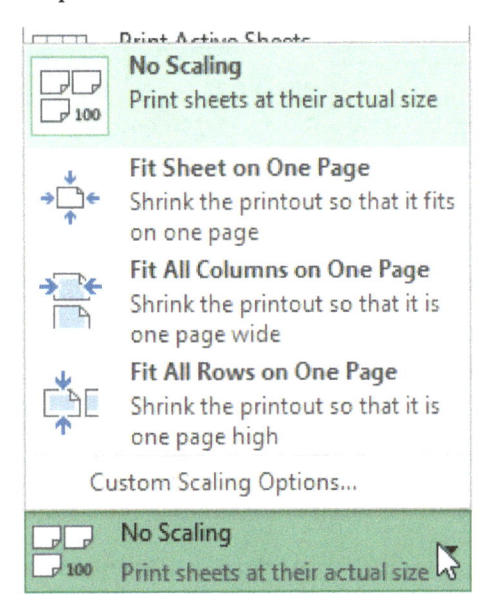

## Chapter Summary

In this chapter, students learned how to create a spreadsheet of data and how to further enhance their data using formulas. They learned how to professionally present their data to co-workers, peers, bosses and clients using formatting, charts, and graphs. Finally, they learned how to perform a statistical analysis of their data as well as answer specific questions about data with multiple variables using pivot tables.

# Exercises

## Exercise 5.1

1. Create the following spreadsheet:

   | | A | B | C |
   |---|---|---|---|
   | 1 | Client | Legal Fees | Disbursements |
   | 2 | John Smith | $ 1,200.00 | $ 236.32 |
   | 3 | Mary MacDonald | $ 750.00 | $ 76.09 |
   | 4 | Lucy Lawson | $ 3,200.00 | $ 237.98 |
   | 5 | Sam Elliott | $ 1,275.00 | $ 125.25 |
   | 6 | Thomas Sinclair | $ 975.00 | $ 98.44 |
   | 7 | Brigitte Fonda | $ 1,050.00 | $ 87.90 |
   | 8 | Jake Rampton | $ 2,350.00 | $ 142.66 |
   | 9 | Rhonda McMaster | $ 3,600.00 | $ 266.99 |
   | 10 | Joe Hall | $ 900.00 | $ 102.87 |
   | 11 | Lane Cleroux | $ 1,500.00 | $ 120.11 |

2. Add the following columns after Disbursements:
   a. Subtotal
   b. HST
   c. Total
3. Add a Totals row after Lane Cleroux
4. Create formulas as necessary and calculate all of the missing fields
5. Ensure your numbers are all formatted using the Accounting format
6. Add a row to the top of your spreadsheet called **Client Totals**
7. Merge and center the title
8. Bold the title and increase the font size to 16pt
9. Add you name to the bottom of the page
10. Add borders to all of the cells in your spreadsheet
11. Add a thick box border to the outside of your data
12. Ensure your exercise fits on all one page (you may need to landscape it) and submit it to your professor

# Exercise 5.2

Create a budget for your company for last year as follows:

1. Label the columns of your spreadsheet as follows:
   a. Item
   b. Q1
   c. Q2
   d. Q3
   e. Q4
   f. Total
2. Label the rows of your spreadsheet as follows:
   a. Rent
   b. Hydro
   c. Gas
   d. Salaries
   e. Photocopier
   f. Advertising
   g. Total
3. Fill in the following data:
   a. Rent is $1,200.00 per month, but in August it increased to $1,250.00 per month (three months in a quarter)
   b. Salaries are $350,000.00 per year (four quarters in a year)
   c. Photocopies expense is $87.25 per month
   d. Advertising is $5,000.00 per year
   e. Use the table below to calculate the gas and hydro amounts for each quarter:

| Month | Gas | Hydro |
|---|---|---|
| January | $125.22 | $234.09 |
| February | 134.11 | 187.95 |
| March | 116.98 | 203.99 |
| April | 145.64 | 217.44 |
| May | 178.32 | 209.11 |
| June | 109.33 | 241.66 |
| July | 111.99 | 272.10 |
| August | 198.01 | 218.00 |
| September | 138.29 | 222.75 |

| Month | Gas | Hydro |
|---|---|---|
| October | 108.99 | 245.61 |
| November | 112.82 | 276.51 |
| December | 118.32 | 215.99 |

4. Calculate the total row and the total column
5. Ensure your numbers are all formatted using the Accounting format
6. Add a row to the top of your spreadsheet called **Annual Budget**
7. Merge and center the title
8. Bold the title and increase the font size to 16pt
9. Add you name to the bottom of the page
10. Add borders to all of the cells in your spreadsheet
11. Add a thick box border to the outside of your data
12. Create a pie chart for your Q1 data
13. Ensure your pie chart has a title and that the amounts are shown in percentages
14. Position your pie chart so that it does not interfere with your data
15. Create another chart using all of your data, with the exception of your totals
16. Choose from the Recommended Charts
17. Ensure your chart has a title and a legend and move it so that it does not overlap your pie chart or your data
18. Ensure your exercise fits on all one page (you may need to landscape it) and submit it to your professor

## Exercise 5.3

1. Search the Internet for the Ottawa Senators' game scores for last season.
2. Create a database of their scores using the following column headings:
    a. Game Number
    b. Opposing Team
    c. Sens Score
    d. Opposing Score
3. Create a statistics section below your data
4. For the Senators, use statistical analysis to calculate:
    a. The average Senators' score for the season
    b. The minimum Senators' score for the season

# Computer Applications for Paralegals

      c. The maximum Senators' score for the season
5. Add a new column called **Win/Loss** beside your data
6. Use the IF function to figure out if the Senators won or lost each game and if they won, display **WIN**, and if they lost, display nothing
7. Add one more column called **Lost By #** beside your **Win/Loss** column
8. Use the IF function to display how many points the Senators lost by, if they lost the game
9. Add a row to the top of your spreadsheet called **Senators' Season Scores**
10. Merge and center the title
11. Bold the title and increase the font size to 16pt
12. Add a title to your stats section, called **Statistics**
13. Merge and center the title above your stats section
14. Bold the title and increase the font size to 16pt
15. Add you name to the bottom of the page
16. Add borders to all of the cells in your spreadsheet
17. Add a thick box border to the outside of your data
18. Ensure your exercise fits on all one page and submit it to your professor

## Exercise 5.4

Create the following database:

| | A | B | C | D | E | F | G | H | I | J |
|---|---|---|---|---|---|---|---|---|---|---|
| 1 | File Number | Clerk | Paralegal | Area of Law | Billable Hours | Rate | Total Fees | | | |
| 2 | 17-001 | June | Alan | Landlord | 37 | | | | | |
| 3 | 17-002 | Josh | Addison | Small Claims | 65 | | | | Rates | |
| 4 | 17-003 | Jess | Amal | Traffic | 18 | | | | Alan | 165 |
| 5 | 17-004 | June | Alan | Criminal | 52 | | | | Addison | 170 |
| 6 | 17-005 | Josh | Addison | Landlord | 79 | | | | Amal | 145 |
| 7 | 17-006 | Jess | Alan | Small Claims | 39 | | | | | |
| 8 | 17-007 | June | Alan | Traffic | 17 | | | | | |
| 9 | 17-008 | Josh | Addison | Criminal | 21 | | | | | |
| 10 | 17-009 | Jess | Amal | Landlord | 108 | | | | | |
| 11 | 17-010 | June | Alan | Small Claims | 64 | | | | | |
| 12 | 17-011 | Josh | Addison | Traffic | 20 | | | | | |
| 13 | 17-012 | Jess | Amal | Criminal | 32 | | | | | |
| 14 | 17-013 | June | Alan | Landlord | 25 | | | | | |
| 15 | 17-014 | Josh | Addison | Small Claims | 30 | | | | | |
| 16 | 17-015 | Jess | Amal | Traffic | 10 | | | | | |
| 17 | 17-016 | June | Alan | Criminal | 8 | | | | | |
| 18 | 17-017 | Josh | Addison | Landlord | 41 | | | | | |
| 19 | 17-018 | Jess | Amal | Small Claims | 28 | | | | | |
| 20 | 17-019 | June | Alan | Traffic | 13 | | | | | |
| 21 | 17-020 | Josh | Addison | Criminal | 30 | | | | | |

1. Use absolute cell references to add the rates to the Rates column
2. Create the necessary formulas to complete the Total Fees column (Billable Hours times Rate)
3. Add a title row to the dataset called **Billable Hours**
4. Merge and center this new title as well as the title of the Rates section
5. Center the data in the Billable Hours section
6. Add borders to both sections
7. Add your name to the spreadsheet
8. Format your spreadsheet to landscape
9. Show your formulas and print all on one sheet, as your first submission
10. Un-show your formulas and continue with this exercise
11. Create pivot tables showing the following:
    a. Billable Hours per Paralegal
    b. Total Fees per Area of Law
12. Print your exercise all on one sheet, as your second submission
13. Hand in both submissions to your instructor

## Exercise 5.5

Create the following spreadsheet:

|    | A         | B     | C     | D     | E   |
|----|-----------|-------|-------|-------|-----|
| 1  | Month     | Sarah | Steve | Sandy | You |
| 2  | January   | 108   | 111   | 101   | 120 |
| 3  | February  | 121   | 115   | 120   | 124 |
| 4  | March     | 122   | 128   | 110   | 125 |
| 5  | April     | 119   | 109   | 129   | 121 |
| 6  | May       | 118   | 122   | 127   | 117 |
| 7  | June      | 130   | 121   | 125   | 115 |
| 8  | July      | 122   | 126   | 126   | 96  |
| 9  | August    | 123   | 119   | 108   | 120 |
| 10 | September | 121   | 118   | 118   | 123 |
| 11 | October   | 118   | 127   | 119   | 124 |
| 12 | November  | 117   | 130   | 123   | 131 |
| 13 | December  | 90    | 141   | 123   | 127 |

1. Instead of "You", change it to your name
2. Add the following columns after your name:
   a. Goal Hours
   b. Over/Under
   c. How Many Over
3. The **Goal Hours** for each paralegal are 120 for each month
4. For the **Over/Under** column, use an IF function to determine if YOUR monthly hours are over or under the goal of 120 – display "Over" if you are over your goal and display "Under" if you are under your goal
5. For the **How Many Over** column, use an IF function to determine how many hours over you are in the months that you are over your goal – display the number of hours over if you are over your goal and display nothing if you are under your goal
6. Add the following rows under December:
   a. MIN
   b. MAX
   c. AVERAGE
7. Calculate the statistics MIN, MAX, and AVERAGE for each of the employees
8. Create formulas as necessary and calculate all of the missing fields
9. Ensure your numbers are all formatted using the Accounting format
10. Add a row to the top of your spreadsheet called **Paralegal Billable Hours**
11. Merge and center the title
12. Bold the title and increase the font size to 16pt
13. Apply a formatted table of your choice to the data (not the title)
14. Ensure your exercise fits on all one page (you may need to landscape it) and submit it to your professor

# Exercise 5.6

Create the following spreadsheet:

| | A | B | C | D |
|---|---|---|---|---|
| 1 | Last Name | First Name | Paralegal | Hours |
| 2 | Abbott | John | Anna | 7.2 |
| 3 | Baker | Mike | Hassan | 10.1 |
| 4 | Corbin | Betty | Victor | 8.5 |
| 5 | Edwards | Carole | Anna | 23.9 |
| 6 | Frankton | Donna | Hassan | 9.5 |
| 7 | George | Charles | Victor | 19.4 |
| 8 | Hill | Sam | Anna | 22.8 |
| 9 | Illiad | Graham | Hassan | 5.3 |
| 10 | Jones | Catrina | Victor | 11.9 |
| 11 | Kang | Wendy | Anna | 12.3 |
| 12 | Longton | Jamie | Hassan | 17.2 |
| 13 | Miller | Casey | Victor | 7.9 |
| 14 | Norbert | Barry | Anna | 5.1 |
| 15 | Outlander | Wally | Hassan | 14.8 |
| 16 | Pianosi | Rose | Victor | 22.1 |

1. Add the following new columns after Hours:
   a. Rate
   b. Legal Fees
   c. HST
   d. Total Billed
2. Add the following row after Pianosi:
   a. Totals
3. Sort your data:
   a. First by paralegal
   b. Second by client's last name
4. Add each paralegal's billable rate as follows to the rate column:
   a. Anna's billable rate is $180.00 per hour

      b. Hassan's billable rate is $160.00 per hour
      c. Victor's billable rate is $200.00 per hour
5. Calculate the Legal Fees column by multiplying the hours by the billable rate
6. Calculate the HST column by multiplying the Legal Fees by 0.13
7. Calculate the Total Billed column by adding the Legal Fees and the HST amounts together
8. Calculate the total of each column at the bottom
9. Ensure your numbers (except hours) are all formatted using the Accounting format
10. Add a row to the top of your spreadsheet called **Paralegal Monthly Billing**
11. Merge and center the title
12. Bold the title and increase the font size to 16pt
13. Select your data (not the title) and apply a formatted table style of your choice
14. Use Conditional Formatting rules to the following:
      a. Identify any client with more than 10 hours of billable time
      b. Apply the Data Bar of your choice to the Legal Fees column
      c. Apply the Icon Set of your choice to the Total Billed column
15. Ensure your exercise fits on all one page (you may need to landscape it) and submit it to your professor

# Chapter 6: Word

## Learning Outcomes

In this chapter, students will:

- Learn how to create the most commonly used formats of external correspondence
- Create internal memos
- Properly format single and multi-page letters and memos
- Create a properly formatted professional report
- Use Word's templates to create fax cover sheets
- Perform a merge using Outlook and Word
- Create tables to add to letters, memos, and reports
- Create new styles and use existing styles, and
- Perform a variety of editing and proofreading techniques so that the best possible product is produced.

## Overview

Word is Microsoft's word processing software and allows you to create a variety of professional-looking documentation that is suitable for the:

- Workplace
- Court
- Tribunals
- Lawyers, judges, justices, paralegals, and other legal professionals
- Clients, and
- Industry professionals, such as courthouse officials and process servers.

Note that each user's version of Word may be configured differently. As such, please make the following changes to your system's settings before working with the precedents and exercises in this text, so that everyone is viewing things in the same way:

- Change your units of measurement to inches, if necessary, by going to the File tab and selecting Options and then Advanced. Once there,

Computer Applications for Paralegals

scroll down to find the section titled Display and change the units of measurement to inches.
- Set your paragraph settings to single spacing (1.0) and ensure that both options at the bottom say "Add" by clicking on the Home tab and selecting the Line and Paragraph Spacing option in the Paragraph grouping.

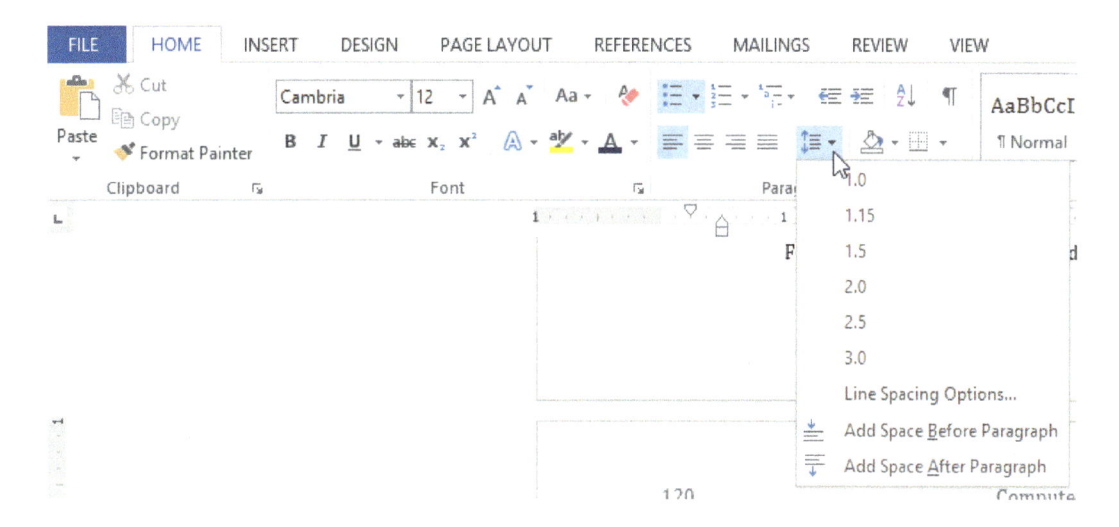

When opening the software for the first time, you have a few choices:

- When you open the software, a new document is automatically on your screen
- To open an existing document, go to the File tab and click Open, then browse to find your existing document
- To create a new document, go to the File tab and click New and then click on the Blank Document option
- To open a document before the software is open, browse your computer to the proper document and double-click on it and it will automatically open in Word, or
- To open a Word document from the Internet or another online source, either double-click on the link and choose open, or right-click on the link and choose open.

# Correspondence

In your career, you will most likely create letters on a daily basis. There are a few different types of letters that are common among legal professionals:

- Full Block Letters, in which all components of the letter are aligned at the left margin of the page
- Modified Block Letters, in which all components of the letter are aligned at the left margin of the page, with the exception of the date and the closing and the writer's name, and title and company, if applicable, which start at the center of the page, and
- Modified Block Letters with Indentation, which is the same as the Modified Block Letter, except that the first line of each paragraph is indented.

In the instructions for each type of letter, you will see these letter components:

| Component | Description |
| --- | --- |
| Letterhead | Section usually at the top of the first page of the letter that contains information about the company sending the letter, such as name, address, phone number, fax number, email, and web address |
| Date | The date the letter was written, found below the letterhead |
| Address Block | The address of the recipient of the letter |
| Confidential Notation | If a letter is to be marked confidential, this notation is located between the date and the address block |
| Greeting | Below the address block is the greeting line, which is usually a standard greeting like, **Dear Mr. Smith:** |
| Reference Line | The reference line (or Re: line or subject line) tells the recipient the topic of the letter and usually contains the file number that the letter relates to |
| Body | The body of the letter is located below the Re: line and contains the main message of the letter |
| Closing | The closing of the letter is located after the body of the letter and is typically a parting phrase such as **Yours very truly,** |

| Component | Description |
|---|---|
| Company Name | Sometimes, letters will contain the name of the company following the closing and before the signature block |
| Signature Block | The signature block contains the writer's name and title |
| Initials | The initials of the writer are included following the writer's name and title and, if the writer and typist are two different people, then both sets of initials are included |
| Enclosure Notation | If there is an enclosure or an attachment, it is noted after the initials |
| Delivery Notation | The method of delivery is included after the enclosure notation, if there is one – note that this can also be where the confidential notation is, however, if there are both, the confidential notation takes precedence |
| Copy Notation | If the letter is to be copied to anyone, they are noted here, at the bottom of the letter |
| Post Script | If there is a PS, it is the last item of the letter |

If your letter will include a bulleted or a numbered list, note that the bullets or numbers should be located at the left margin of the letter.

To get a bulleted list to start at the left margin, start a bulleted list by clicking on the bullets icon in the Paragraph grouping of the Home tab. Before you start typing the text that will follow the bullet, click on the Decrease Indent button in the Paragraph grouping of the Home tab to move the bullet back to the left margin.

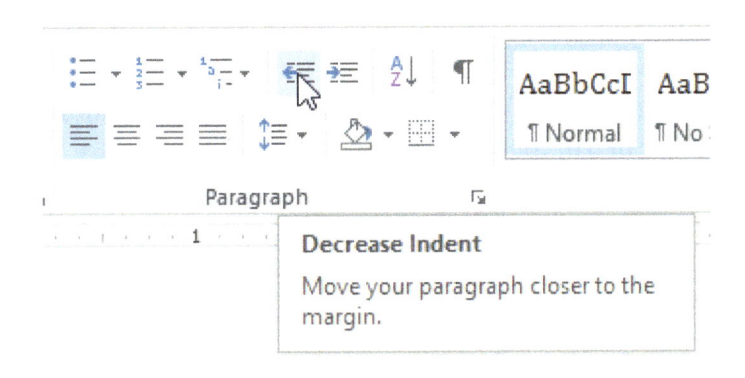

## Full Block Letters

There is an instructional video for students on this topic at:
Webpage: http://www.asselingroup.com/paralegals
Password: paralegals

An example of a full block letter is included on the following page. Please note the following:

- There is consistently one blank space between components of this letter, with the exception of the following:
    o There are four to five blank spaces after the date
    o There are four to six blank spaces after the closing
    o There are no spaces between the "housekeeping" items at the bottom of the letter
- All of the components of the letter are aligned at the left edge of the letter
- The top, bottom, right, and left margins of the letter are all set at one inch
- Since there is a confidential notation in this letter, there is one blank space before the confidential notation and two blank spaces after
- If your letter is just more than one page in length and you would like to amend it so that it is only one page, you may:
    o Reduce the number of spaces after the date, however, there should be at least two blank spaces
    o If there is a confidential notation, you can reduce the number of spaces after it to one blank space
    o You can reduce the number of spaces in the signature block, however, there should be at least three blank spaces to properly hold a physical signature
    o You could reduce the font size, however I wouldn't go below 10pt or 10.5pt font size, and
    o You could reduce the size of the margins, however, I wouldn't go below 0.8" for each of the top, bottom, right, and left margin

> **Paralegals' Professional Corporation**
> 1 Paralegal Private
> Ottawa, Ontario K2K 2K2
> T (613) 555-9999 F (613) 555-8888
> www.ParalegalsProfessionalCorporation.com
>
> June 30, 2017
>
> CONFIDENTIAL
>
> Mr. John Smith
> 1 Smith Street
> Ottawa, Ontario K1N 5A1
>
> Dear Mr. Smith:
>
> RE:  Smith v. MacDonald
>         Our File No. 44425-17
>
> I am pleased to advise that this matter is now complete.
>
> In accordance with your instructions, we have commenced an action against Mr. MacDonald and served him with the filed documents. Further to the receipt of our documentation, Mr. MacDonald retained his own representation who contacted us to discuss a possible settlement. We arrived at a settlement, which was paid by Mr. MacDonald and deposited into our trust account. We held enough back to cover our account and forwarded the balance to you.
>
> Please find enclosed our Statement of Account and Trust Statement. It outlines all of the time and disbursements on your file, as well as payment in full. Don't hesitate to contact me if you have any questions regarding this account, or if you require any legal assistance in the future.
>
> Yours very truly.
>
>
> Barb Asselin, MBA
>
> BLA/yi
> Enclosure
> By Regular Mail

There are two types of punctuation used in legal correspondence: open and mixed. They refer to the punctuation that following the greeting line and the closing of the letter. Here are the differences:

- Open punctuation has no punctuation after either the greeting line or the closing of the letter, and
- Mixed punctuation has a colon after the greeting line and a comma after the closing of the letter.

The Full Block Letter is a common style of letter used in paralegal firms. However, some firms use one of the modified styles referred to below.

The goal of any business is to have every letter that leaves its office be consistent and have the same professional look. You may work for a firm that uses full block with open punctuation. Or, you may have a firm that uses modified block with indentation and mixed punctuation. It is best to know all of the options, so that you can adhere to the company's standards once you start working, or choose which one you'd like for your firm.

## Modified Block Letters

There is an instructional video for students on this topic at:
Webpage:     http://www.asselingroup.com/paralegals
Password:    paralegals

Here is an example of a Modified Block Letter so that you may compare it to the Full Block Letter reviewed previously.

Please note that the date and the signature block both start at the center of the letter and move towards the right of the letter. In order to accomplish this, first turn on your ruler. You can do that by going to the View tab and clicking on the Ruler checkbox.

**Paralegals' Professional Corporation**
1 Paralegal Private
Ottawa, Ontario K2K 2K2
T (613) 555-9999 F (613) 555-8888
www.ParalegalsProfessionalCorporation.com

There is a small box to the far left of the ruler. By default, there is an L in the box, which is the symbol for a left tab. To set a left tab at the center point in your letter, do the following:

- Place your curser at the beginning of the line where you want the date

- Click in the ruler at the 3.25" mark (the page is 8.5" wide minus 2" for the right and left margins, leaving 6.5" and the middle of that is 3.25")
- This will put an L at the 3.25" point in your ruler, which is a left tab
- To access the tab, press your TAB button once on your keyboard
- Your curser should move to the middle of the page and you can add the date, and
- Repeat these steps once you get to the closing and name and title of the sender.

### Paralegals' Professional Corporation
1 Paralegal Private
Ottawa, Ontario K2K 2K2
T (613) 555-9999 F (613) 555-8888
www.ParalegalsProfessionalCorporation.com

June 30, 2017

CONFIDENTIAL

Mr. John Smith
1 Smith Street
Ottawa, Ontario K1N 5A1

Dear Mr. Smith:

RE: Smith v. MacDonald
Our File No. 44425-17

I am pleased to advise that this matter is now complete.

In accordance with your instructions, we have commenced an action against Mr. MacDonald and served him with the filed documents. Further to the receipt of our documentation, Mr. MacDonald retained his own representation who contacted us to discuss a possible settlement. We arrived at a settlement, which was paid by Mr. MacDonald and deposited into our trust account. We held enough back to cover our account and forwarded the balance to you.

Please find enclosed our Statement of Account and Trust Statement. It outlines all of the time and disbursements on your file, as well as payment in full. Don't hesitate to contact me if you have any questions regarding this account, or if you require any legal assistance in the future.

Yours very truly,

Barb Asselin, MBA

BLA/yi
Enclosure
By Regular Mail

## Modified Block Letters with Indentation

There is an instructional video for students on this topic at:
Webpage: http://www.asselingroup.com/paralegals
Password: paralegals

The only difference between a Modified Block Letter with Indentation and the previous example is that each paragraph in the body is indented. The example shows a 0.5" indentation, which is accomplished by placing your curser at the beginning of each paragraph and pressing the TAB key.

**Paralegals' Professional Corporation**
1 Paralegal Private
Ottawa, Ontario K2K 2K2
T (613) 555-9999 F (613) 555-8888
www.ParalegalsProfessionalCorporation.com

June 30, 2017

CONFIDENTIAL

Mr. John Smith
1 Smith Street
Ottawa, Ontario K1N 5A1

Dear Mr. Smith:

RE:   Smith v. MacDonald
      Our File No. 44425-17

      I am pleased to advise that this matter is now complete.

      In accordance with your instructions, we have commenced an action against Mr. MacDonald and served him with the filed documents. Further to the receipt of our documentation, Mr. MacDonald retained his own representation who contacted us to discuss a possible settlement. We arrived at a settlement, which was paid by Mr. MacDonald and deposited into our trust account. We held enough back to cover our account and forwarded the balance to you.

      Please find enclosed our Statement of Account and Trust Statement. It outlines all of the fee and disbursements on your file, as well as payment in full. Don't hesitate to contacte if you have any questions regarding this account, or if you require any legal assistance in the future.

                              Yours very truly,

                              Barb Asselin, MBA

BLA/yi
Enclosure
By Regular Mail

# Multi-Page Letters

There is an instructional video for students on this topic at:
Webpage:     http://www.asselingroup.com/paralegals
Password:    paralegals

Some of your letters will be more than one page in length. In this case, note that only the first page of the letter will be on letterhead. The second and subsequent pages will be on regular paper. Alternatively, your firm may use a cream-colored paper for their letterhead, or another light color that is not quite white. If this is the case, then the second and subsequent pages will be on blank paper of that color.

In this example of a multi-page letter, please notice the following:

- It is a Modified Block Letter
- The address block is to a company rather than a person – note that there is an attention line following the address of the company
- The signature block includes the company name of the sender and this is placed between the closing and the name and title of the sender,

with one blank space before the company name and at least three blank spaces after the company name
- In Modified Block Letters, the company name in the signature block is also set to start at the center of the page
- This letter example includes a cc, or a copy notation indicating that a copy of the letter will be sent to someone else as well
- There is a post-script, or PS – note that the TAB function is used to line up the lines of the message that make up the PS
- When there is more than one page to a letter, the entire signature block PLUS at least two lines of text, or one full sentence must be on the final page, and
- The second and subsequent pages have a header that includes the name of the recipient, the page number, and the date.

To add a header to the second and subsequent pages, first go to Insert > Header and click on Blank Header.

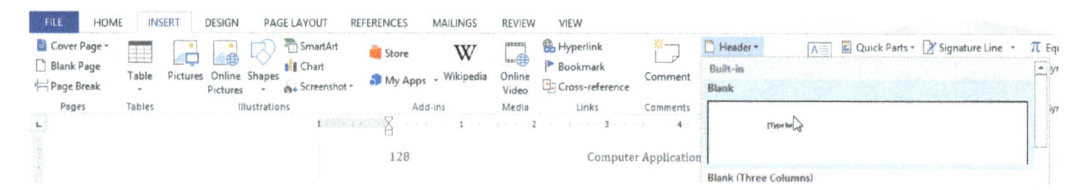

A Header & Footer Tools Design tab will open up at the far right of your ribbon.

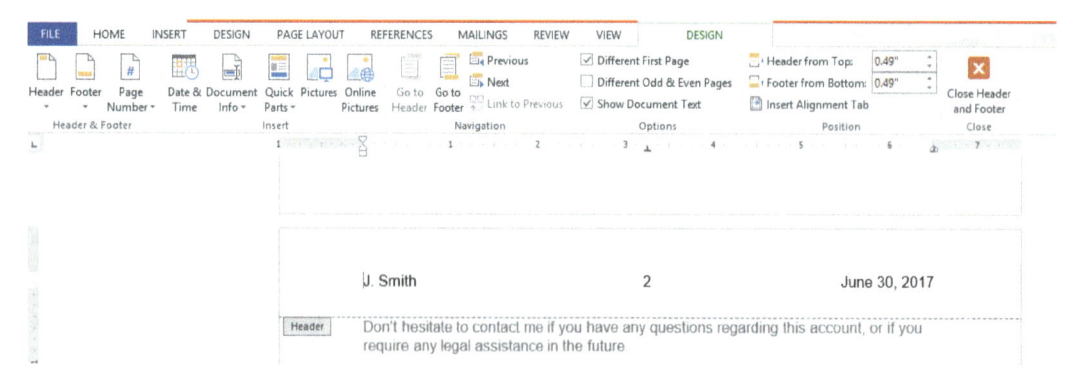

If you are using the template provided with this textbook, you will notice that the Header & Footer Tools Design tab opens up automatically if you double click in the letterhead portion of the letter. The letterhead portion of the letter is the first page header. The Options grouping has Different First Page and Show Document Text selected.

Computer Applications for Paralegals

Scroll from the first page to the second page. You will see that the first page has a first page header (with the letterhead) and a first page footer (blank). The second page has just header and footer, both of which are blank.

Notice on your ruler that there are symbols at the left margin (a left tab), the center (a center tab), and the right margin (a right tab). On the second page you can add a second page header by following these steps:

- Click in the header for page two at the left margin
- Add the name of the recipient of the letter
- Press the TAB button to go to the center tab
- Add the page number by going to Header & Footer Tools tab and clicking on Page Number > Current Position > Plain Number

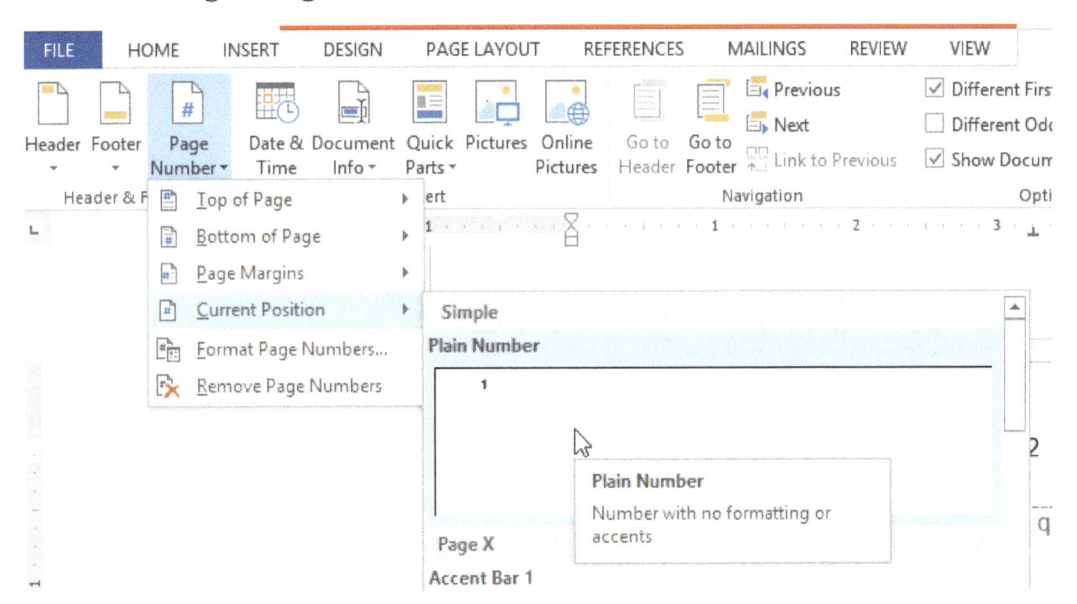

- Press the TAB button to go to the right margin
- Type the date of the letter, and
- Click the red X to close the Header & Footer Tools Design tab.

Note that this is the header for multi-page Modified Block Letters.

Next, we will look at an example of a multi-page Full Block Letter. Note the differences in the second page header. To create a header for the multi-page Full Block Letter, complete the following steps:

- Open the header by double-clicking in the header area of the letter

- Place your curser in the second page header at the left margin
- Type the name of the recipient of the letter
- Press ENTER
- Type the word Page and then type a space
- Add the page number by going to the Header & Footer Tools tab and clicking on Page Number > Current Position > Plain Number
- Press ENTER
- Add the date of the letter, and
- Press the red X to close the Header & Footer Tools Design tab.

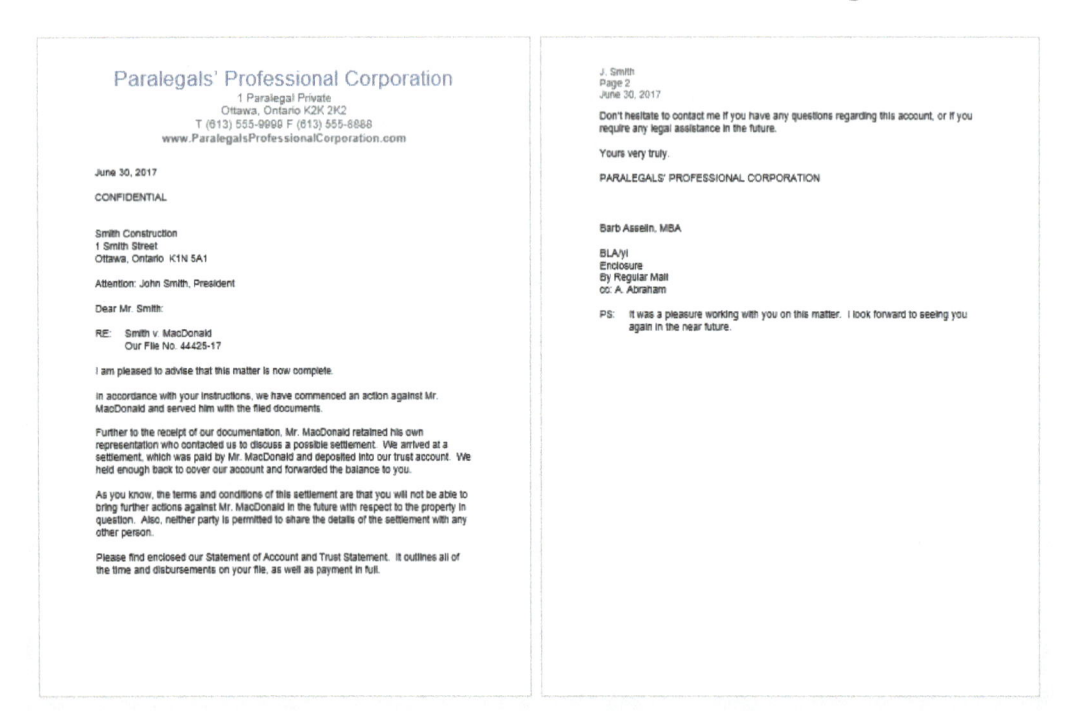

## Envelopes and Labels

There is an instructional video for students on this topic at:
Webpage: http://www.asselingroup.com/paralegals
Password: paralegals

Most letters need either an envelope or a label. To print an envelope, follow these steps:

- Place your curser at the beginning of the first line of the address block

Computer Applications for Paralegals 191

- Go to the Mailings tab and click on Envelopes
- Make sure there is an envelope in your printer
- The address from your letter should automatically appear in the Delivery address box of the Envelopes and Labels dialogue box
- If necessary, add your company's return address in the Return address box, and
- Click Print.

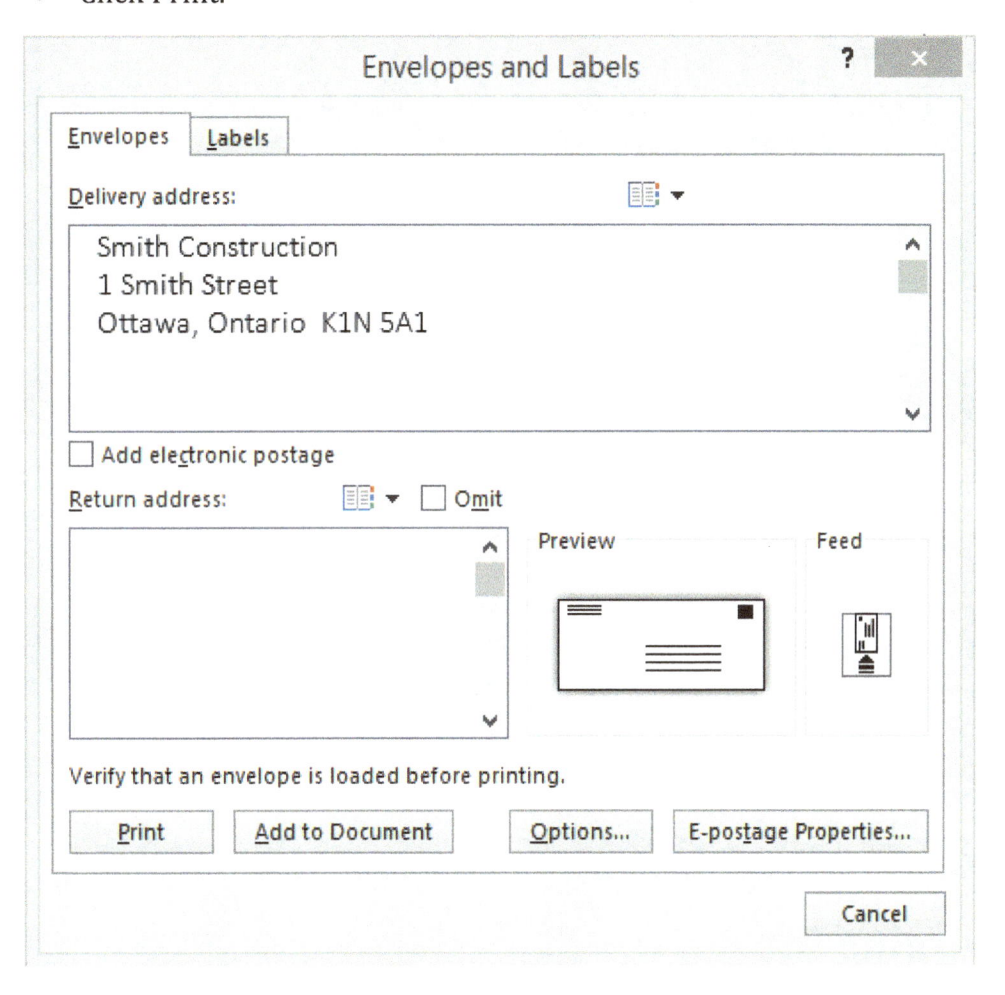

To print a label, follow these steps:

- Place your curser at the beginning of the first line of the address block
- Go to the Mailings tab and click on Labels
- The address from your letter should automatically appear in the Delivery address box of the Envelopes and Labels dialogue box

- Make sure your sheet of labels is in your printer
- If necessary, click on Options and select the correct brand and number of labels you are using
- Choose single label and the location of the label you want to print, and
- Click Print.

## Merging

There is an instructional video for students on this topic at:
Webpage:     http://www.asselingroup.com/paralegals
Password:    paralegals

Merging is a tool that combines Word with either Excel or Outlook to save a great deal of time. It is often used when you want to send the same letter, or close to the same letter, to a number of people separately. For example, if our office was moving to a new location, we could send a letter about the new location to all of our clients and be able to customize the letter that each client receives.

To complete a merge, we will be using the Mail Merge Wizard, which is found on the Mailing tab by clicking Start Mail Merge > Mail Merge Wizard.

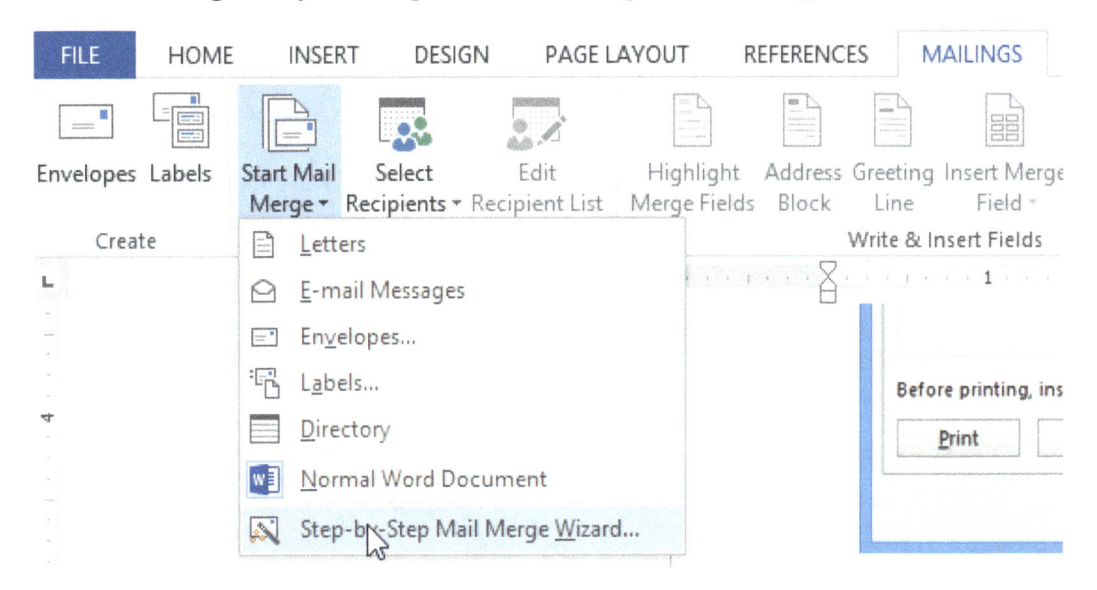

The Mail Merge task pane will open up on the right side of your screen. There are six steps to completing a mail merge. Four of the steps are really easy and two of them are lengthier.

Notice that there are three sections to the task pane. The first section usually gives you a choice of items for whatever step you are on.

The middle section will explain the selection that you have made.

The last (bottom) section allows you to navigate back and forth through the six steps of the mail merge.

For this example, I will create a letter to be sent to our firm's clients advising them on our upcoming new office location.

## Step 1

In step 1, you will select the type of document that you would like to create. The options are letters, e-mail messages, envelopes, labels, and directory. We will choose Letters, which should automatically be selected.

The middle section of the task pane explains that we will send a letter to multiple people.

Now, click the **Next: Starting Document** link at the bottom of the task pane.

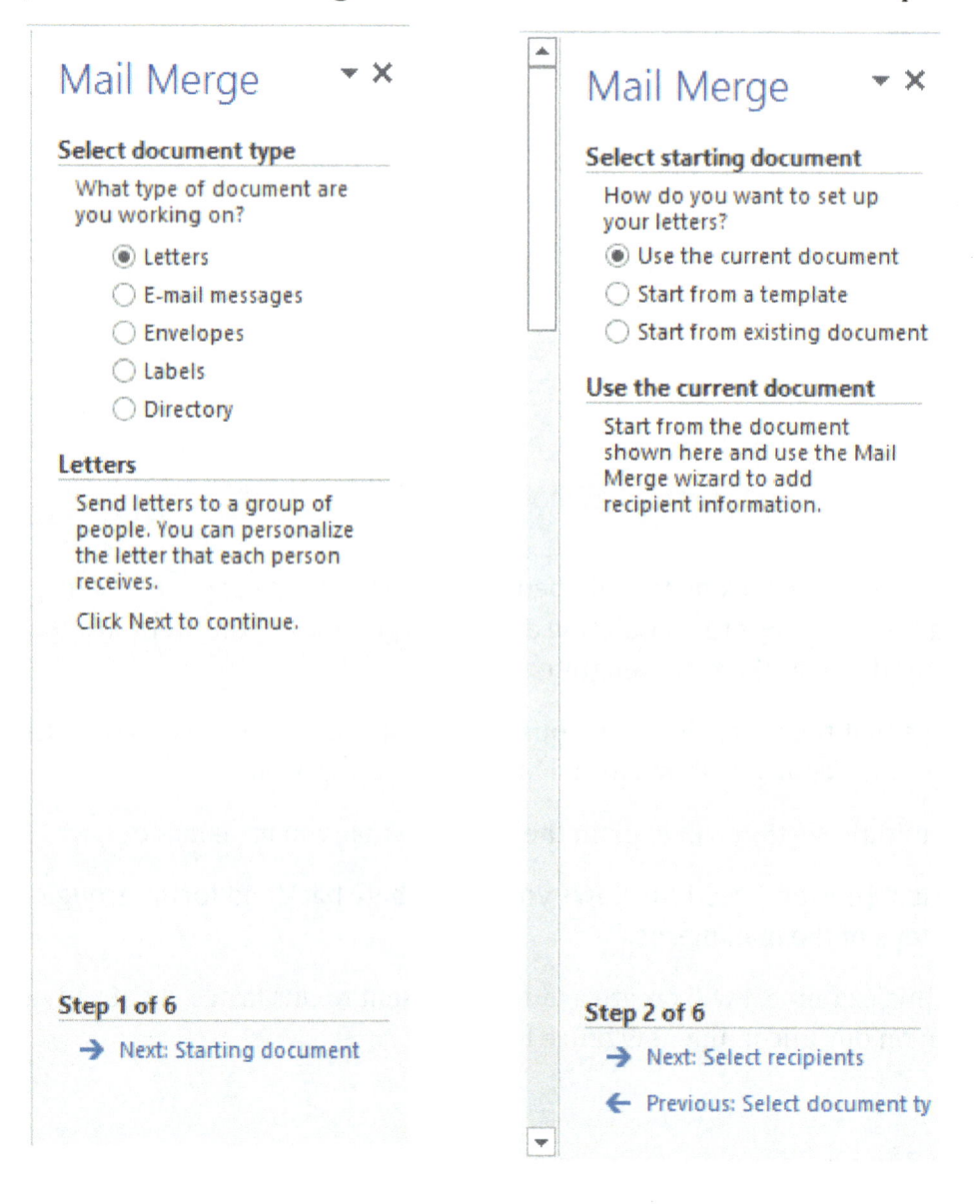

## Step 2

In step 2, you choose the document you want to start with. Your options are:

- To start with the document that is currently on your screen. This is the option I chose since I have the letterhead template from the text already displayed on my computer.
- To start using one of Word's pre-designed templates (see the templates section later in this chapter), or
- To start using a document on your computer. If you have the letterhead from the text saved on your computer, you can choose this option and click Open to browse your computer to find it.

Now, click the **Next: Select Recipients** link at the bottom of the task pane.

## Step 3

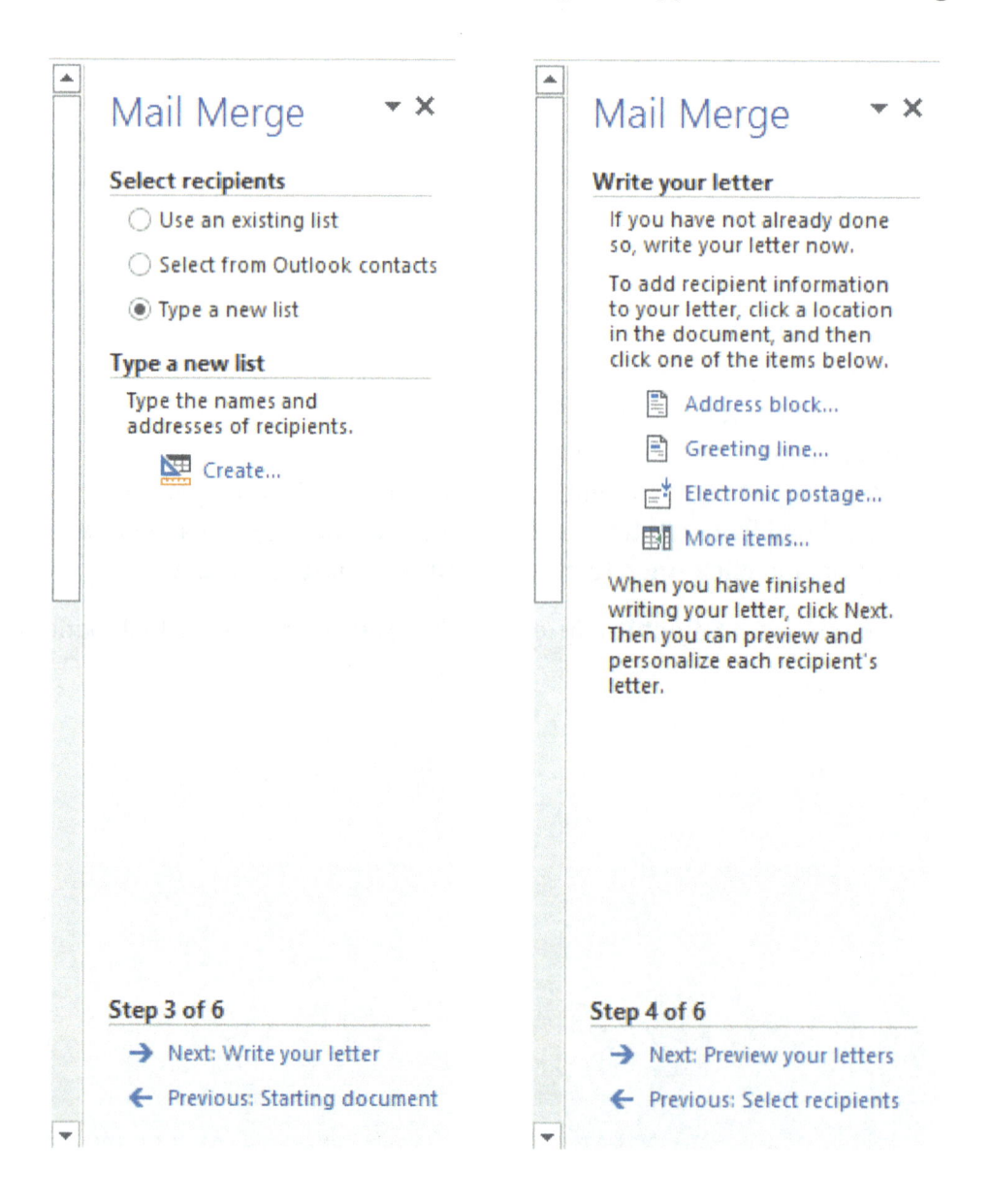

There are three options in step 3:

- You can use an existing list that you may have already created either in Word or in Excel. If you select this option, you can browse to find your file of contacts.

Computer Applications for Paralegals

- You can select your contacts from Outlook, or
- You can create a new list, which is the option I have chosen.

In the middle section, the only thing you can really do is click on the **Create** link. Once you click on that link, a dialogue box opens up where you can add information about the recipients of your letter.

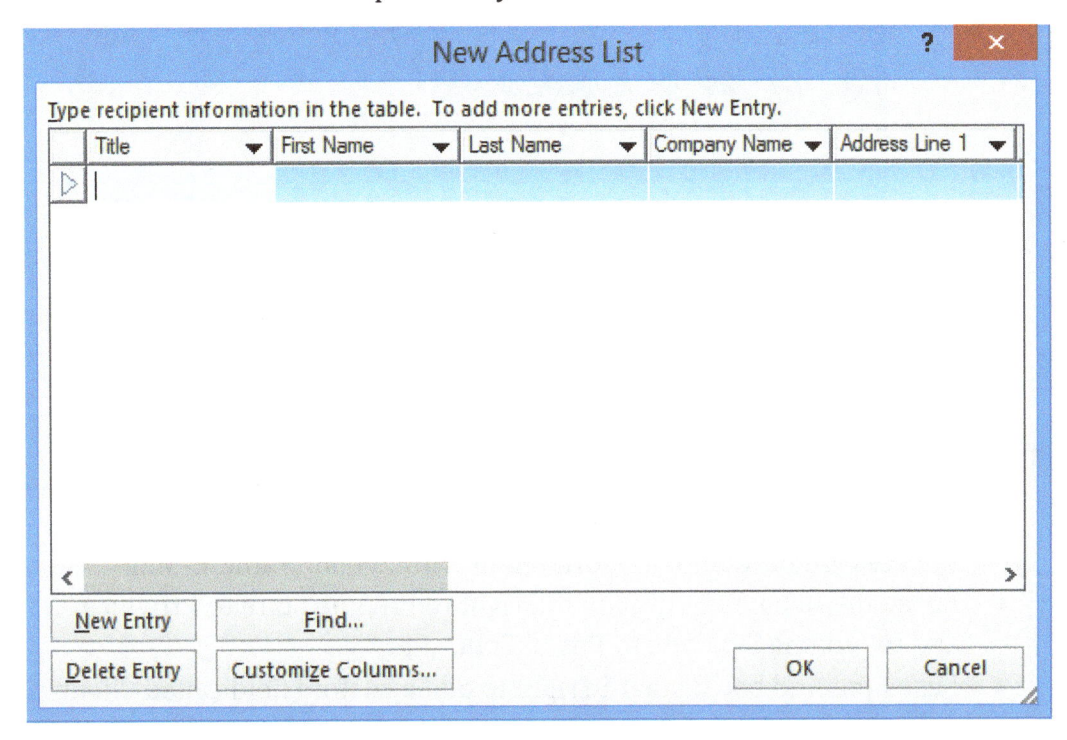

If you scroll across the categories of information, you will see many more than you need in order to send a letter by mail. Click on the Customize Columns button at the bottom of the dialogue box change the categories to only those that you need.

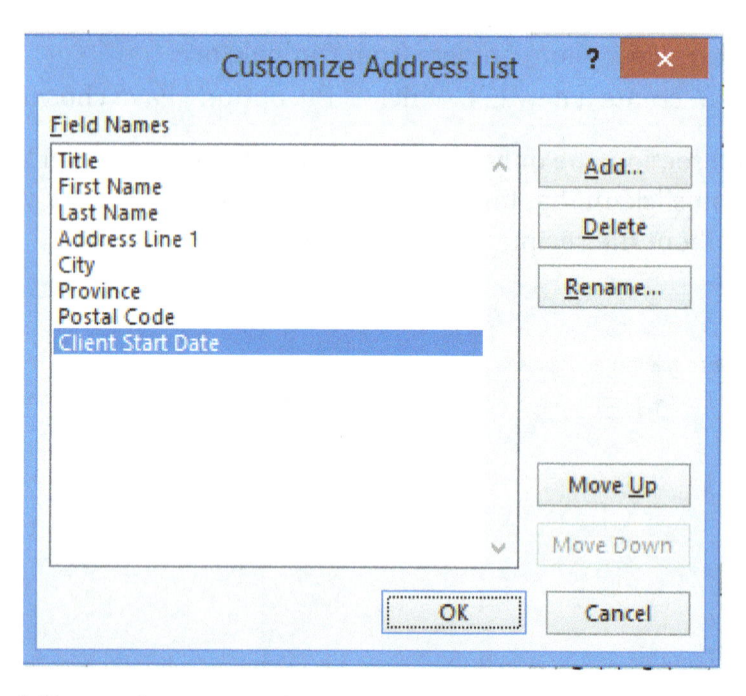

[Screenshot of "Customize Address List" dialog box showing Field Names: Title, First Name, Last Name, Address Line 1, City, Province, Postal Code, Client Start Date (highlighted), with buttons Add, Delete, Rename, Move Up, Move Down, OK, Cancel.]

Mine looks different from yours because I made the following changes:

- I used the Delete button on the right to delete these fields: Company, Address Line 2, Country, Work Phone, Home Phone, and E-Mail
- I used the Rename button on the right to rename State to Province and to rename Zip Code to Postal Code, and
- I used the Add button on the right to add a custom field called Client Start Date.

The custom field allows me to send a more customized and personalized letter to each recipient. In this field, I will enter the date when each client joined our firm so that I can add that piece of information to each client's letter.

Once you are finished customizing the Field Names, click OK. Now you can add your recipient information. You can see from the example that I have added three clients and their information, including their start date.

Once you have added a few recipients, click OK. This will prompt you to save your database of clients. There are three things to save when performing a merge and this is the first.

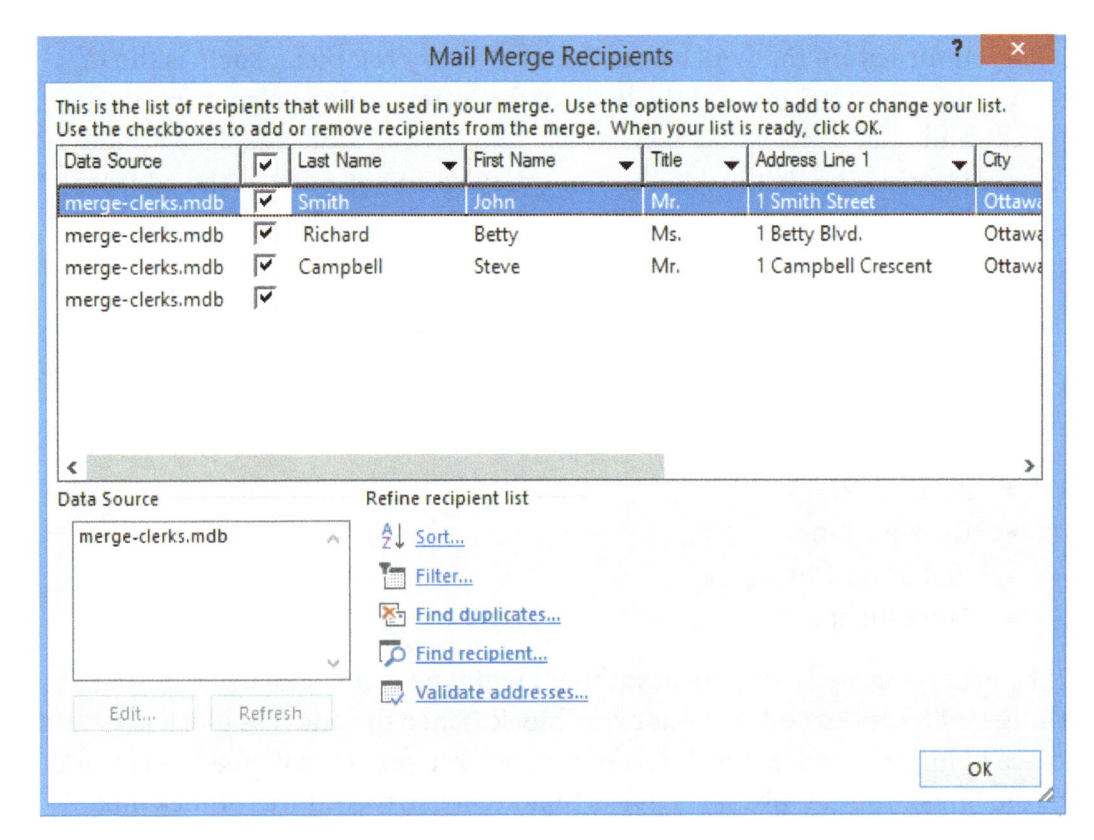

Once you save it, the list will appear in the above format. All of your recipients are selected with checkmarks. Notice that I have a blank entry at the bottom that I should uncheck. If you notice any mistakes in your entries, you will not be able to fix them on this screen. To edit your database, you will need to click on the file in the Data Source box on the bottom right and then click Edit. Make the necessary changes and save again. Once you are satisfied with your recipients, click OK.

Now you should notice that Step 3 on your mail merge task pane shows that you are using recipients from an existing list and that the file you saved is listed in the middle portion of the task pane.

Click the **Next: Write Your Letter** link at the bottom of the task pane.

## Step 4

In Step 4, you will write your letter. It is important to remember that there are two types of information in any letter that you create with a merge:

- Information that will be the same for every recipient, such as the re: line, the date, most of the body of the letter, and the signature block, and
- Information that is different for every recipient, such as the address block, the greeting line, and customized parts of the body of the letter.

It is easy to add the common elements to your letter. You simply type them. The customized parts, though, are added differently.

On the Step 4 task pane, the instructions are to type your letter now and that customized information can be added using the following links:

- Address Block
- Greeting Line
- Electronic Postage, and
- More Items.

If I start typing my letter, the first thing I will type is the date. The second thing I will want to add is the address block. Since the address block is a piece of information that is different for each recipient, I will need to use one of the links. You can probably guess that I will use the Address Block link.

To add the Address Block code to your letter, click in your letter in the spot where you want the address block to go. Then, click the Address Block link.

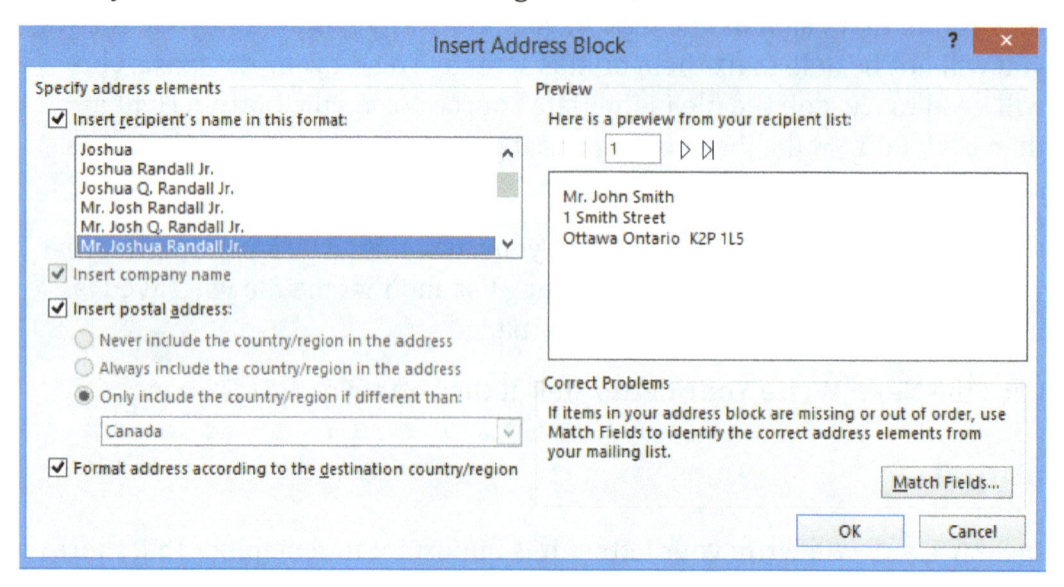

The dialogue box that pops up shows you a variety of different ways to show your recipients. The preview box on the right will give you a sample using one of your recipients. If you like how it looks, click OK. If you see that a field is in the wrong place in the address, click the Match Fields button and see if one of your fields is mismatched. Then click OK. That will place the Address Block code into your letter.

**Paralegals' Professional Corporation**
1 Paralegal Private
Ottawa, Ontario K2K 2K2
T (613) 555-9999 F (613) 555-8888
www.ParalegalsProfessionalCorporation.com

June 30, 2017

«AddressBlock»

Next, I will continue with my letter to add the greeting line. Again, this is customized content and I will use the Greeting Line link in the task pane.

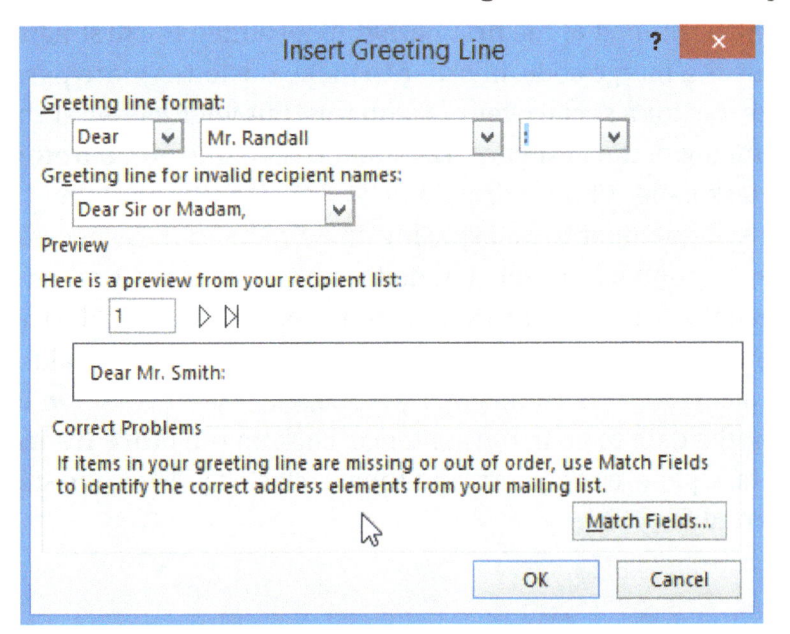

**Insert Greeting Line**

Greeting line format:
Dear | Mr. Randall | :

Greeting line for invalid recipient names:
Dear Sir or Madam,

Preview
Here is a preview from your recipient list:

Dear Mr. Smith:

Correct Problems
If items in your greeting line are missing or out of order, use Match Fields to identify the correct address elements from your mailing list.

Match Fields...

OK | Cancel

The dialogue box shows a preview of one of your contacts. The only change I made is to change the comma to a colon after the greeting line. This is because I am writing a business letter with mixed punctuation. I would choose nothing if I were writing a business letter with open punctuation. I would choose a comma if I were writing a personal letter.

If you are happy with how your preview looks, click OK. Now you have inserted the Greeting Line code.

> June 30, 2017
>
> «AddressBlock»
>
> «GreetingLine»

Continue with your letter as most of it now will be similar content for all of your recipients.

You will see from the following completed letter that most of the letter is the same for everyone. There are two areas where I added merge codes to customize the letter for each client:

- At the beginning of the first paragraph, I added the first name of the client as a merge code, in order to make the letter more personal, since it is for a social event. To do this, put your curser at the beginning of the first paragraph and click of the **More Items** link in the task pane. Choose first name and then click insert and then click close. Remember to add spacing and punctuation, as necessary, and
- In the second paragraph, I added a merge code to say when the client joined the firm. This further customizes the letter for the individual client and I get to use the custom field I created when making my recipient list. To add this merge code, place your curser where you want the date to go in the sentence, click on the **More Items** link in the task pane, click insert, and then click close. The code should be inserted for you.

> **Paralegals' Professional Corporation**
> 1 Paralegal Private
> Ottawa, Ontario K2K 2K2
> T (613) 555-9999 F (613) 555-8888
> www.ParalegalsProfessionalCorporation.com
>
> June 30, 2017
>
> «AddressBlock»
>
> «GreetingLine»
>
> Re:   New Office Grand Opening
>
> «First_Name», we are pleased to announce that our office is expanding and moving to a new location at 123 Success Street, effective September 1st. I am enclosing a map showing our new location.
>
> We are holding a client appreciation day on September 1st for all of our preferred clients. Since you have been a valued client since «Client_Start_Date», we'd love it if you could attend. Feel free to bring your partner and/or family. There will be delicious snacks, a local band, and even a magician!
>
> Please RSVP by August 20th with the number of attendees. The party starts at 1:00 p.m.
>
> We look forward to celebrating with you.
>
> Yours very truly,
>
>
>
> Barb Asselin, MBA
>
> /ba
> Enclosure

This is the second thing that you will save as you are completing a merge. Save the coded letter on your computer or USB.

You are now ready to move to Step 5. Click the **Next: Preview Your Letters** link at the bottom of the task pane.

## Step 5

Congratulations! You have completed the two most time-consuming steps and now there are only two quick steps left until you are finished.

Step 5 performs your merge for you based on your letter (with merge codes) and your list of recipients. It displays one of your letters to one of your recipients on the main part of your screen. Check it over to see if it is accurate. Especially note the spacing and punctuation around your merge code fields and see if it is correct.

If you see errors that need to be fixed, click on the **Previous: Write Your Letter** link and go back to Step 4. Make the necessary changes and then go to Step 5 again to see if the errors have been fixed.

If you are happy with how your first sample letter looks, you can use the arrows in the top portion of the task pane to scroll through all of your recipients to see if each of the letters looks good.

Notice that, in this step, you can still edit your recipient list, or go back to edit your letter. Once you have finished with a step, you can always go back to change it.

You are now finished with Step 5. Click the **Next: Complete the Merge** link at the bottom of the task pane to move on to the final step.

## Step 6

Step 6 allows you to create one file that will have all of your merged letters in it, one after the other. This is the document that will save you lots of time, as you can simply press print once and get all of your letters.

To get all of your letters, do the following:

- Read the instructions in the Step 6 task pane
- Click on the **Edit Individual Letters** link in the task pane, and
- A new document will open up on your computer that will have all of the letters in it, one after the other.

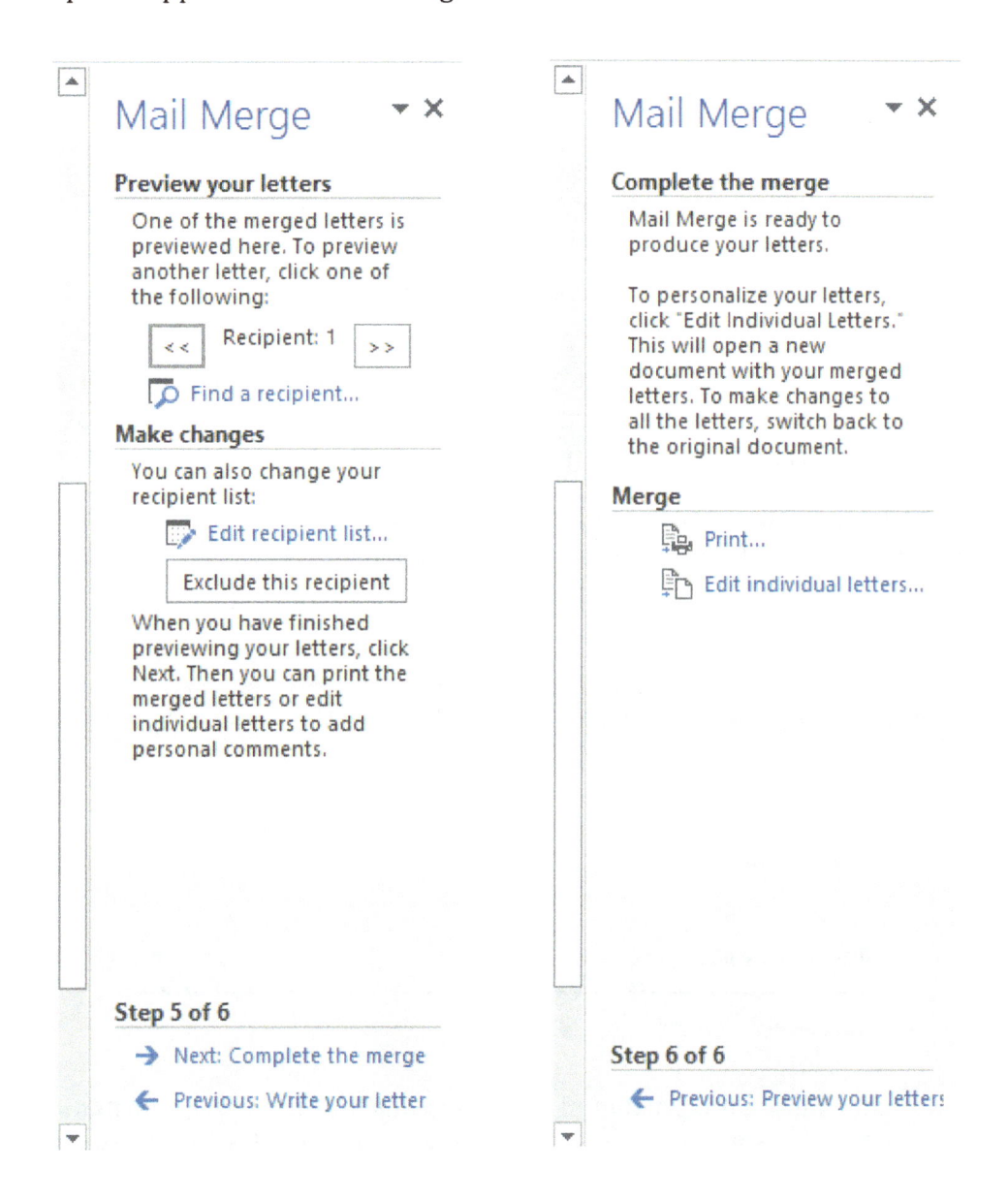

This new document is the third and final document that you will save as part of a mail merge. Click File > Save As and save the document to your computer or USB.

Now, you are ready to print your letters.

# Memos

There is an instructional video for students on this topic at:
Webpage:    http://www.asselingroup.com/paralegals
Password:    paralegals

A memo is a form of internal office communication that is sent from one member of a firm to another member of a firm.  The document is less formal than a letter (external communication) and is on a type of letterhead that typically has less information on it than regular letterhead.

A memo letterhead is available for students to download from the private textbook webpage.  It will be used in this demonstration.

**Paralegals' Professional Corporation**
Interoffice Memorandum

TO:     Here
FROM:   Here
DATE:   Here
RE:     Here

Body of memo

You will see that the top portion of the memo has four pieces of information: To, From, Date, and Re: (reference line).  Tabs are used to line up the words "here" after each of the labels, which is where you will type your information.

The top portion of the memo is separated from the bottom portion of the memo by a line.  The line is not necessary but serves as a visual between the top and bottom sections and is often used in memo templates.

The letterhead used for the memo has only the name of the firm and the words Interoffice Memorandum.  Other companies may use the word Memo, or Memorandum, or Office Memo, or some other phrase.  Note that there is no address, phone number, website, email, or other contact information contained in the letterhead portion of the memo. This is because it is used for internal communications. Both parties (the sender and the recipient) work for the same company so both parties already know where the office is located.

There are two blank spaces below the letterhead and one blank space between each of the pieces of information on the top portion of the memo.

An example of a memo that you may write would be to the Human Resources officer of your firm asking for holidays to be approved. The next image is an example of such a memo.

## Paralegals' Professional Corporation
### Interoffice Memorandum

TO:     Caroline Weber

FROM:   Barb Asselin

DATE:   June 30, 2017

RE:     Upcoming Holiday Request

Further to our departmental meeting last Tuesday, I am submitting my request for holidays prior to the deadline of July 4, 2017.

I am entitled to three weeks of holidays and I have carried forward seven days from 2016. To date in 2017, I have already taken nine days off. I would like to request the following additional holidays during the remainder of 2017:

- August 1 – 4, inclusive
- August 14 – 18, inclusive
- December 22, and
- December 27 – 29, inclusive.

I believe this additional holiday schedule will use my remaining 13 days of holidays.

Could you please let me know at your earliest convenience if the above-noted holidays are approved?

Thank you very much.

/ba

cc: Marc Bourque

Notice the following about this memo:

- There is no greeting, such as Dear Ms. Weber
- There is no closing, such as Yours very truly

- There is no signature block
- Memos have the same format as a Full Block Letter in that each paragraph is left-aligned, and not indented
- The memo is cc'd to Marc Bourque, a clerk in my department, so that he is aware of my request for holidays
- There is consistently one blank space between paragraphs, and
- In the bulleted list, the bullets start at the left margin.

To get a bulleted list to start at the left margin, start a bulleted list by clicking on the bullets icon in the Paragraph grouping of the Home tab. Before you start typing the text that will follow the bullet, click on the Decrease Indent button in the Paragraph grouping of the Home tab to move the bullet back to the left margin.

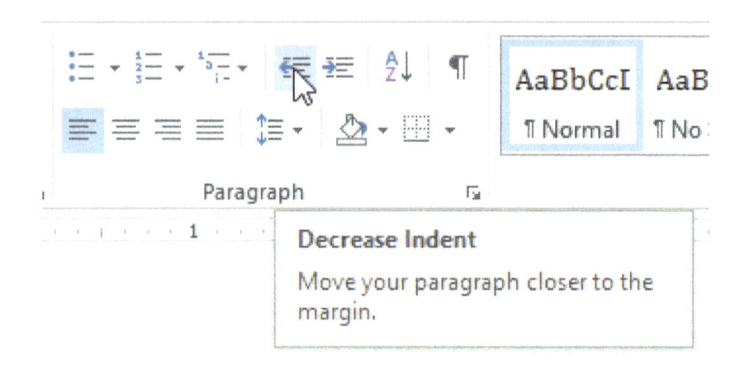

## Multi-Page Memos

There is an instructional video for students on this topic at:
Webpage: http://www.asselingroup.com/paralegals
Password: paralegals

A multi-page memo is similar to a multi-page letter in that it is almost exactly the same as a single-page memo, except that on the second and subsequent pages, you will have a header.

The header for a multi-page memo is formatted the same way as a header for the multi-page Modified Block Letter.

To add a header to the second and subsequent pages, first go to Insert > Header and click on Blank Header.

Computer Applications for Paralegals

A Header & Footer Tools Design tab will open up at the far right of your ribbon.

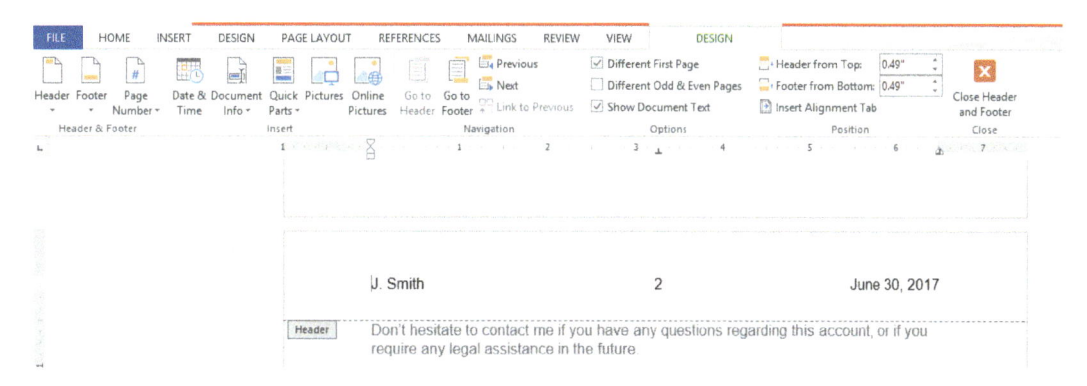

If you are using the template provided with this textbook, you will notice that the Header & Footer Tools Design tab opens up automatically if you double click in the letterhead portion of the memo. The letterhead portion of the memo is the first page header. The Options grouping has Different First Page and Show Document Text selected.

Scroll from the first page to the second page. You will see that the first page has a first page header (with the letterhead) and a first page footer (blank). The second page has just header and footer, both of which are blank.

Notice on your ruler that there are symbols at the left margin (a left tab), the center (a center tab), and the right margin (a right tab). On the second page you can add a second page header by following these steps:

- Click in the header for page two at the left margin
- Add the name of the recipient of the memo
- Press the TAB button to go to the center tab
- Add the page number by going to Header & Footer Tools tab and clicking on Page Number > Current Position > Plain Number

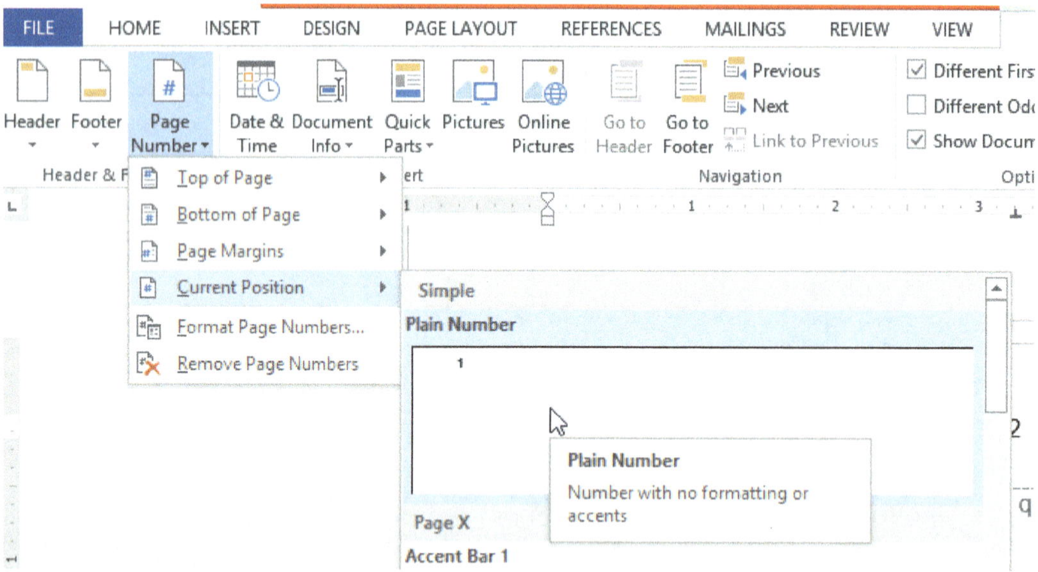


- Press the TAB button to go to the right margin
- Type the date of the memo, and
- Click the red X to close the Header & Footer Tools Design tab.

Voila! You now have a properly formatted multi-page memo.

# Fax Cover Sheets

There is an instructional video for students on this topic at:
Webpage: http://www.asselingroup.com/paralegals
Password: paralegals

Word contains a number of pre-designed documents for use in the business world. A useful one is a fax cover sheet.

To create a fax cover sheet, go to the File tab and click on New.

# Computer Applications for Paralegals

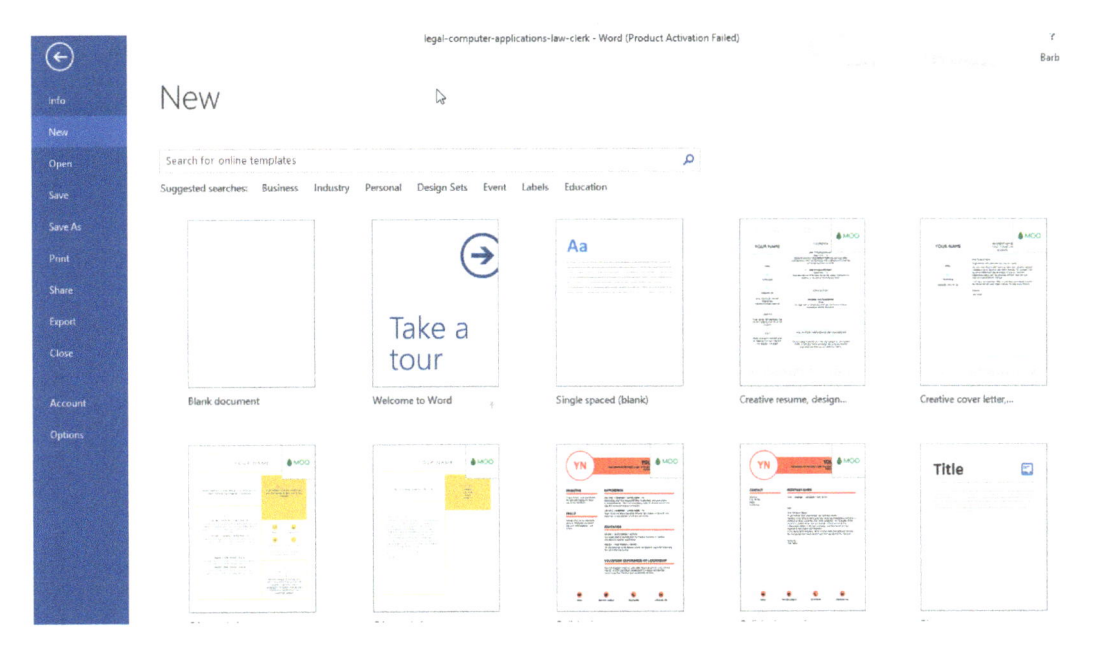

211

You can scroll through the documents that automatically appear on the next screen, or, if you know what you are looking for, you can use one of the search terms at the top of the screen, or you can use the search bar.

Try typing fax cover sheet in the search box and see what comes up.

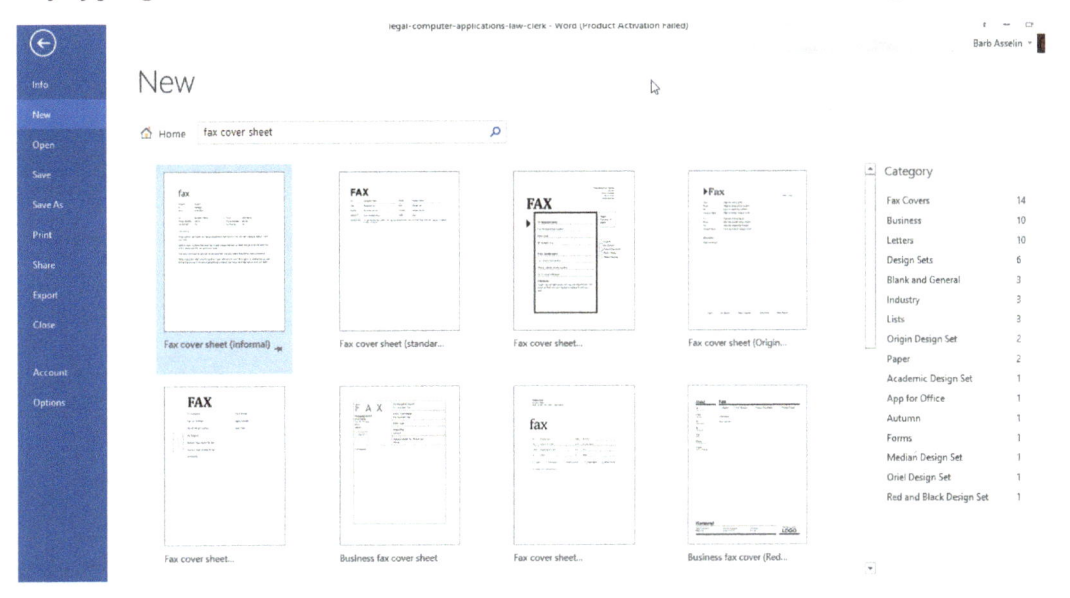

As you can see, there are a number of options available to you. On the right, you will see links to other business documents that you can choose from instead or either narrow or broaden your search.

212                                         Computer Applications for Paralegals

I am going to choose the Business fax cover sheet, which is second one in on the second row.  Once I make my choice, I get the following dialogue box:

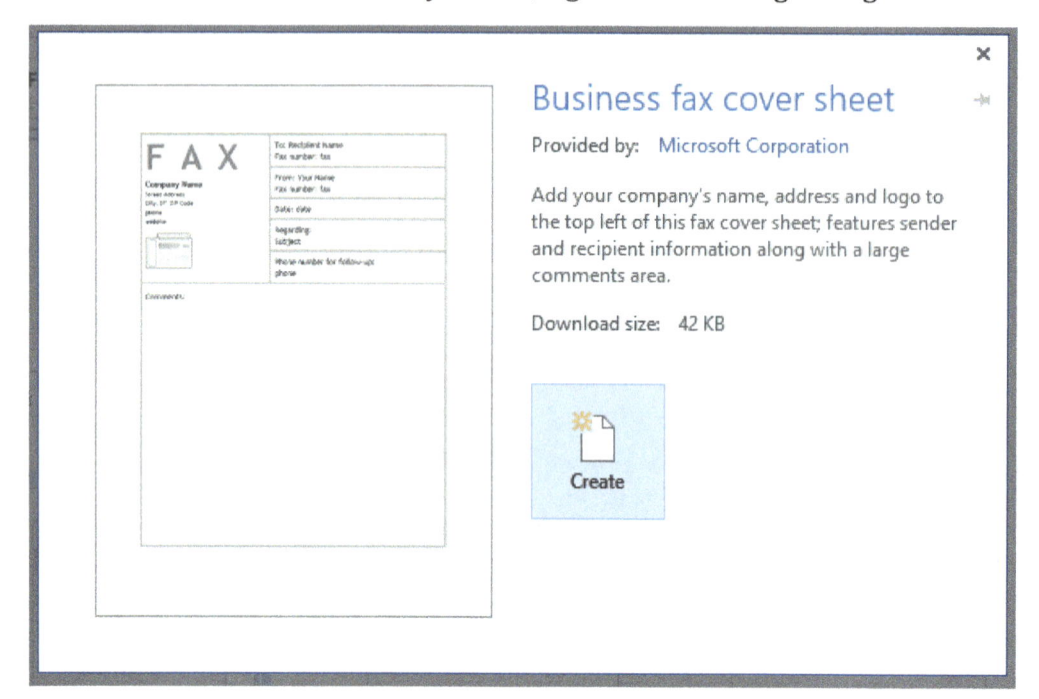

This dialogue box tells me briefly what this template is and how I can use it and customize it.  I will click Create to open a new document with this fax cover sheet in it.

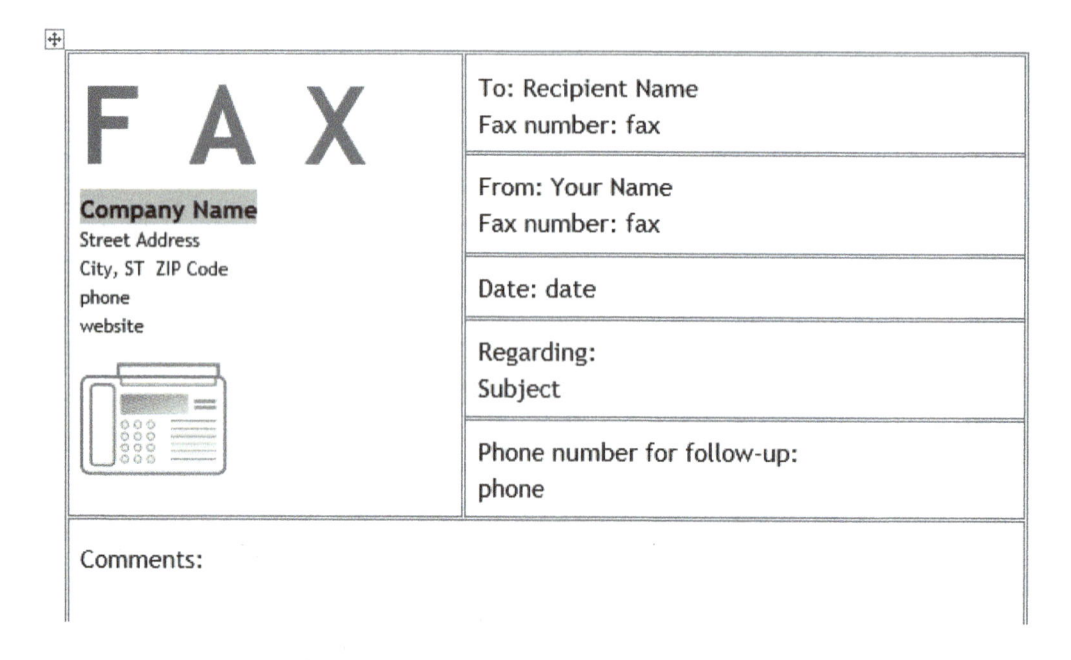

Computer Applications for Paralegals 213

Each template is different and contains different information. This particular example has a spot on the left where I can add my company name and contact information. On the right, I will enter the specifics about who I am sending my fax to, their fax number, my name, my fax number, the date, the subject of the fax, and my phone number.

Each one of these pieces of information is similar to a PowerPoint slide in that each field is a "placeholder" where you can click and type the proper response. In the previous graphic, I have selected the Company Name field. You can see that it is gray, which indicates that it has been selected. Once I have selected a field, I simply need to type in my response to complete that portion of the document.

On the bottom half of this document, there is a section for comments. Here, I would make a brief statement about the contents of the fax. Something like, "Please find enclosed the form we spoke about earlier today. Kindly complete the form and return a signed copy to our office by Friday."

Once you are finished with your fax cover sheet, you can save it in your client's folder on your computer.

Note that you can create a precedent for your firm that includes your firm contact information and then save the new precedent to be used whenever you need a fax cover sheet. That way, you will always be using the same form, which gives your firm a consistent and professional appearance to the public.

If you go to work for a firm, they will have a similar precedent that they use for all of their outgoing faxes and you will use that template.

## Templates

There is an instructional video for students on this topic at:
Webpage:    http://www.asselingroup.com/paralegals
Password:   paralegals

Fax cover sheets are not the only templates in the Word program. There are lots of others that can be found when opening a new document from the File tab. They include:

- Resumes
- Reports
- Menus
- Letters
- Cover letters
- Budgets
- Flyers, and
- Much more.

Each template you choose works the same way the fax cover sheet did in the previous example. There are placeholders for information. As you click on each placeholder, you can type in it to replace the descriptive words that are in the template.

Here is an example of an event template that you could choose to advertise an upcoming seminar for law students.

Small firms without a graphic designer and looking for a quick design for an upcoming event could use such a template. Click Create and see what we can come up with.

Computer Applications for Paralegals                    215

Upon opening, there are some administrative fields that you could complete.

By closing the upper section (click the x at the top right), you can complete the event flyer.

In the example below, I completed the flyer for a seminar to be held at our offices to attract articling students to apply to article at our firm.

In no time at all, you can have a professionally designed flyer ready to go.

You could further customize a document like this by adding your company logo to the document somewhere such as the top right corner.

## Reports

There is an instructional video for students on this topic at:
Webpage:   http://www.asselingroup.com/paralegals
Password:   paralegals

Word's templates can also help us prepare professional reports for our firm, our clients, and other industry professionals.

To create a report, first create a new document, by going to the File tab and choosing New. Then, click in the search bar and type report.

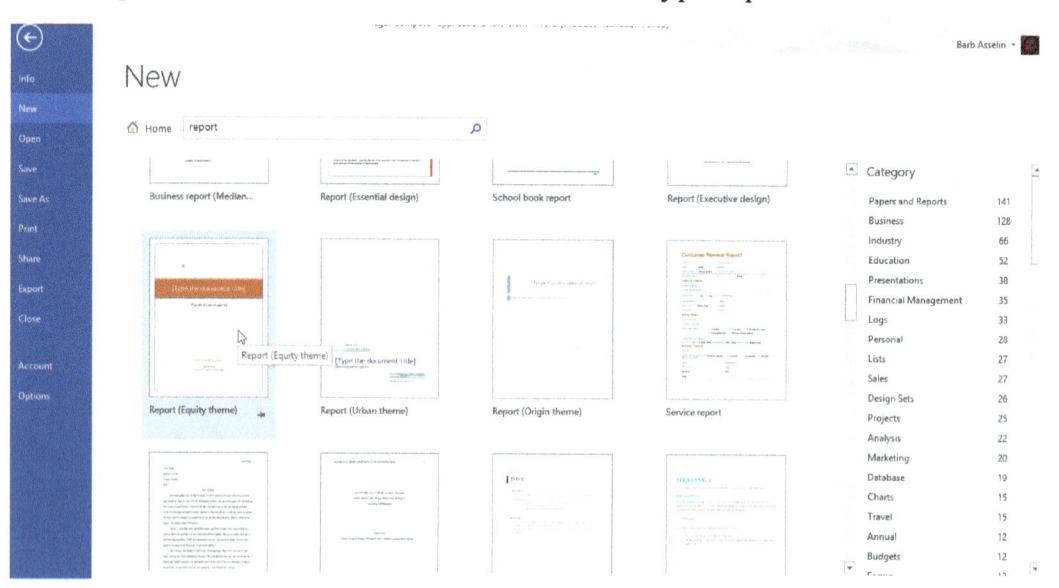

Choose a report from the options available. If you want to choose the same one I chose, it is the Report (Equity theme).

You should see the following dialogue box that allows you to generate the report by clicking Create.

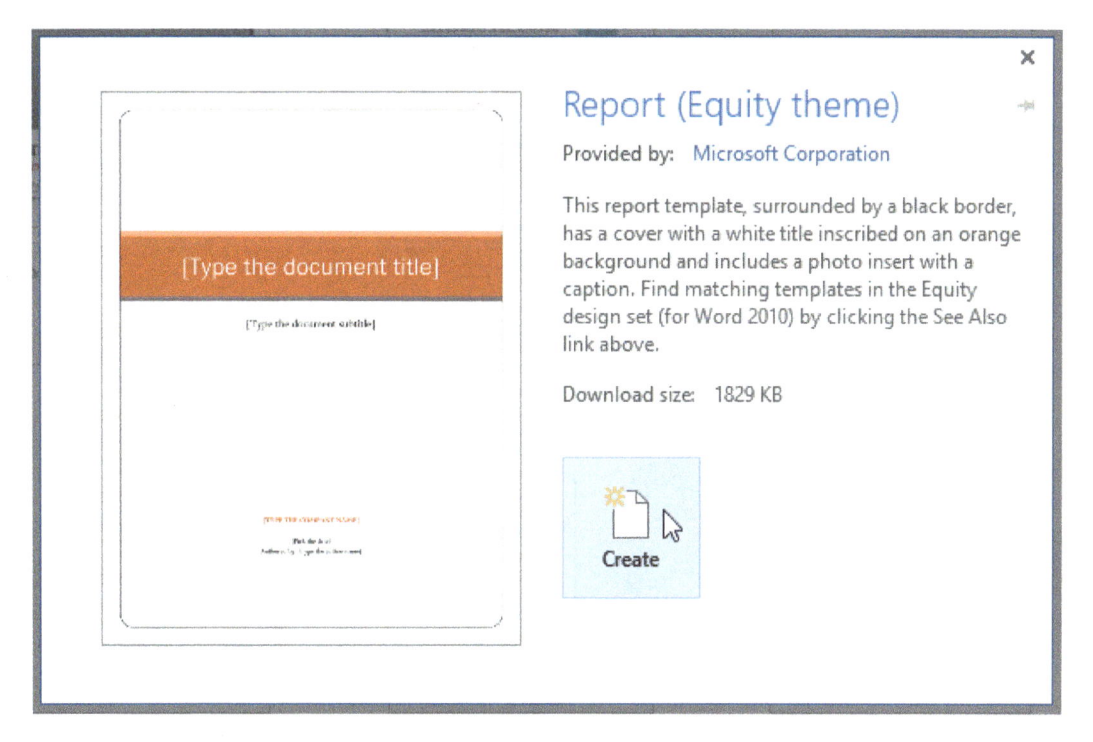

Your report will open in a new document on your computer.

This report template is similar to the fax cover sheet and the flyer templates we have already looked at, wherein it uses placeholders for the various pieces of information.

There are two pages to the report. The first page is the title page and the second page is the body of the report. Since we don't have a report yet, the body of the report is just text explaining how the report template works.

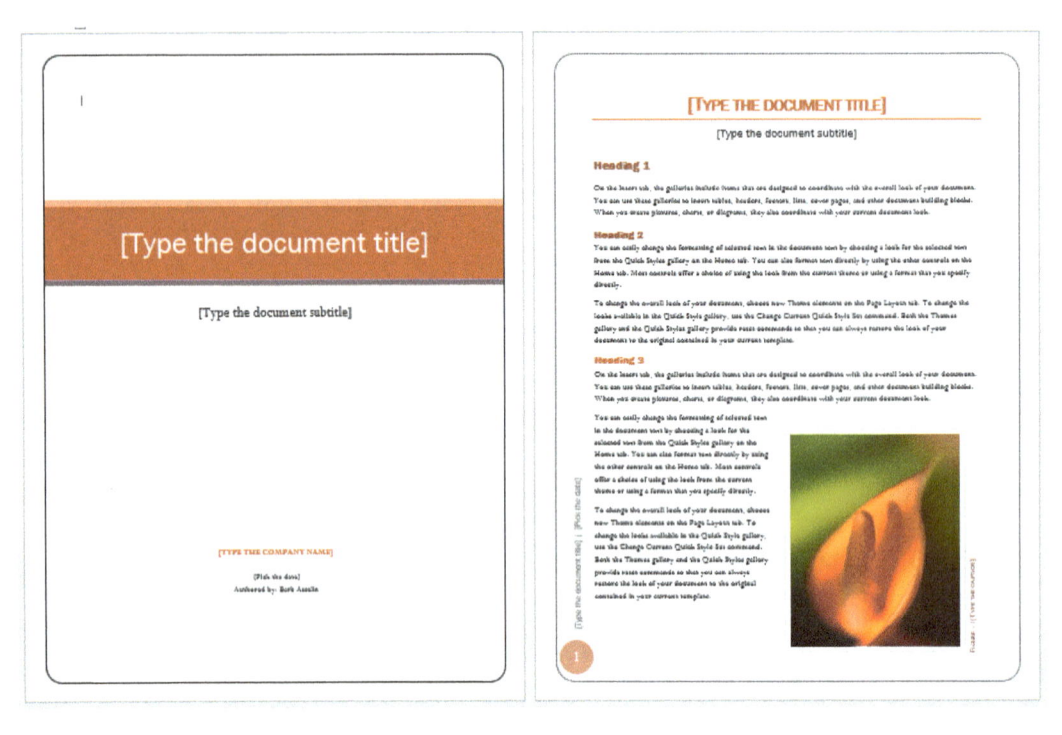

I'm going to create a report about using MS Office Suite, so that I can show you how the various elements of the report work.

I'll start by adding the title **How to Use MS Office Suite** and the subtitle **A Guide for Paralegal Firm Employees**. I will add my name as the author and today's date and the company name.

> **How to Use MS Office Suite**
>
> A Guide for Paralegal Firm Employees
>
> PARALEGALS' PROFESSIONAL CORPORATION
>
> June 30, 2017
> Authored by: Barb Asselin

The next step is to look at the second page. Nearly the entire page is a placeholder for the body of the report. Notice how the title and subtitle have been inserted into the top of the page.

> Barb Asselin
>
> **How to Use MS Office Suite**
>
> A Guide for Paralegal Firm Employees

Also, notice that the Styles grouping on the Home tab is filled with orange heading styles so that they will match the design we have chosen.

If you have already researched a report or have the content of a report, you could copy and paste it into this report. If you are copying and pasting, be careful how to paste. There are usually at least three or four different ways to paste into a document. Right-click and under the paste options, try placing your mouse on each one and see how the pasted document looks. Basically, you want to keep the formatting of the new document and not the formatting of the previous or original document.

## If Your Copy and Paste Doesn't Work

Depending on your version of Word, when you copy and paste the body of your report into the template, it may cut off the text at the bottom of the first page. This is because your version of the template has a new text box for each page of text and most of your report is "hiding" below the edge of the text box on the first page.

If this is the case for your document, you may wish to create your own custom report using a Cover Page template and then adding additional pages as necessary.

## Using a Cover Page Template

To use a pre-designed Cover Page Template, simply start with a new, blank document, click on the Insert tab, and choose Cover Page. Scroll through the options until you find a design you like and that fits your topic and color scheme.

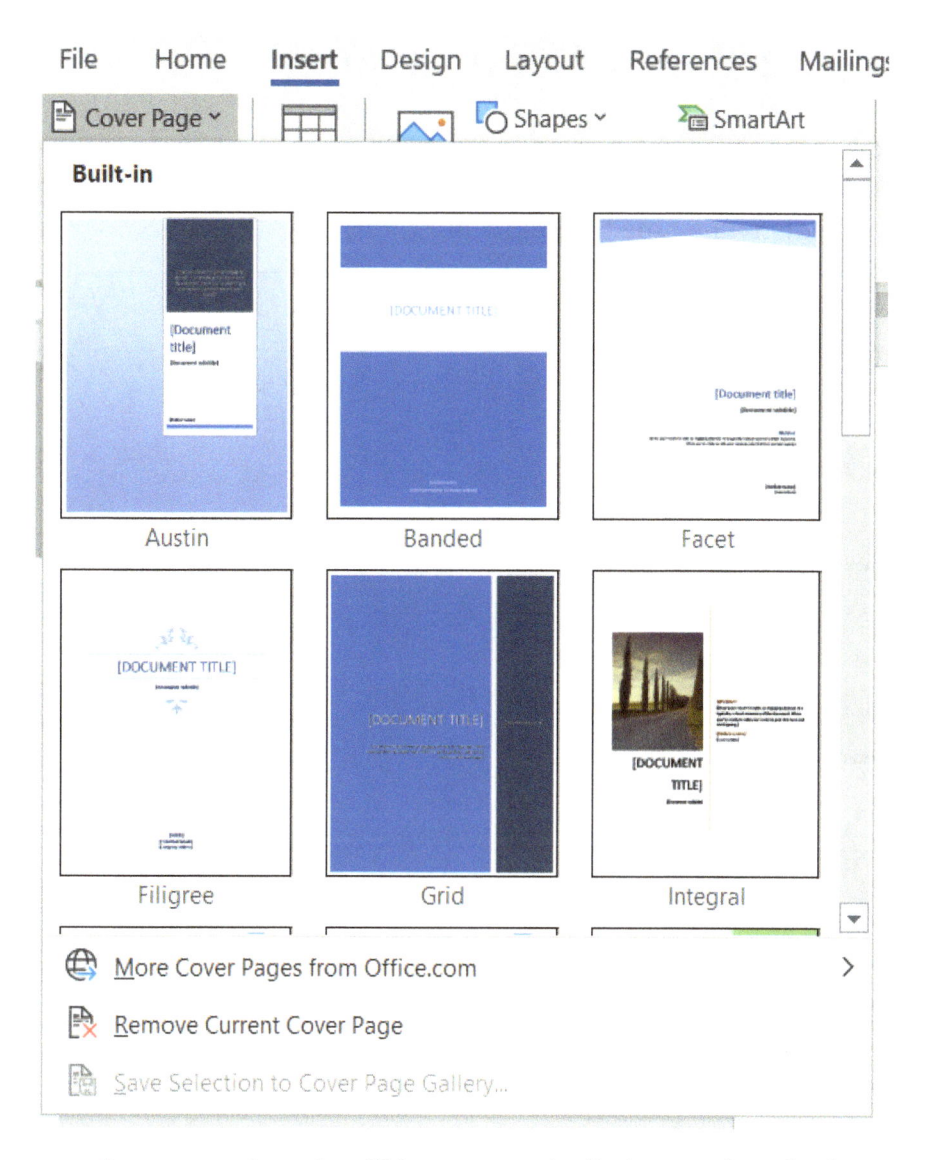

Once you select a template, it will be automatically inserted as the first page of your document.

Next, add the title, subtitle, author, date, and other information required to complete your new cover page.

## Typing the Body of Your Report

Since I don't have a researched report to paste in, I will be typing my document from scratch. If you are following along with me, click in the body of your document and type the following:

> # How to Use MS Office Suite
> 
> A Guide for Law Firm Employees
> 
> MS Office Suite intro
> 
> Word
> 
> Information on Word
> 
> Excel
> 
> Information on Excel
> 
> PowerPoint
> 
> Information on PowerPoint
> 
> Outlook
> 
> Information on Outlook
> 
> Conclusion

I have added the title of each software in the MS Office Suite. I would like to make each of these software titles a Heading 1 style. To do that, select each title and click on the Heading 1 style in the Styles grouping on the Home tab. It should look like this:

# How to Use MS Office Suite

A Guide for Law Firm Employees

Introduction

## Word
Info

## Excel
Info

## PowerPoint
Info

## Outlook
Info

## Conclusion
Info

Applying these styles will help us out later in the report-making process when we want to add additional elements such as a Table of Contents.

Now, let's add some sub-headings under one of the headings. I will add the following sub-headings in the Word section: Letters, Memos, Faxes, Reports, and Tables. Then, I will apply the Heading 2 styles by selecting each sub-heading and clicking on the Heading 2 style in the Styles grouping of the Home tab.

Introduction

**Word**
Info

**Letters**
Here

⊿ **Memos**
Here

**Faxes**
Here

**Tables**
Here

⊿ **Reports**|
Here

**Excel**
Info

I have now outlined some of my report. Let's assume that we now have a fully written report and now we'd like to add some elements to it.

## Graphics

Let's add a graphic. To add a graphic, put your mouse where you would like the graphic to be placed and go to the Insert tab and choose Online Pictures. I will choose a Word graphic.

# Computer Applications for Paralegals

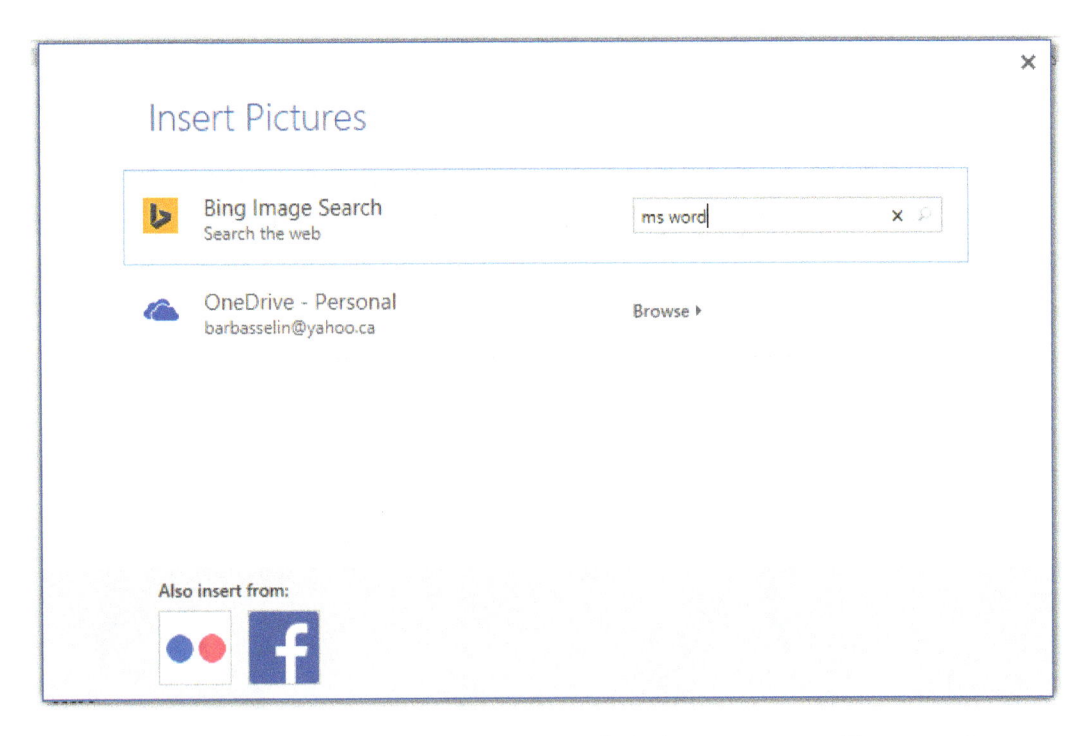

225

Choose one of the graphics that appear and click Insert. It will appear in your document under your curser. Click on your picture and you will see the Picture Tools Format tab at the top of the ribbon. Use the Position or Wrap Text or Align options to align your picture to the right so that the text wraps around it.

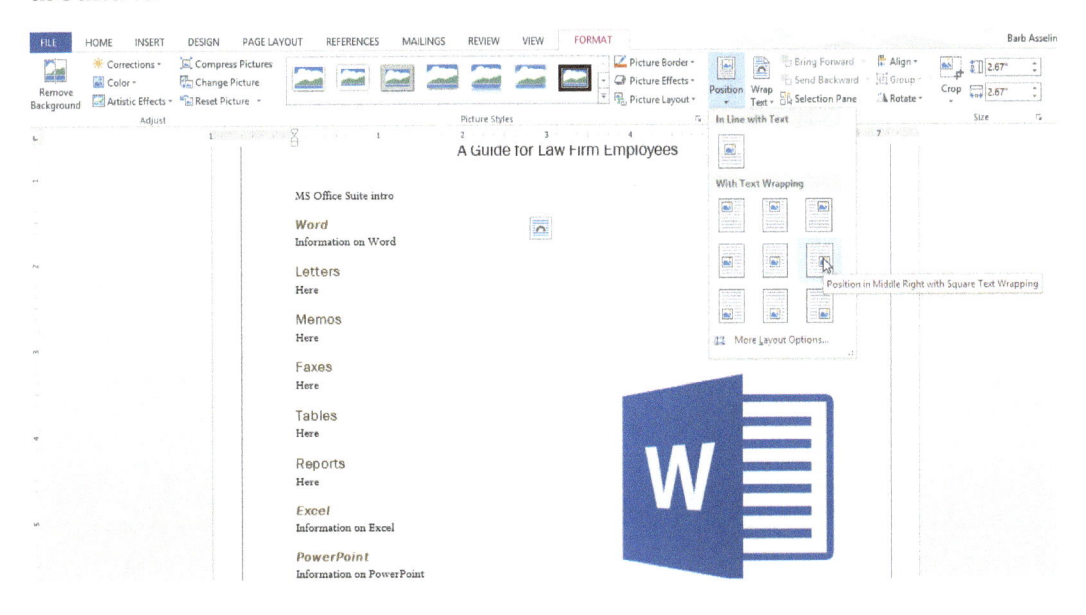

Resize the picture, if necessary, by clicking on one of the eight control handles and clicking and dragging it either bigger or smaller.

**SmartArt Graphic**

We can also add SmartArt graphics to our reports. Let's add one to the end of the report.

To add a SmartArt graphic, place your curser where you want to insert the graphic and go to the Insert tab. Click on SmartArt and choose a graphic that is meaningful considering the information you would like to display.

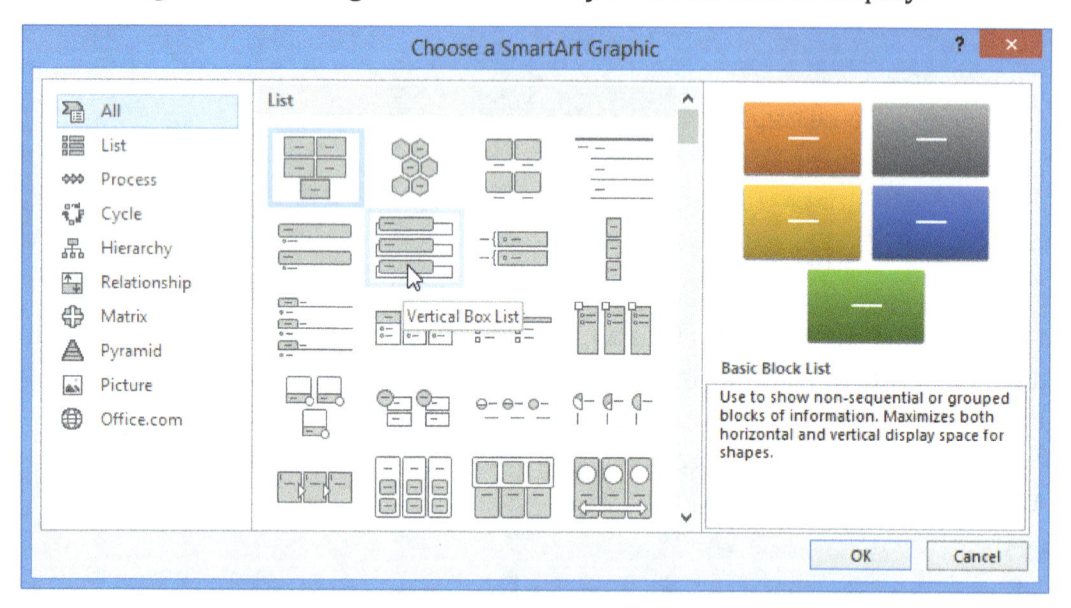

I would like to display a list of the programs within MS Office Suite, so I will choose the Vertical Box List.

Computer Applications for Paralegals 227

- Word
- Excel
- PowerPoint
- Outlook

Notice that as you choose your SmartArt graphic, it automatically matches the color scheme of your report.

**Header and Footer**

Next, let's add a header and footer to the report. There are actually headers and footers already added into the report, but we can access them two different ways:

- Go to the Insert tab and click on either Header or Footer, or
- Double-click in the header or footer that is already present in your document.

The footer actually is along the left side of the bottom of the document and to access it, double click in the footer area at the bottom of any page of your document.

Once you are in your document, you should notice the Header and Footer Tools Design tab. You should have Different First Page selected in the Options grouping.

Try adding your name to the header (not the first page header). Then close the Header and Footer Tools Design tab by clicking the red X at the far right of the ribbon.

## Table of Contents

Our report is starting to look more professional now. Let's add a Table of Contents to the front of the report, just after the title page and before the body of the report. The Table of Contents could have its own page after the title page, but since this is a short report, we can just put it after the title and subtitle on page two (the first page of the body of the report).

The Table of Contents is very easy to add, but only because the body of our report uses Heading 1 and Heading 2 styles. If we did not use these styles, we would not be able to generate a Table of Contents.

To add a Table of Contents, place your curser where you want the Table of Contents to go. Then go to the References tab and drop down the arrow beside Table of Contents.

The Table of Contents options will appear, and you can choose one of the options. I will choose Automatic Table 2.

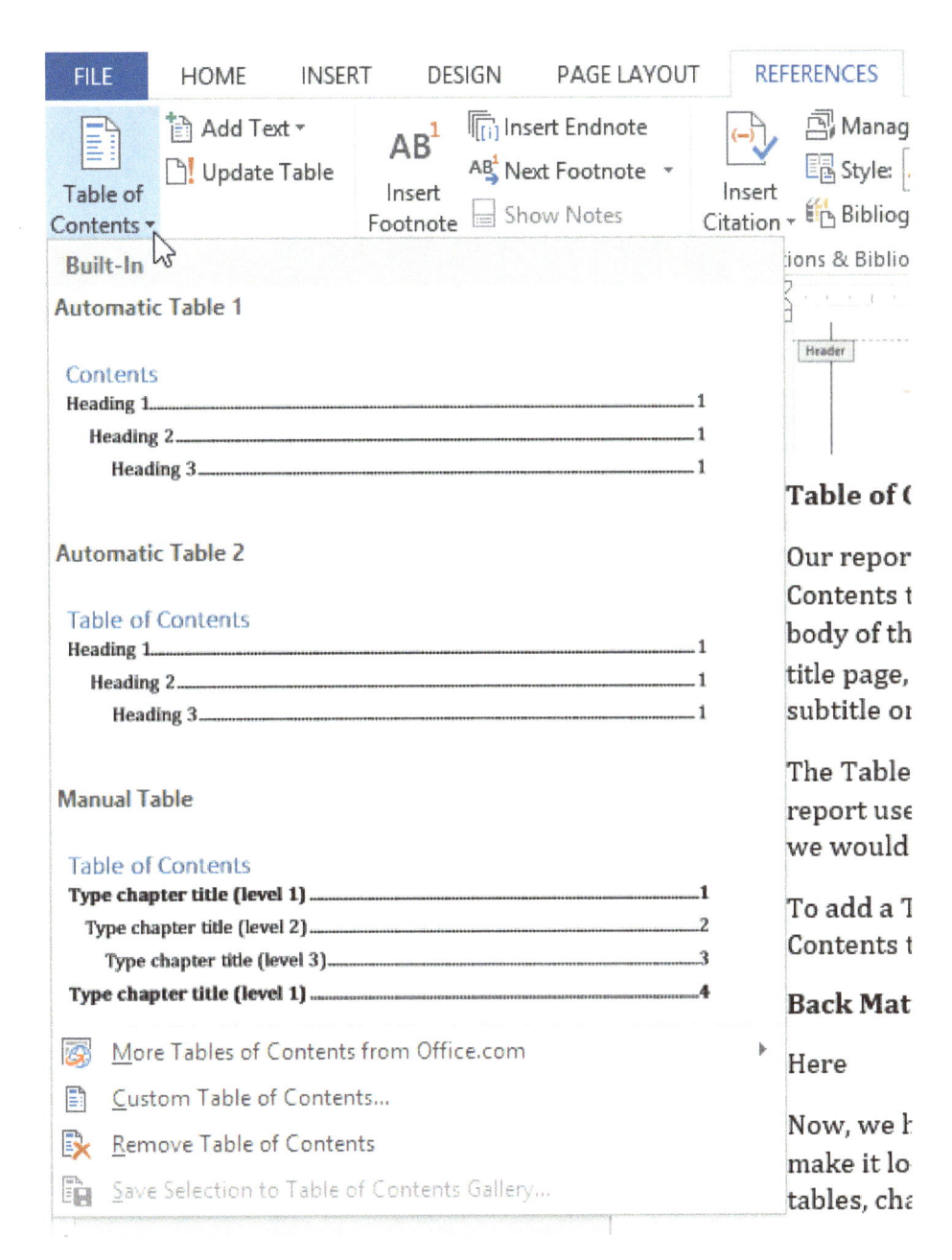

This will insert a Table of Contents at the beginning of my report.

Notice how each of the Heading 1 and Heading 2 styles are formatted in the Table of Contents. Each heading has a dotted leader line that leads up to the page number. The Heading 2 style headings are indented slightly to show that they are subheadings.

> Barb Asselin
>
> # How to Use MS Office Suite
>
> A Guide for Paralegal Firm Employees
>
> **Table of Contents**
>
> WORD ............................................................................ 1
>     LETTERS ..................................................................... 1
>     MEMOS ....................................................................... 1
>     FAXES ......................................................................... 1
>     TABLES ....................................................................... 1
>     REPORTS ..................................................................... 1
> EXCEL ............................................................................ 1
> POWERPOINT ................................................................. 2
> OUTLOOK ...................................................................... 2
> CONCLUSION ................................................................. 2

**Back Matter**

The last thing we will add to our report is back matter. Back matter consists of items such as a bibliography or an index. These items are found on the References tab.

When you research a report, you should keep track of the sources that you use and cite them properly. On the References tab, there is a Citations & Bibliography grouping. Note that the requirements of the McGill Guide citation format should always be used for this program.

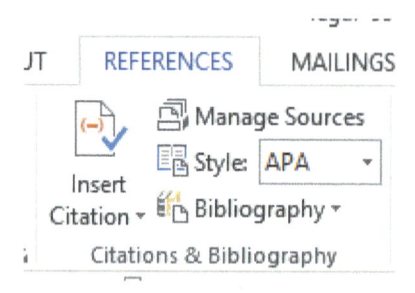

The first step is to add a citation and a source. This can be done by following these steps:

- Place your curser at the end of the sentence you want to add a citation to
- Click on Insert Citation on the References tab

- Choose Add New Source, and
- Fill in the blanks depending on the source you used and click OK.

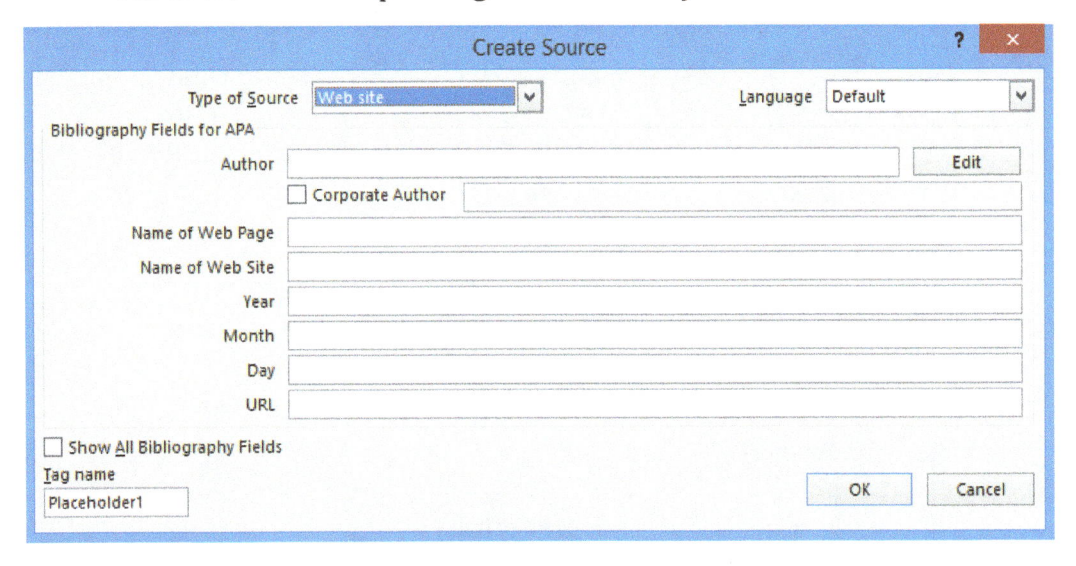

This will add the proper citation at the end of the sentence you chose.

Now that you have a source, you can create a bibliography.

To add a bibliography, go to the end of your report and create a new page. Add the title Bibliography and apply the Heading 1 style to your title.

Next, go to the References tab and drop down the arrow beside Bibliography and choose one of the options.

Once you make your choice, the sources you entered will be added to the new Bibliography page.

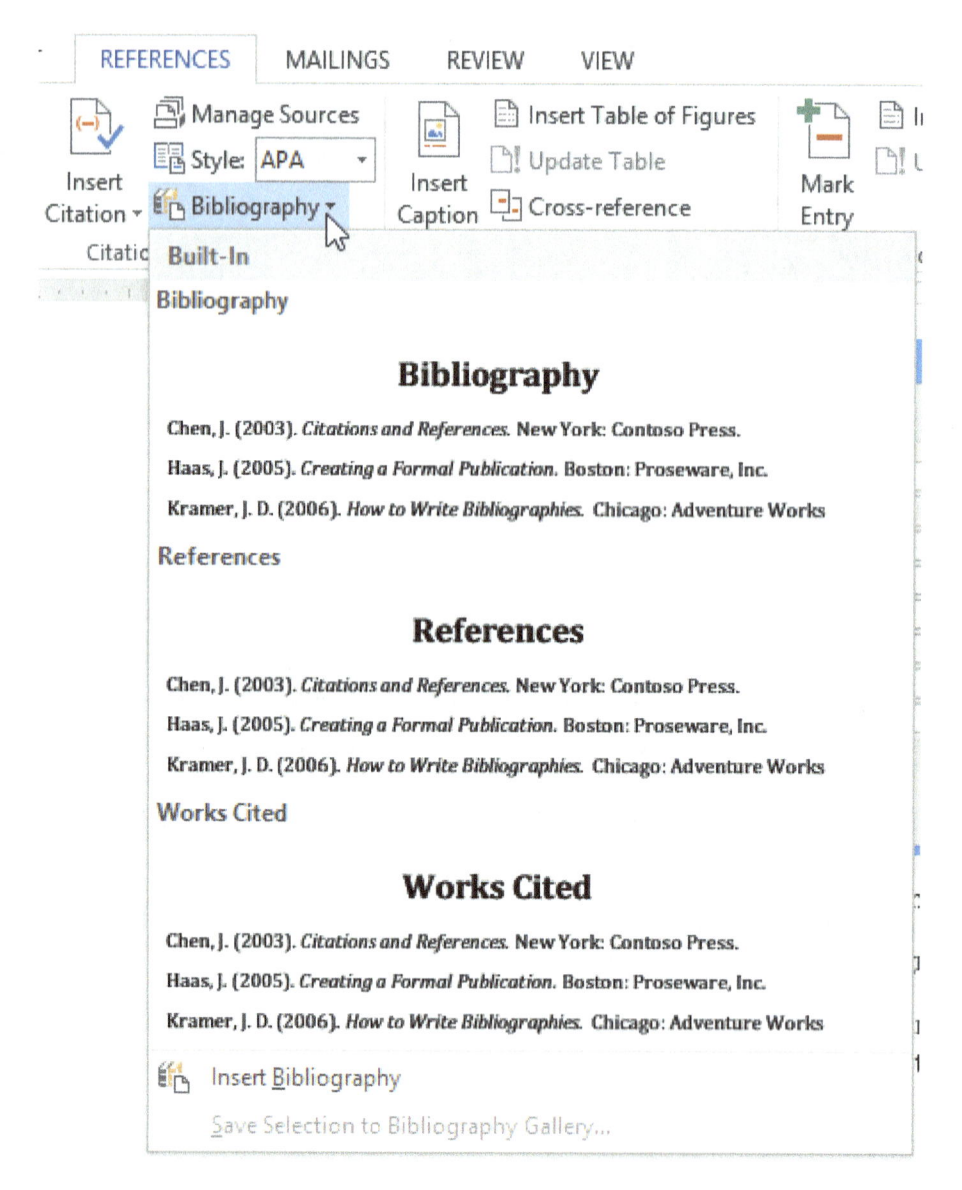

Now, we have added a variety of word processing elements to our report to make it look professional. Other items you could add would be bulleted lists, tables, charts, and objects.

There are a couple of final steps to take before your report is finalized.

Once you have added all of the elements you plan on adding, take a final run-through of your report from the beginning and make sure there are no "widows or orphans". These are headings by themselves at the bottom of a page, or single lines of text by themselves at the top of a page. The rule of thumb is that there should be at least two lines of text after each heading and at the top of a page. Take whatever action is necessary to fix these issues.

The final step is to re-generate the Table of Contents to account for added elements and to update page numbers.

To update the Table of Contents, right-click in the Table of Contents and choose Update Table at the top left of the Table of Contents. Choose Update Entire Table and it will automatically update.

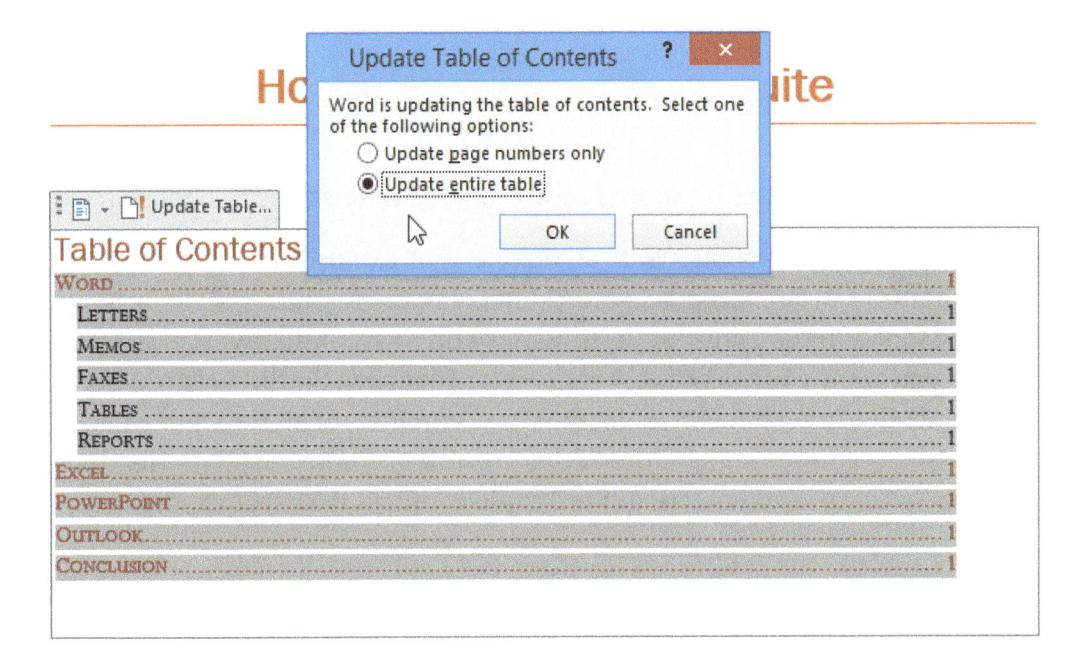

## Styles

We learned about styles in the previous section on reports, however, the examples we looked at were pre-set styles that were the result of a report template that was used.

You can customize the styles that you use in your documents using the Styles grouping on the Home tab.

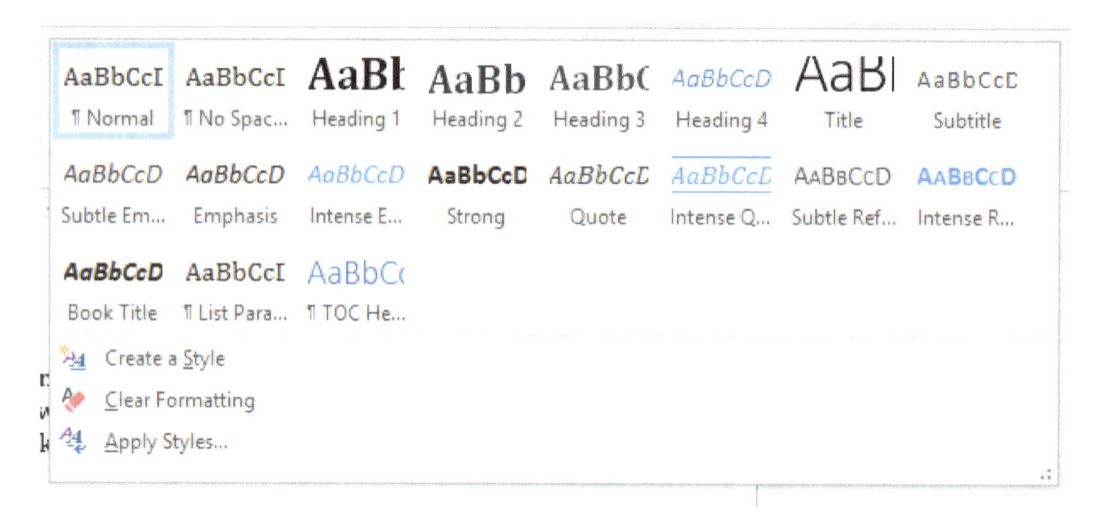

As you can see, there are a number of pre-determined styles to choose from.

Alternatively, you can create your own style. For example, if your company's color scheme is green and blue, you can make your Heading 1 style dark blue and 18pt font and bold and centered. Once you have some text that is just the way you want your Heading 1 style to be, just click on the Create a Style option and give it a name. Or, select the text you just formatted and right-click on the Heading 1 style in the Styles grouping. Choose Update Heading 1 to Match Selection and your Heading 1 style is officially customized.

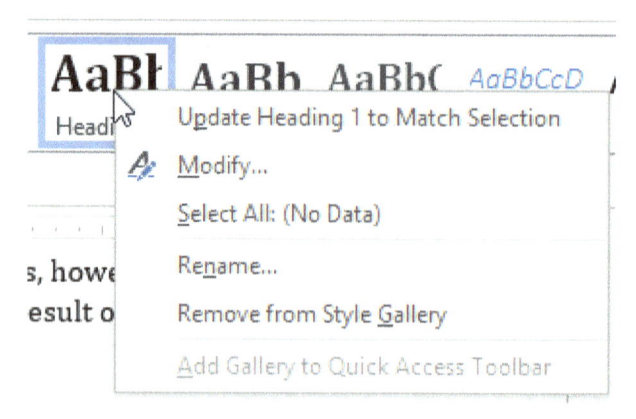

Similar steps can be taken for any of the styles in the Styles grouping, allowing you to create a custom report template for all of your firm's reports that matches your company color scheme.

# Tables

> There is an instructional video for students on this topic at:
> Webpage: http://www.asselingroup.com/paralegals
> Password: paralegals

Tables are a great way to consolidate data into a format that is easy to digest.

There are many ways to add a table to a document:

- Go to the Insert tab and click on the table icon – choose how many rows and columns you would like using the displayed grid
- Go to the Insert tab and drop down the arrow below the Table option – type in how many rows and columns you would like
- Go to the Insert tab and drop down the arrow below the Table option and choose Draw Table – use your curser to draw the lines of your table, or
- Go to the Insert tab and drop down the arrow below the Table option and choose one of the options in the Quick Tables section.

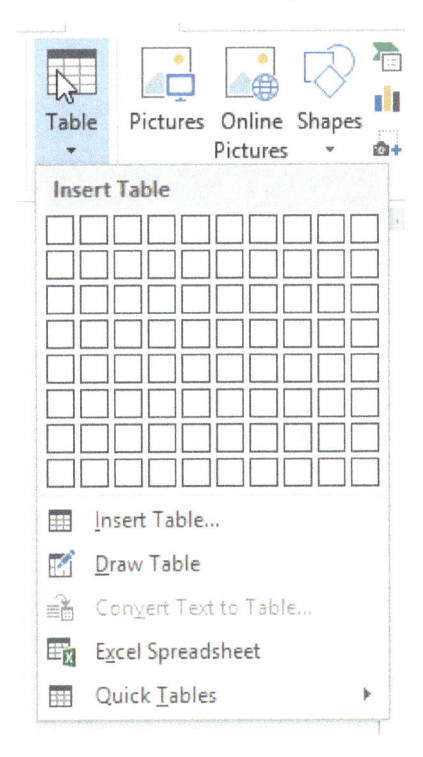

Once you have added a table to your document, you will notice that there are two new tabs at the top of the ribbon. They are the Table Tools Design and Layout tabs.

The Design tab allows you to change the design and color scheme of your table as well as add and remove and change border lines.

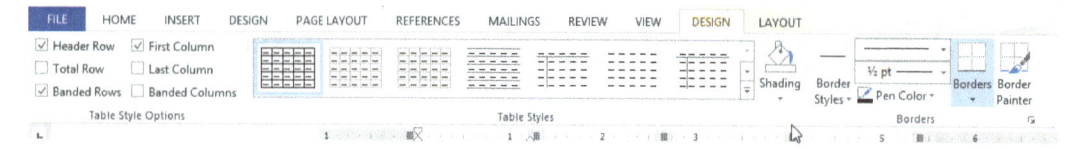

The Layout tab allows you to delete or add rows or columns, merge cells, split cells, align content within cells, and change text direction. You can also select the headings in the top row and choose the Repeat Header Row option. This is great for long tables that span more than one page of a document as the header row will be repeated at the top of each new page.

Here is an example of a table of time dockets per paralegal for the first quarter of a year:

| Paralegal | January | February | March |
|---|---|---|---|
| Jane | 120 | 108 | 112 |
| James | 115 | 118 | 98 |
| John | 101 | 110 | 124 |
| Jenny | 97 | 101 | 126 |

I can add a title row to this table by placing my curser in the first row and going to the Table Tools Layout tab and choosing Insert Above.

| | | | |
|---|---|---|---|
| Paralegal | January | February | March |
| Jane | 120 | 108 | 112 |
| James | 115 | 118 | 98 |
| John | 101 | 110 | 124 |
| Jenny | 97 | 101 | 126 |

Then, I can choose to merge the cells together in the new top row, once they are all selected, so that I can type in my table's title.

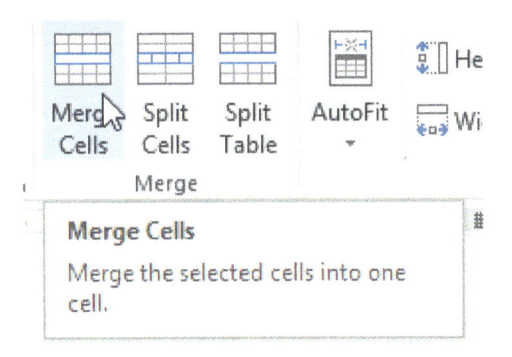

| First Quarter Billable Hours | | | |
|---|---|---|---|
| Paralegal | January | February | March |
| Jane | 120 | 108 | 112 |
| James | 115 | 118 | 98 |
| John | 101 | 110 | 124 |
| Jenny | 97 | 101 | 126 |

If you are adding a table to a letter, memo, or report, the format of your table should change slightly. The width of your table should be less than the width of the text of your letter, memo, or report.

To change the width of your table, click within your table. Once your table is active, you should be able to put your curser at the top left corner of the table and click on the four-way arrow to select your entire table. Now, right-click on your table and choose Table Properties from the menu.

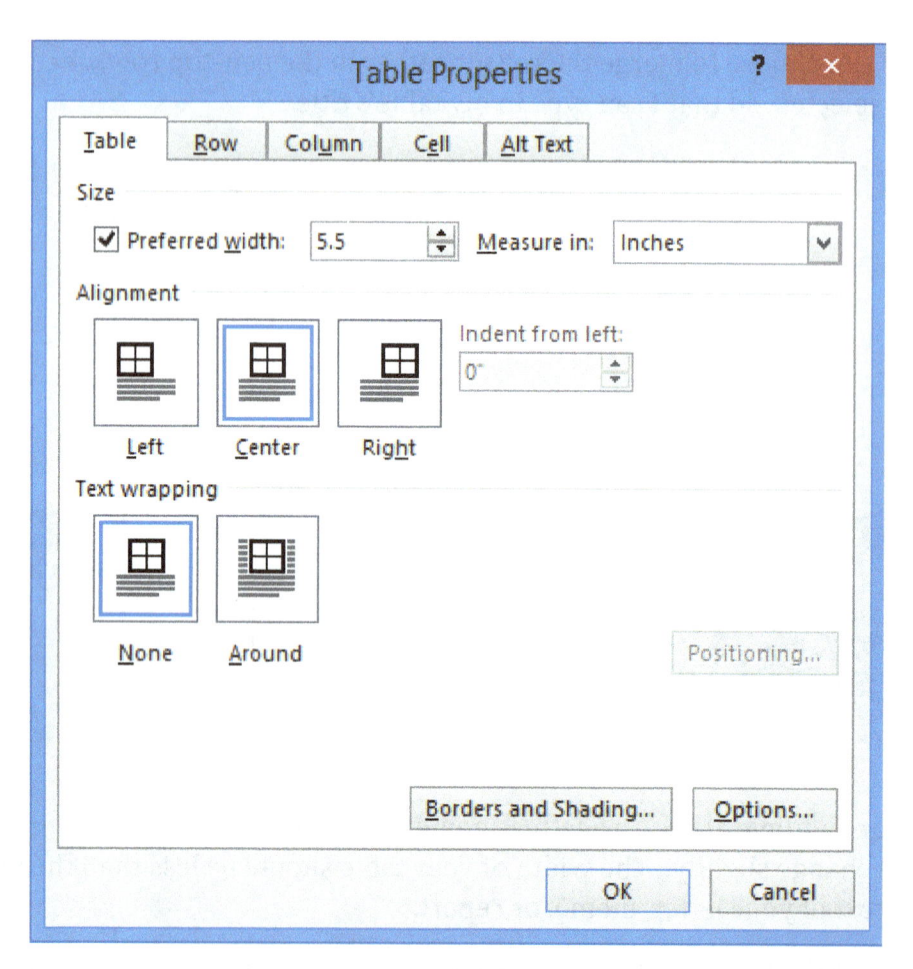

The width of a letter, memo, or report is 8.5" with a 1" margin on the left and right sides. In order for your table to be inside those margins, you will need to click Preferred Width on the Table tab and type in 5.5". Then, choose to have the table centered. The resulting table will look like this:

| Paralegal | First Quarter Billable Hours | | |
|---|---|---|---|
| | January | February | March |
| Jane | 120 | 108 | 112 |
| James | 115 | 118 | 98 |
| John | 101 | 110 | 124 |
| Jenny | 97 | 101 | 126 |

This is the proper way to display a table in a letter, memo, or report.

# Editing

Editing is a very important part of any document you create in the workplace. Whether it is an internal document such as a memo, or an external document such as a letter or a report, accuracy is a big part of whether or not you and your firm will be seen as professional or sloppy. Of course, all firms want to be seen as professional and so every document that you produce should be error-free.

If you can regularly produce documents that do not have to be revised, you can bet that you will be the employee that your company will keep if downsizing, or promote when the opportunity arises.

## Proofreading

Proofreading is the first step to creating and sending an error-free document. A document that is conceived, drafted, reviewed, and sent in one sitting is rarely error-free.

Using Word's built-in spellchecker and grammar checker should be your first actions when completing a new document. To access them, go to the Review tab and choose Spelling & Grammar. The software will go through your document checking for spelling and grammatical mistakes.

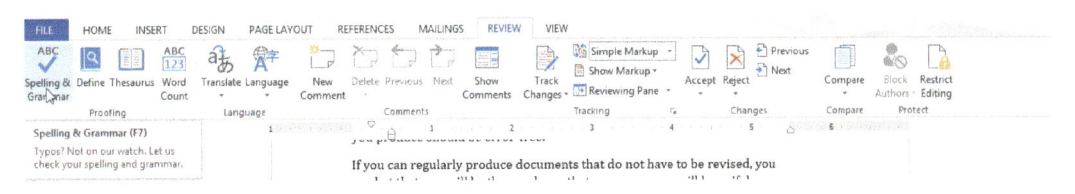

Word's spellcheck features won't fix words that are wrong but are not caught because they are still words. For example, if you write form instead of from, Word may not catch that mistake. Here are some tips to help you produce and send the highest quality document your company expects:

- Print your document and proofread it before you send it out
- If you want to save paper, try reading it out loud before you send it to anyone
- If you are drafting and finalizing your document in one sitting, take a step back from it – try working on something else for a few minutes,

or take a quick walk to get some water – anything so that your eyes will be "fresh" when you look at it again
- Try reading it from the bottom to the top, or in a different order than from top to bottom – a tip that may help you see errors, and
- Have someone else read it over for errors.

## Find and Replace

There is an instructional video for students on this topic at:
Webpage: http://www.asselingroup.com/paralegals
Password: paralegals

If you are working on a document and you find that you have consistently spelled the client's name wrong (hopefully not!), there is a feature on the Home tab that can help. Instead of reading through your document looking for the same phrase that needs to be changed and perhaps missing one or two references, you can use the items in the Editing grouping on the Home tab.

If you just have a long document and you know you need to change one paragraph and you know that the word partnership is in that section, you can use the Find feature to search for the correct section in your long document.

Go to the Home tab and click on the Find feature. A Navigation task pane will open on the left-hand side of your screen. You can type your search word or phrase into the search field and that should help you narrow down your search quickly.

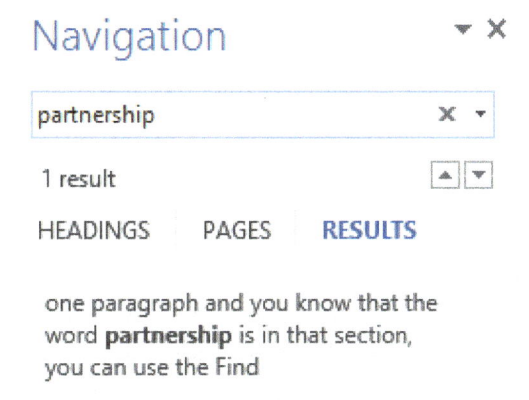

Navigation panel showing search for "partnership" with 1 result under RESULTS tab.

In this example, I searched this text's file for the word partnership and the result is this exact section of the textbook. I just need to click on the result and Word will take me to that section of my document so that I can edit it.

Replace is another feature and one that is helpful for those misspelled client names. If you click on the Replace option on the Home tab, the Find and Replace dialogue box will appear. It will allow you to search for a word or phrase that you misspelled and replace each instance with the correct spelling.

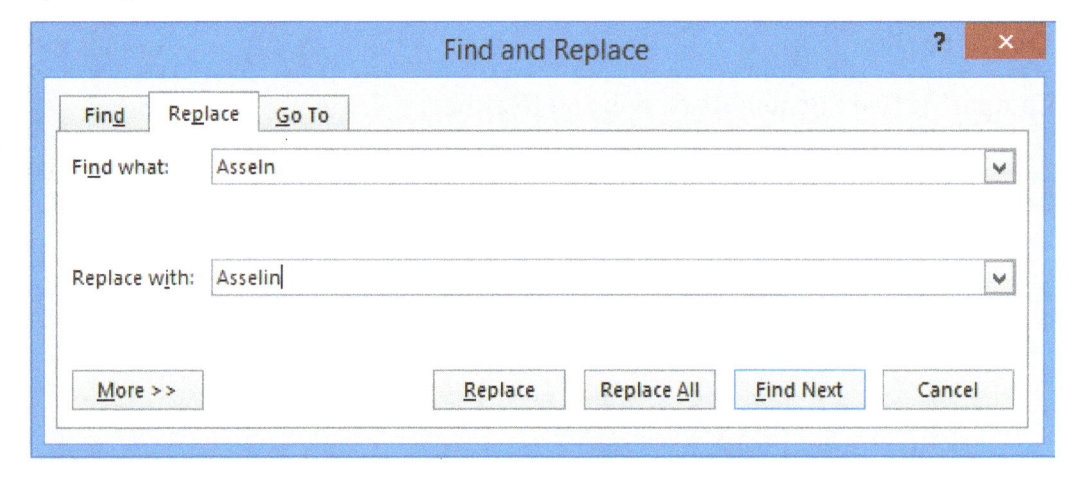

Find and Replace dialog box with Find what: "Asseln" and Replace with: "Asselin".

In the example, I have searched for an incorrect spelling of my name and, in the Replace With field, I have entered the correct spelling of my last name. If I want to just replace them, I will click on Replace All. If I want to monitor the results, I will click on Find Next and replace the ones that need to be fixed.

## Compare, Comment, and Track Changes

There is an instructional video for students on this topic at:
Webpage: http://www.asselingroup.com/paralegals
Password: paralegals

In various areas of law, you may work on a document that two or more people are editing. Examples include agreements, reports, and research papers. If you are working on such a document, it can be complicated to know which version you are working on, or if you have the most recent version. Luckily, Word has some features that let multiple people comment on and make changes to the same document. The changes and comments do not take effect in the document until they are approved by all of the editors of the document.

These features are found in the Review tab.

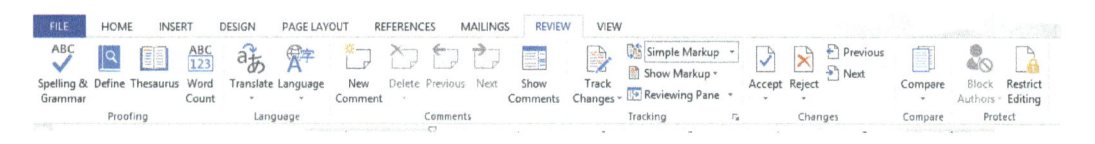

### Compare

Comparing two documents allows you to either:

- Open two documents side by side and compare one with the other, or
- Combine two documents into one.

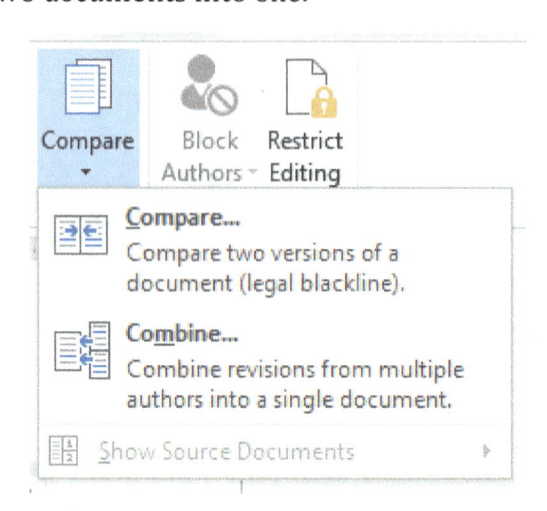

Computer Applications for Paralegals 243

This option would be useful if you have lost track of which version of a document is more recent, or if the Track Changes option was not used when revising a document.

**Comment**

While reviewing a document that was created by or edited by someone else, you can make comments where you may have questions, but the author is not available to answer your questions right away.

To make a comment, go to the Review tab and click on New Comment.

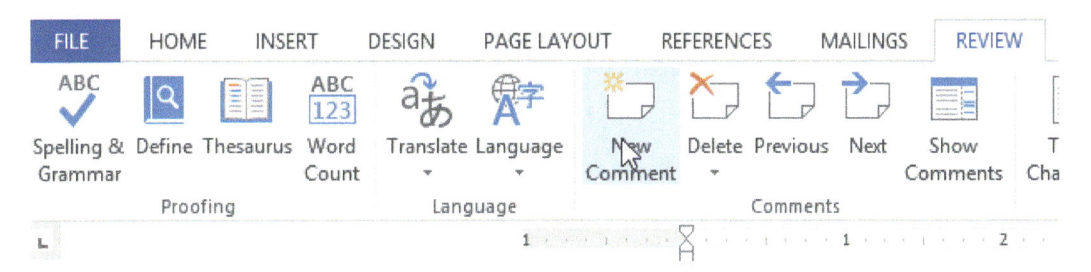

A Comment box will open up on the right margin of your document where your curser is.

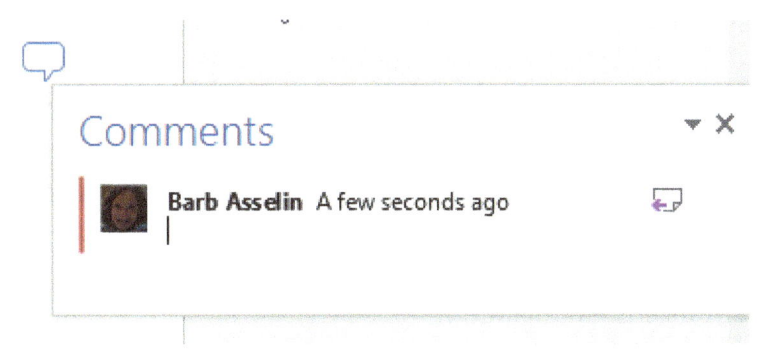

You can type your question or comment and click on the X in the upper right corner of the Comments box to close it. A small speech bubble will stay in the right margin of your document. That speech bubble is notice to the next reviewer that you have a comment or a question. The next reviewer can either respond to your question or delete the comment altogether.

All comments should be addressed and removed before the final document is sent to the recipient.

To delete a comment, click on it and then choose Delete in the Review tab.

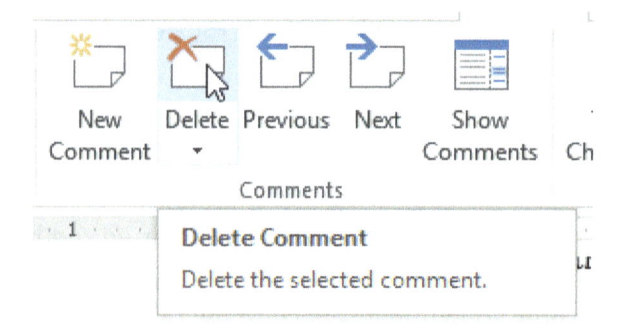

## Track Changes

When two or more people are working on the same document, making changes, it is useful for each editor to track their changes. You can do this by using the Track Changes option on the Review tab.

Take these steps when tracking changes:

- Turn on Track changes by going to the Review tab, dropping down the arrow beside Track Changes, and choosing Track changes
- Go through your document and add or delete and generally make the changes you want
- You will see that your deletions are crossed out instead of deleted and your additions are added in colored font so that they can be seen by the other editor or editors
- Save your edited document
- Forward it to the other editor or editors
- Each editor will use a different color for editing the text
- When you get the document back, you will make sure your Track Changes option is turned on and start reviewing the document's changes
- Go to the first change and either accept it or reject it using the Accept and Reject buttons on the Review tab
- Click Next to go to the next change, and
- Continue until you have either accepted or rejected all proposed changes.

These steps will be taken by each editor until everyone agrees on the content of the document.

When reviewing changes, note your computer's settings in the Tracking grouping of the Review tab. If you display All Markup, you will see all of the changes.

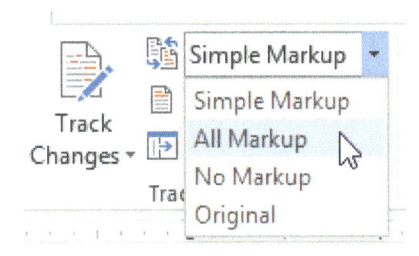

Similarly, you should ensure that all options are checked in the Show Markup drop down list.

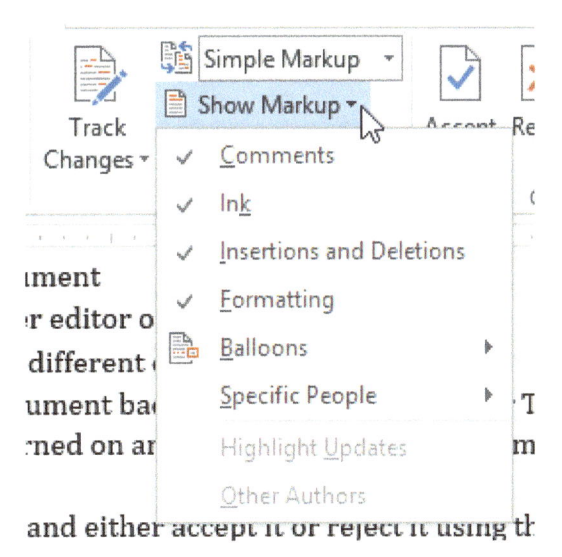

# Saving

When saving a new document for the first time, go to the File tab and choose Save. Choose Computer and Browse and you will see the following dialogue box:

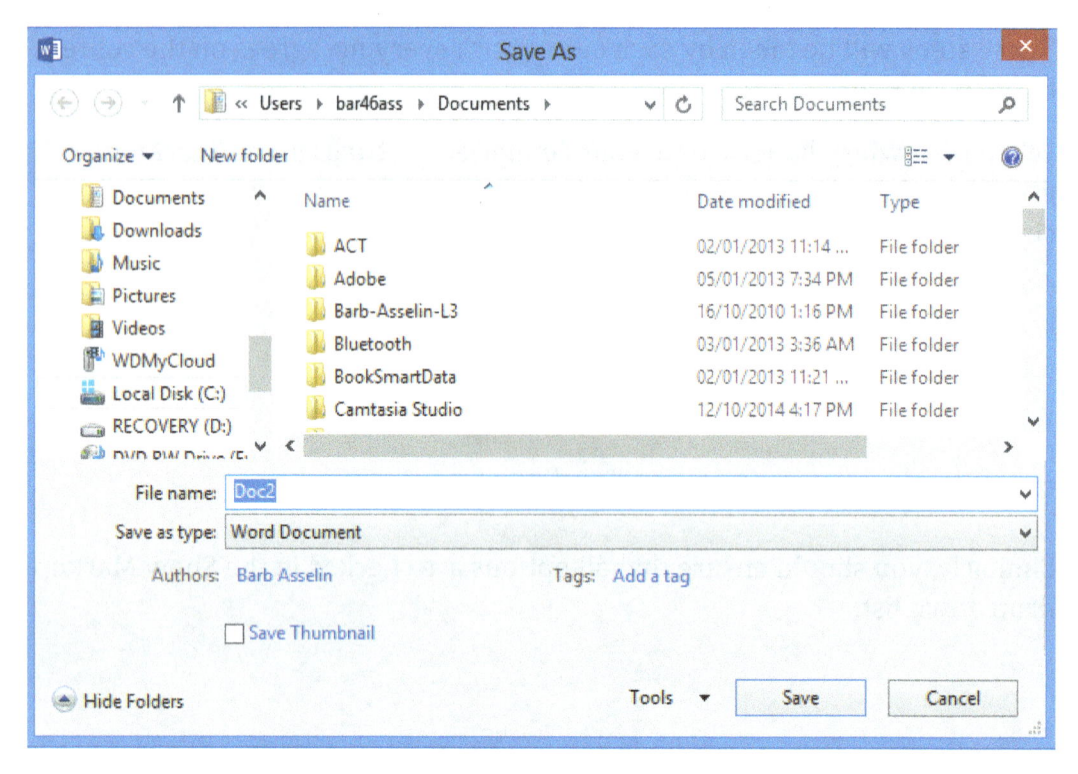

The different locations on your computer are shown on the left and, as you choose a location, the folders and documents within that location will show on the right. Type an appropriate name in the File Name box. It will automatically save as a Word Document (.docx file). Click the Save button.

If you are working on a precedent and want to save it as a different file so that you can save your precedent without the changes you are making to it, go to the File tab and choose Save As. Type your new file name in the File Name box and click Save.

Sometimes, you may wish to save a document and forward it to someone but you don't want them to be able to change it. In this case, consider saving your document as a PDF file. To save a document as a PDF file, first save it as a Word document. Then, go to the File tab and click Save As. Choose the location where you want to save your PDF. In the Save as Type box, drop down the options and choose PDF. Click Save.

# Printing

To print a document, go to the File tab and select Print. There are a number of options available for you on this screen. They are all listed on the left. A preview of the current page of your document is displayed on the right. You are able to:

- Choose the number of copies you would like to print
- Select the proper printer, if more than one is available
- Choose to print all pages, or just the current page, or selected multiple pages of a document
- Collate or not (i.e., print more than one copy of a multi-page document as 11, 22, 33, or 123, 123, 123
- Change the orientation of the document from portrait to landscape, or vice versa
- Change the size of the paper to letter size, legal size, a custom size, or other standard sizes
- Change the margins of your document, or
- Scale the printing of your document to one page per sheet, two pages per sheet, up to 16 pages per sheet, or to fit the size of your current paper.

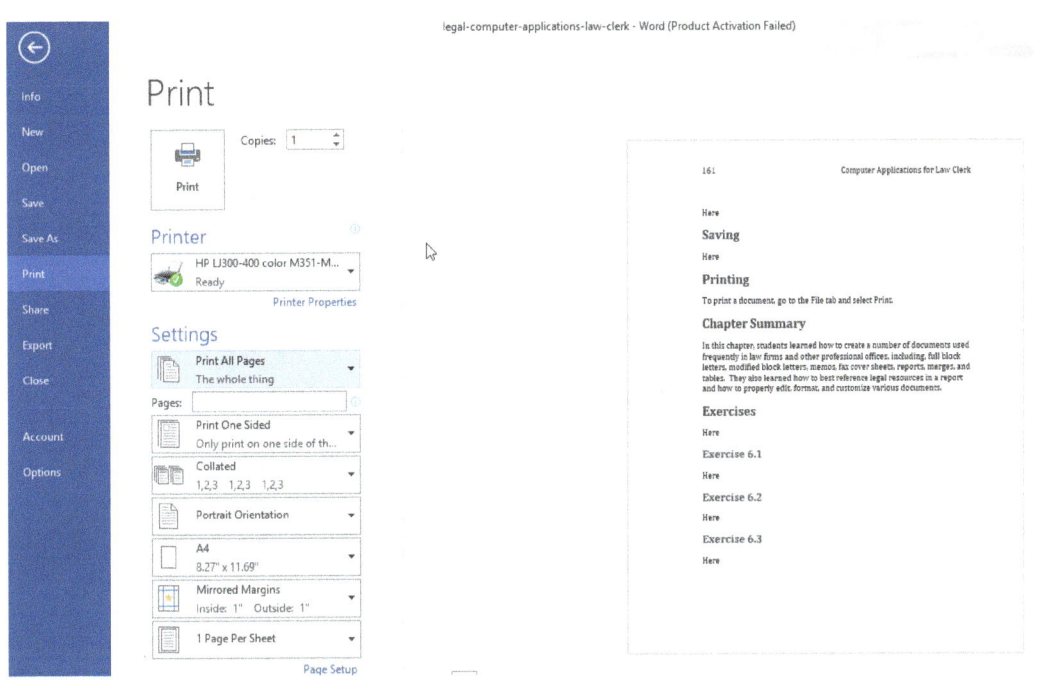

## Chapter Summary

In this chapter, students learned how to create a number of documents used frequently in law firms and other professional offices, including full block letters, modified block letters, memos, fax cover sheets, reports, merges, and tables. They also learned how to best reference legal resources in a report and how to properly edit, format, and customize various documents.

# Exercises

## Exercise 6.1

1. Using the letterhead posted on the textbook's webpage, create a letter
2. The letter will be full block style with open punctuation
3. The letter is to your client, Troy Nesbitt, from you, regarding his initial consultation with you last week
4. Troy Nesbitt's address is 75 Buckingham Street, Ottawa, Ontario, K7S 3G8
5. The letter is confidential, will be sent by courier, and is dated today's date
6. Create an appropriate re: line – the file number is 20-345
7. The contents of the letter are as follows

This letter is further to your meeting with Marc Bourque and me at our offices last week.

You confirmed that you are ready to proceed with having us assist you in performing your ongoing landlord duties on your new apartment building located at 21 Main Street.

Our first step will be to create a database of all units, their current tenant or tenants, the current amount of monthly rent, and the anniversary date of each tenancy.

You will contact us if any tenant is late on their rent, and we will prepare a Notice of Non-Payment of Rent to be sent to the tenant forthwith.

You have advised that the following tenants are currently in arrears:

- Unit 201, John and Jane Smith are in rental arrears of $780.00, and
- Unit 306, Charles and Leslie Potter are in rental arrears of $1,275.00.

We will prepare the necessary notices and contact you once they are ready for signature.

We look forward to assisting you in the creation and delivery of the required landlord documents for your new property.

# Exercise 6.2

1. Using the letterhead posted on the textbook's webpage, create a letter
2. The letter will be modified block style with mixed punctuation
3. You are filling in for the small claims court paralegal who is on holidays this week
4. The letter will be to your clients, Paul and Susan Layman, 48 Springtown Street, Ottawa, Ontario, K3H 7G6
5. The letter will be from you and will be dated today's date
6. The letter will be confidential and delivered by fax
7. Choose an appropriate re: line – the file number is 20-896
8. The contents of the letter are as follows

This letter is regarding your property at 1788 High Meadow Park and your current dispute with your neighbor at 1790 High Meadow Park.

You have advised us of an incident that occurred recently. We wish to confirm the following information that you have provided us with:

- On August 1st, a large oak tree from your neighbor's property split in half and part of it fell on the ground and damaged the fence in between your properties
- On August 2nd, your neighbor tried to cut down the remainder of the tree with his chainsaw
- As your neighbor was cutting down the remainder of the tree with his chainsaw, a large portion of the tree split off from the main trunk and fell on your vehicle, a 2017 Honda Civic
- Your neighbor neglected to secure the tree prior to cutting it down
- The damage to your vehicle was valued at $3,450.00

Please discuss these items with each other and contact me to advise if you are prepared to proceed with your action against the neighbor, or if you have any questions regarding any of these items.

# Exercise 6.3

1. Using the memo letterhead posted on the textbook's webpage, create a memo
2. You are helping out in the small claims department today since their paralegal is on holidays
3. The memo will be to one of your firm's law clerks, Ernie MacLellan, from you on today's date
4. Choose an appropriate re: line
5. The memo will be cc'd to Margaret Childs
6. In the memo, tell Ernie that you would like him to do some research on a new file for the department
7. Your client is Marcus Winchester and the file number is 20-1021
8. Mr. Winchester slipped and fell in the local Walmart parking lot and broke his left leg, right arm, and two ribs
9. He also suffered a concussion
10. Ask him to research similar cases where the judge ruled in favor of the plaintiff, where the total amount claimed was $25,000 or less, as well as slip and fall cases where freezing rain was involved
11. Tell him you need the research completed on or before next Friday
12. Enclose your notes from your initial meeting with the client

# Exercise 6.4

1. Using the memo letterhead posted on the textbook's webpage, create a memo
2. The memo will be from you to the firm's Human Resources manager, Caroline Weber and it will be dated today
3. You have completed the self-reflection and performance evaluation that is required on the anniversary of your hiring date
4. Write a memo to Ms. Weber noting that you have completed the evaluation form and that it is enclosed
5. Ask if you can schedule a time to meet with her to discuss the completed form and suggest three different upcoming days
6. Also, request your annual vacation time and list three weeks during the following year that you would like to be on holidays
7. Choose an appropriate re: line

8. The memo will be cc'd to the firm's managing partner, Lisa Picolo.

## Exercise 6.5

1. Using the letterhead template provided on the textbook's webpage, create a merge
2. You are helping out in the immigration department today and you have been advised of four upcoming hearings
3. The merged letters will be to four different clients from you using the full block style with mixed punctuation

    a. Mr. Jim McKenna
       1 McKenna Street
       Ottawa, Ontario K1P 8G4
       Hearing Date: March 1
       File No.: 20-567
       Country: Brazil

    b. Ms. Gloria Caulfield
       1 Caulfield Crescent
       Ottawa, Ontario K3G 7D8
       Hearing Date: March 8
       File No. 20-498
       Country: Pakistan

    c. Mr. Steven Patterson
       1 Patterson Private
       Ottawa, Ontario K8D 3H7
       Hearing Date: March 12
       File No. 20-193
       Country: Italy

    d. Ms. Tianna Brown
       1 Brown Blvd.
       Ottawa, Ontario K1H 9D2
       Hearing Date: March 4
       File No. 20-201
       Country: Germany

4. The details of the letter are as follows (note that this is only the body of the letter and that your letter should include all of the parts of a letter):

Re: &lt;first name&gt; &lt;last name&gt; Immigration from &lt;country&gt;
File No. &lt;file number&gt;

I am writing to advise you that I have received notice of your hearing date in your immigration from &lt;country&gt;.

Your hearing date has been set for &lt;hearing date&gt;.

I will contact you as your hearing date approaches so that I can arrange an appointment for you to come in and meet with Anna Bengali to prepare for the hearing. At that time, we will prepare you for your participation in the hearing.

If you have any questions regarding this matter, please do not hesitate to contact me.

# Exercise 6.6

1. Download the Report Exercise Unformatted from the textbook's webpage
2. Make changes to the report as follows:
    a. Download the title page template of your choice and add it to the beginning of your new document
    b. The title of the report will be **Do I Need a Lawyer or a Paralegal?**
    c. The subtitle will be **A Guide for Clients**
    d. You are the author, and you will use today's date
    e. If your report template requires a blurb, briefly review the downloaded document and come up with a one or two sentence summary of the document
    f. In the Design tab, choose a design and a color scheme
    g. Change all bold headings to Heading 1 style
    h. Change all italicized headings to Heading 2 style
    i. There are three reference URLs in the downloaded document

- i. Create a citation at the end of the last paragraph preceding each reference URL, using the information obtained from the webpage from each URL
- ii. Once you have entered all three citations, delete the URLS from the body of the report

j. Add a SmartArt graphic at the end of your report that includes the following. Use the "stacked list item" from SmartArt. The text for the two column titles (circles) will be **Lawyer** and **Paralegal.** Under the **Paralegal** column, enter the following 4 items:
   - i. small claims court
   - *ii.* traffic court
   - iii. summary conviction
   - iv. various tribunals

k. Add additional shapes where necessary. There should be four items on each side, after the title. Under the **Lawyer** column, enter the following 4 items:
   - i. family law
   - ii. corporate law
   - iii. wills and estates law
   - iv. real estate law

l. Add items where necessary.

m. Add a graphic to your report on either the first or second page
   - i. Choose an online picture by searching the word "lawyer" or "paralegal"
   - ii. Right align the picture and make sure the text wraps around it

n. Create a bibliography page at the end of your report that will include the three citations

o. Create a Table of Contents after the title page and before the first paragraph of your report

p. Go through your report and fix any formatting issues such as widows and orphans

q. Revise your Table of Contents, if necessary

r. Submit your completed report to your instructor

# Exercise 6.7

1. Using the memo template provided on the textbook's webpage, create a memo
2. The memo will be to Simon Leblanc in your firm's administration department – Simon is the editor of your firm's monthly newsletter, the PPC Times
3. The memo will be cc'd to the other members of the newsletter committee: Sharon Wong, Julie Broadbent, Kendall Pink, Justin Terris, and Xavier Brethour
4. In the memo, tell Simon that you have some ideas for upcoming issues of your firm's newsletter and that you would like to be considered as a contributor to the periodical as you love to write
5. Make up a few credentials of your past writing experiences
6. Using a table, list your ideas for articles for the next six months
7. Give your table a title row that is merged and centered with an appropriate title
8. Ask Simon to let you know if any of your ideas are acceptable to the committee and, if you are allowed to write them, what the first deadline will be
9. Submit your completed memo to your instructor

# Exercise 6.8

1. Using the memo template provided on the textbook's webpage, create a memo
2. The memo will be to Tabitha Gunther and Marc Bourque from you dated today regarding hiring a new assistant to help out Sharon Wong in your department
3. In the memo, indicate that you have held interviews with five potential assistants and that you have chosen your preferred candidate
4. List the name and best qualities of your candidate in the hopes of convincing the others to agree with you (make up some information and a name)
5. Suggest a starting date and a salary for your candidate and ask them to let you know their thoughts on or before a deadline (choose a date)

6. Submit your completed memo to your instructor

# Exercise 6.9

1. Using the letterhead template provided on the textbook's webpage, create a merge
2. You have been advised of four upcoming hearings for clients of yours that are landlords
3. The merged letters will be to four different clients from you using the full block style with mixed punctuation

   a. Mr. Tim Kocialek
      1 Kocialek Crescent
      Ottawa, Ontario K4G 8K0
      Hearing Date: November 1
      File No.: 20-123
      Tenant: Alida Tourian

   b. Ms. Robin Smith
      1 Smith Street
      Ottawa, Ontario K9J 2D2
      Hearing Date: November 8
      File No. 20-543
      Tenant: Cody Ayotte

   c. Mr. James Farmer
      1 Farmer Private
      Ottawa, Ontario K8F 3F7
      Hearing Date: November 12
      File No. 20-821
      Tenant: Roland Hedges

   d. Ms. Catrina Boyle
      1 Boyle Blvd.
      Ottawa, Ontario K6F 1D7
      Hearing Date: November 4
      File No. 20-555
      Tenant: Roberta Kelly

4. The details of the letter are as follows (note that this is only the body of the letter and that your letter should include all the parts of a letter):

Re:   <first name> <last name> tenancy dispute with <tenant>
      File No. <file number>

I am writing to advise you that I have received notice of your hearing date in your Landlord and Tenant Board hearing with <tenant>.

Your hearing date has been set for <hearing date>.

I will contact you as your hearing date approaches so that I can arrange an appointment for you to come in and meet with me to prepare for the hearing. At that time, we will go over the process and what you can expect during the proceedings.

If you have any questions regarding this matter, please do not hesitate to contact me.

## Exercise 6.10

1. Using the letterhead posted on the textbook's webpage, create a letter
2. The letter will be modified block style with mixed punctuation
3. The letter is to your client, Greg Townley, from you, regarding his initial consultation with you last week
4. Greg Townley's address is 100 Townley Terrace, Ottawa, Ontario, K9H 1S1
5. The letter will be sent by registered mail, and is dated today's date
6. Create an appropriate re: line – the file number is 20-991
7. The contents of the letter are as follows

This letter is further to your recent appointment at our offices last week.

You confirmed that you are ready to proceed with having us assist you in your claim to have the tenants move out of the two rental properties that you are selling.

To confirm, the two rental properties are:

- 88 William Street, and

- 198 Bell Street.

The closing date for both properties is May 10th. The purchasers for each property have indicated that they wish to move into each property themselves. As such, we will prepare the required form N12 indicating to the tenants that they must vacate the properties on or before April 30th. The reason given will be that you have sold each property and that the purchasers are planning to live there. Please keep in mind the following:

- The notices will have to be delivered to each tenant on or before February 28th
- The tenant's last month rent will be used for April's rent
- You are required to give each tenant one month of rent in lieu of this notice and since you are not able to offer them any other units to move into, and
- You have decided to not collect rent for the month of March in lieu of this month of rent that you owe each tenant.

You have also decided to go ahead and file form L2 for each property, in the event that the tenants decide to exercise their right to not vacate the properties. We will also prepare the required form L2 for each property.

We will contact you once the documentation is prepared so that you can make an appointment to attend at our offices to sign the documents. Please contact me or my assistant, Sharon Wong, if you have any questions.

# Chapter 7: Combining Software

## Learning Outcomes

In this chapter, students will learn how to combine software from the MS Office Suite by:

- Embedding either a Word document or a PowerPoint slide show into an Excel spreadsheet
- Embedding either a Word document or an Excel spreadsheet or chart into a PowerPoint presentation, or
- Embedding either a PowerPoint presentation or an Excel spreadsheet or chart into a Word document.

## Overview

Now that you have seen all of the MS Office Suite software covered by this textbook, you have probably noticed some similarities, such as:

- Each program has a ribbon at the top of the screen, the contents of which are controlled by which tab is chosen above the ribbon
- Each program has "housekeeping" commands such as Open, Close, Save, Save As, and Print in the Home tab
- Each program has formatting commands such as Font, Cut, Copy, Paste, Bullets, and Numbering in the Home tab, and
- Each program has an Insert tab that allows you to add various visual and other options into your document.

As we learn to embed documents from one program into documents of another program, we will be using the Object option on the Insert tab.

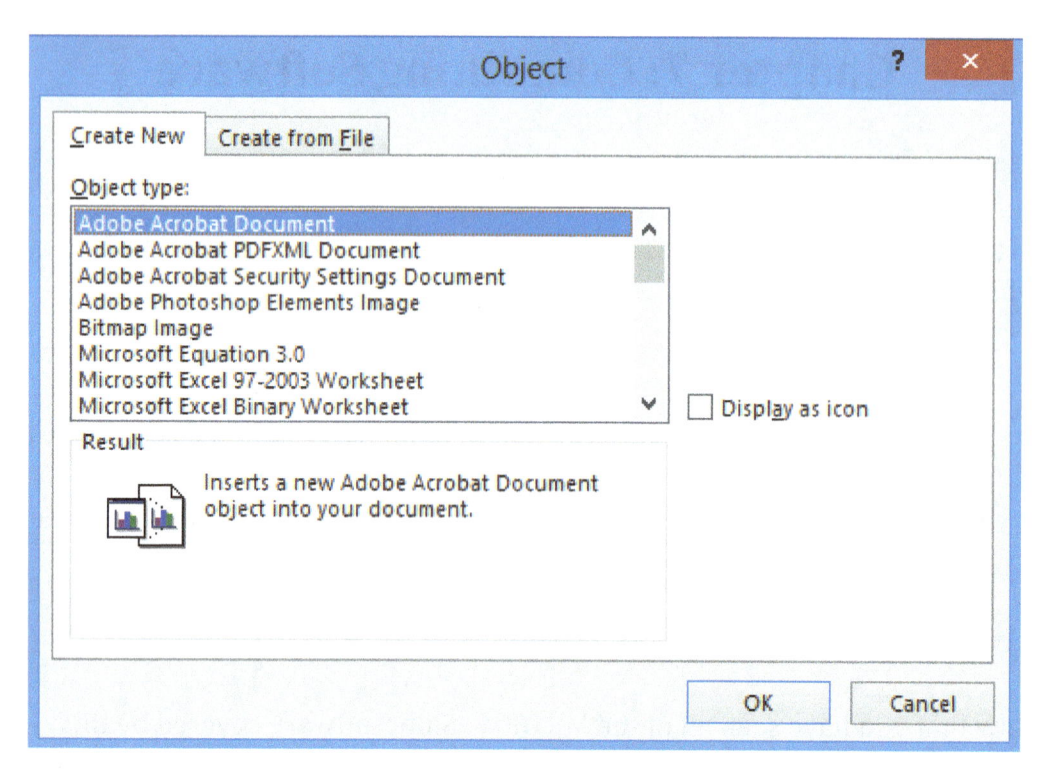

You may be wondering why someone would want to embed a document from one program into a document from another program. There are lots of reasons why, but they all involve having access to a "live" version of one document while working with another document.

For example, an employee may embed an Excel chart into a PowerPoint presentation. The presentation is being given to an audience and, throughout the presentation, the presenter is referencing data and a chart is shown on a slide representing that data. If the data in the chart is data that is changing, for example, each month, our current docketed time is being added to a yearly total and the presentation was prepared in February (with February's totals), but the presentation is being given in April (so it should have March's totals), you can solve that problem by linking the chart to an Excel spreadsheet that is updated each month. As the spreadsheet is updated, the chart automatically updates since it is linked to the spreadsheet. As the chart automatically updates, the PowerPoint slide automatically updates since it is linked to the chart in the Excel file.

## Embedding Into Word

There is an instructional video for students on this topic at:
Webpage: http://www.asselingroup.com/paralegals
Password: paralegals

To embed into Word, you need to create the Word document as well as the Excel or PowerPoint file that you want to embed into your Word document.

For the Word file, let's start with the memo template that is found on the textbook webpage. I created this memo for us to start with.

### Paralegals' Professional Corporation
### Interoffice Memorandum

TO: Anna Bengali

FROM: Barb Asselin

DATE: June 30, 2017

RE: Training Materials

You have asked me to provide some training materials to the new legal assistants that have been hired.

Here is a slide I created which outlines our department's needs from the legal assistants:

Here is an excel pie chart that outlines what percentage of the firm's document production is used in each department:

Please confirm if I may use these examples in my training package.

/ba

In the memo, you can see that I plan to embed a PowerPoint slide and an Excel pie chart. Now, let's make those. Here is my PowerPoint slide.

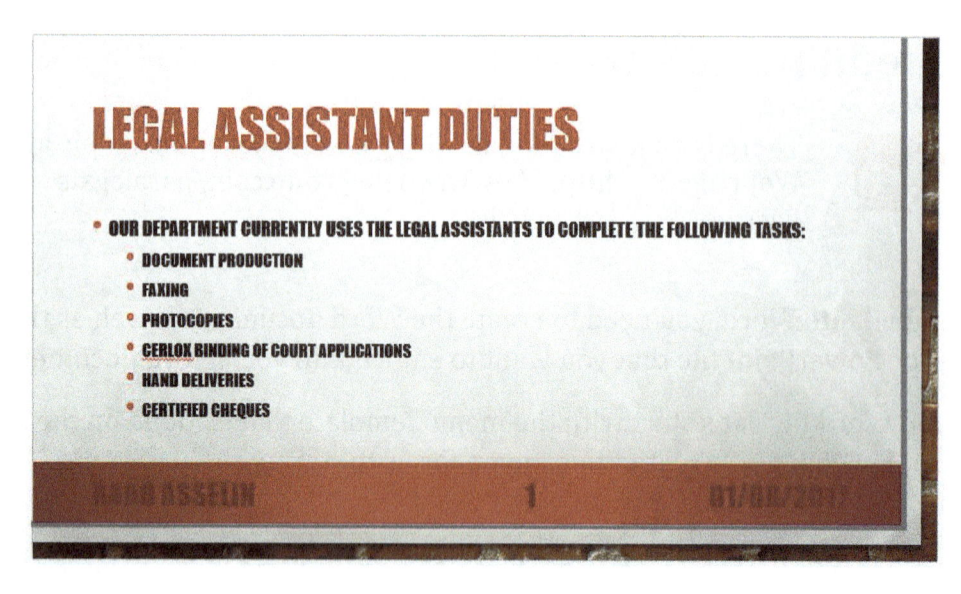

**LEGAL ASSISTANT DUTIES**

- OUR DEPARTMENT CURRENTLY USES THE LEGAL ASSISTANTS TO COMPLETE THE FOLLOWING TASKS:
  - DOCUMENT PRODUCTION
  - FAXING
  - PHOTOCOPIES
  - CERLOX BINDING OF COURT APPLICATIONS
  - HAND DELIVERIES
  - CERTIFIED CHEQUES

Save your presentation/slide and close it. If you only want to embed one slide, be sure that your presentation is only one slide as the first one will be the one that shows. If you want to link your entire presentation, then you will simply create a link to the presentation instead of showing just one slide.

To embed your slide into the memo, click in the memo where you want the slide to go. Then, go to the Insert tab and click on Object. Choose the tab Create from File and click Browse to go and get your slide. Select the Link to File option. Then, click OK.

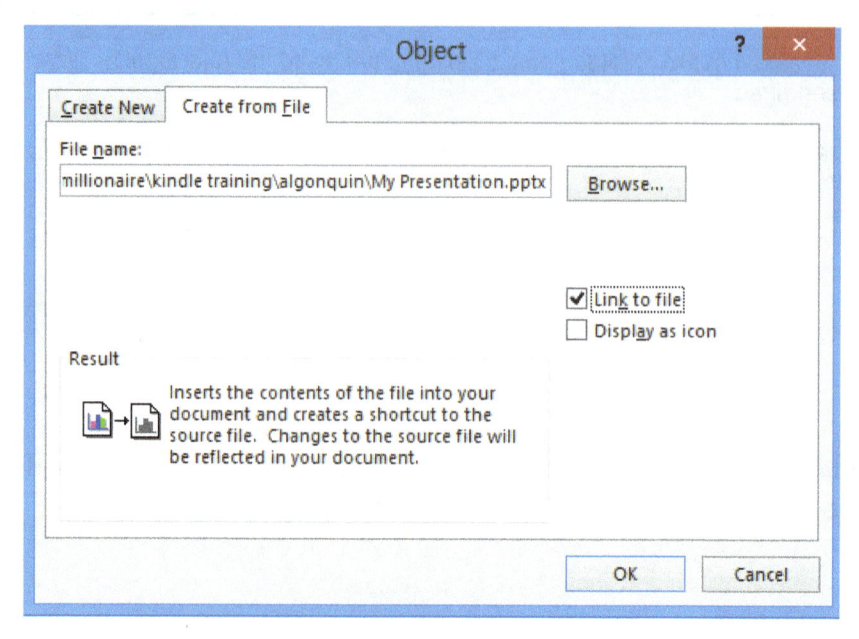

Computer Applications for Paralegals 263

The result is that the slide will appear in your memo.

> **Paralegals' Professional Corporation**
> **Interoffice Memorandum**
>
> TO: Anna Bengali
> FROM: Barb Asselin
> DATE: June 30, 2017
> RE: Training Materials
>
> You have asked me to provide some training materials to the new legal assistants that have been hired.
>
> Here is a slide I created which outlines our department's needs from the legal assistants:
>
> **LEGAL ASSISTANT DUTIES**
>
> - OUR DEPARTMENT CURRENTLY USES THE LEGAL ASSISTANTS TO COMPLETE THE FOLLOWING TASKS:
>   - DOCUMENT PRODUCTION
>   - FAXING
>   - PHOTOCOPIES
>   - CERLOX BINDING OF COURT APPLICATIONS
>   - HAND DELIVERIES
>   - CERTIFIED CHEQUES
>
> BARB ASSELIN          1          01/08/2017
>
> Here is an excel pie chart that outlines what percentage of the firm's document production is used in each department:
>
> Please confirm if I may use these examples in my training package.
>
> /ba

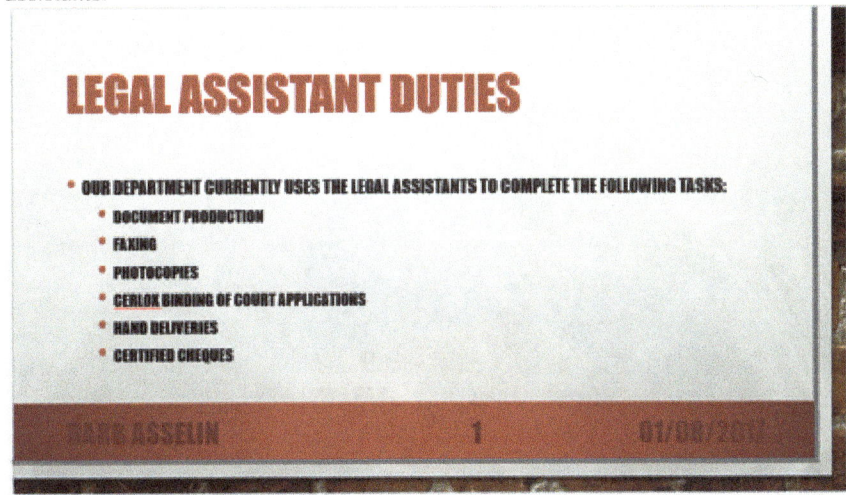

Now to add the Excel portion into our memo.

First, create the following Excel dataset:

| | A | B |
|---|---|---|
| 1 | Department | Percent of Document Production |
| 2 | Small Claims | 28 |
| 3 | Immigration | 24 |
| 4 | Criminal | 8 |
| 5 | Employment | 7 |
| 6 | Landlord | 11 |
| 7 | Traffic | 22 |
| 8 | Total | 100 |

Now, create a pie chart using the data (but not the total) and copy the pie chart to a new tab in the same spreadsheet.

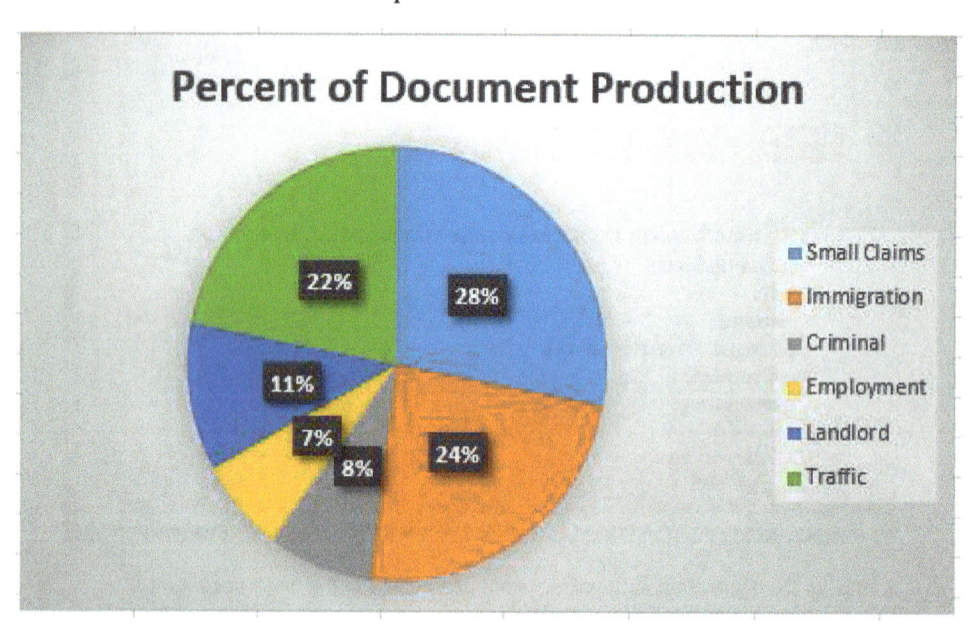

**Percent of Document Production**

- Small Claims: 28%
- Immigration: 24%
- Criminal: 8%
- Employment: 7%
- Landlord: 11%
- Traffic: 22%

Be sure that the tab that contains the pie chart is the open tab, then save your Excel file, and close it.

To embed the Excel pie chart into your memo, following the same steps as for the PowerPoint slide. Go to the Insert tab and choose Object. Select the Create from File tab and browse to find your pie chart. Click OK to insert it.

Computer Applications for Paralegals                                                          265

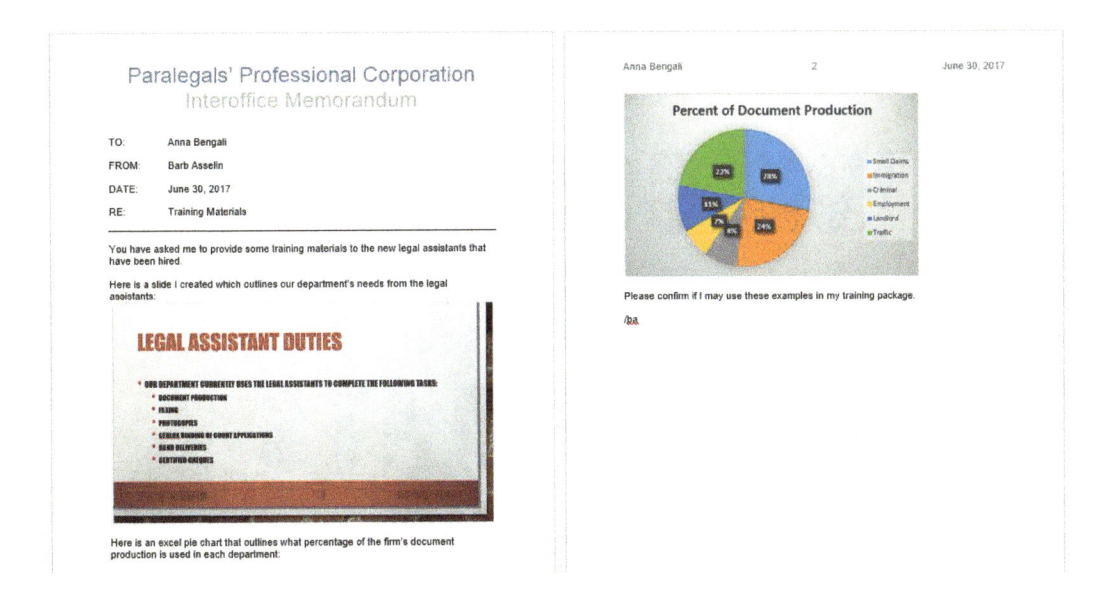

# Embedding Into PowerPoint

> There is an instructional video for students on this topic at:
> Webpage:     http://www.asselingroup.com/paralegals
> Password:    paralegals

To embed into PowerPoint, you need to create a PowerPoint presentation as well as the Excel or Word file that you want to embed into your PowerPoint document.

First, let's create a new PowerPoint presentation.

I'm going to create a new presentation for the legal assistants that are starting at our firm. Here is the title slide:

**WELCOME NEW LEGAL ASSISTANTS**

BARB ASSELIN

Here is the second slide, where I will embed the Excel pie chart from the previous example:

**WHICH OF OUR DEPARTMENTS USES THE LEGAL ASSISTANTS THE MOST**

- Click to add text

For the content of this slide, I will go to the Insert tab and choose Object. I will select from file and browse to find my Excel pie chart.

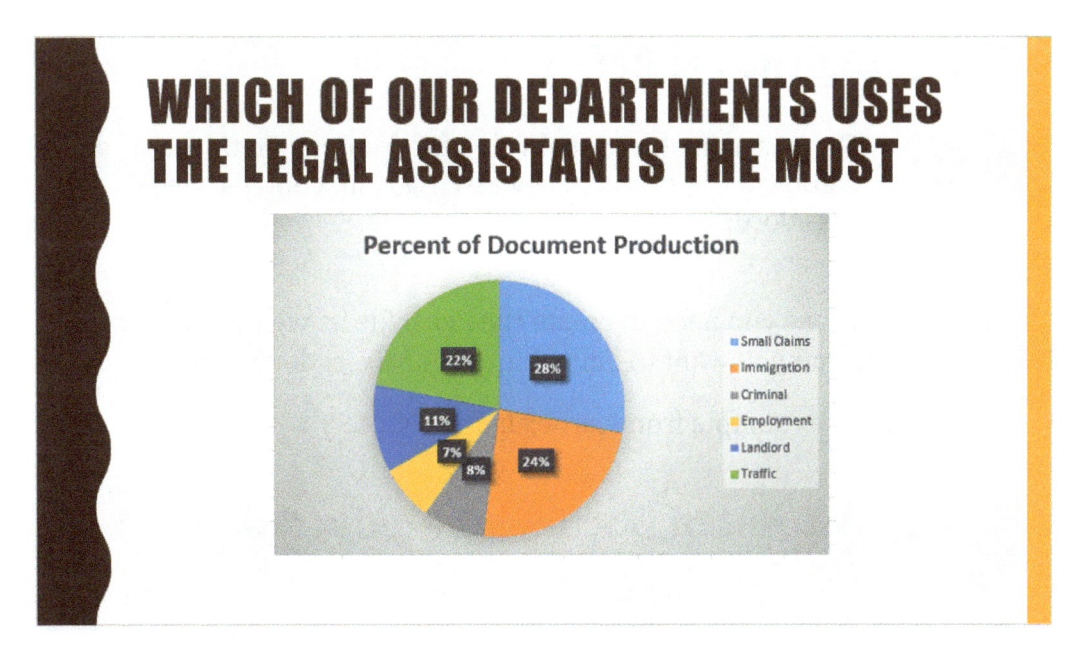

Computer Applications for Paralegals 267

## WHICH OF OUR DEPARTMENTS USES THE LEGAL ASSISTANTS THE MOST

**Percent of Document Production**

- Small Claims: 28%
- Immigration: 24%
- Criminal: 8%
- Employment: 7%
- Landlord: 11%
- Traffic: 22%

Now that I have embedded my Excel into the PowerPoint presentation, let's add the Word document. I will embed the blank memo template provided on the textbook webpage.

Use the same steps to create a new slide with the title **What a Memo From our Department Looks Like**. For the content of the slide, go to the Insert tab and click on Object. Browse to find your memo that you have saved on your computer or USB drive.

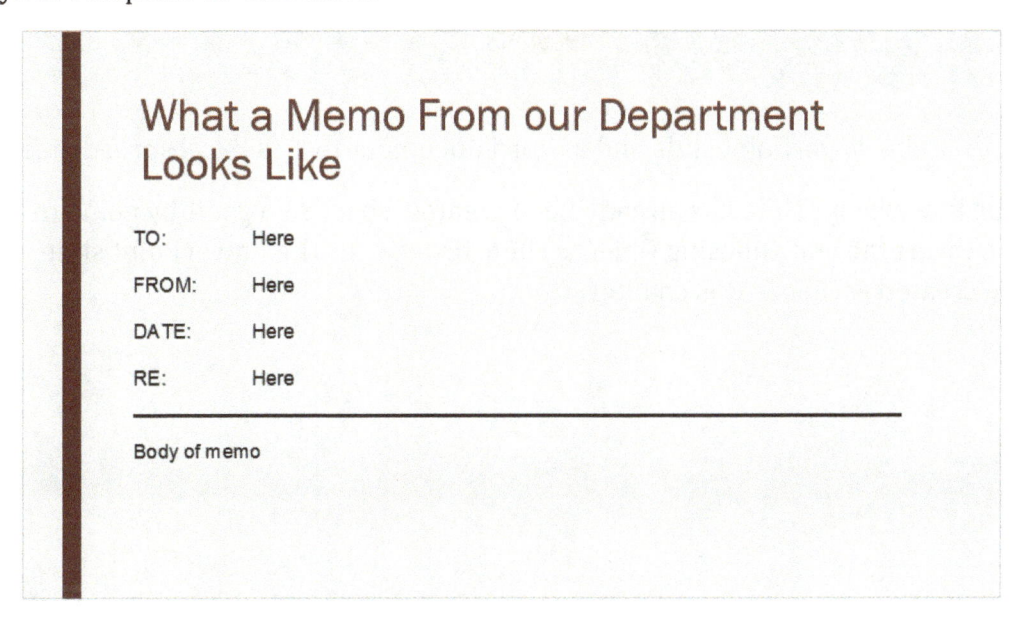

### What a Memo From our Department Looks Like

TO: Here
FROM: Here
DATE: Here
RE: Here

Body of memo

## Embedding Into Excel

There is an instructional video for students on this topic at:
Webpage:   http://www.asselingroup.com/paralegals
Password:   paralegals

To embed into Excel, you need to create the Excel file as well as the Word or PowerPoint file that you want to embed into your Excel document.

Let's start with the example from earlier in the chapter:

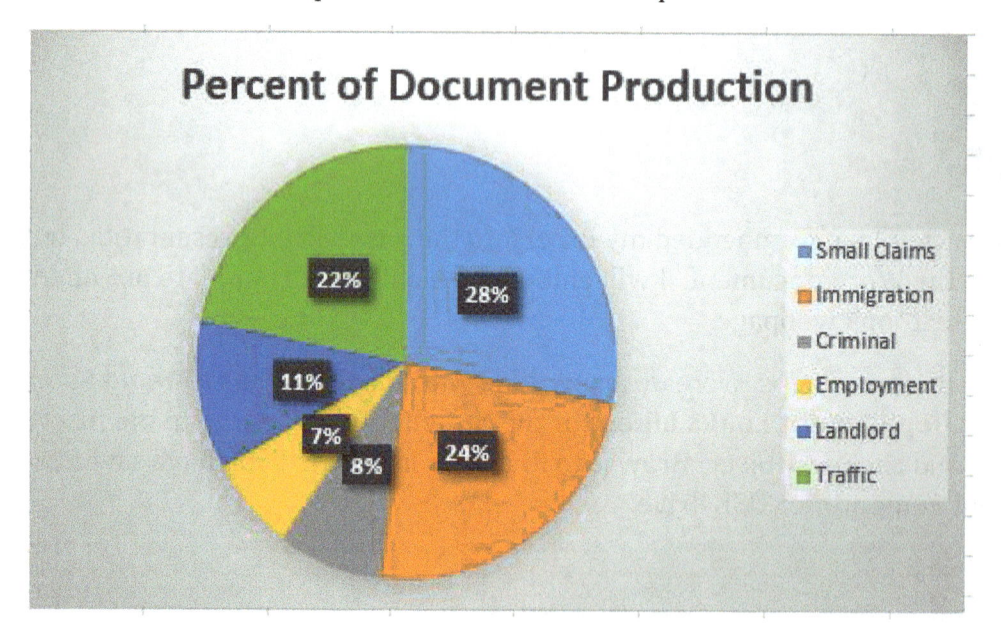

Let's add a PowerPoint slide and a Word document to this Excel spreadsheet.

Our PowerPoint slide has already been created, so let's go get it by going to the Insert tab and choosing Object. Then, browse for the PowerPoint slide we created earlier in this chapter.

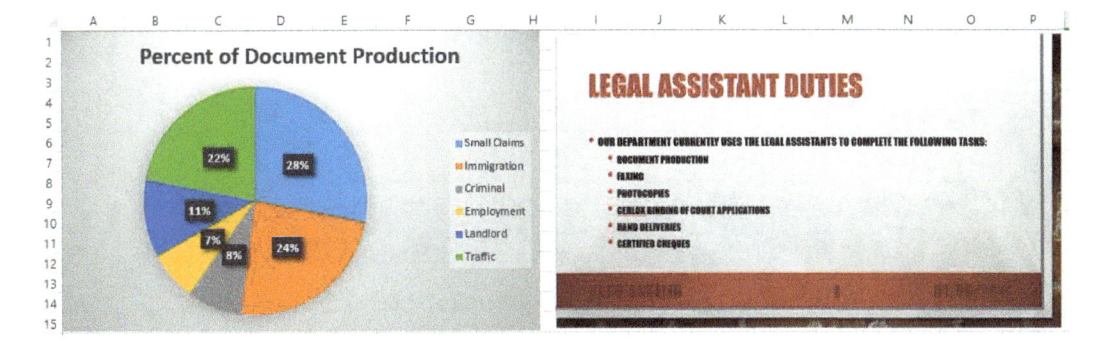

Computer Applications for Paralegals 269

We could re-size the two graphics on this page so that they are similar to one another. Also, this may be a good time to simply link to the PowerPoint presentation and display it as an icon.

Let's add the Word document as an icon to see how that works. I will link to our firm policy document that the user could click on to open the linked document. To do this I will follow the same steps by going to the Insert tab and choosing Object. Then, I will browse to find my document but I will choose Display as Icon and then click OK.

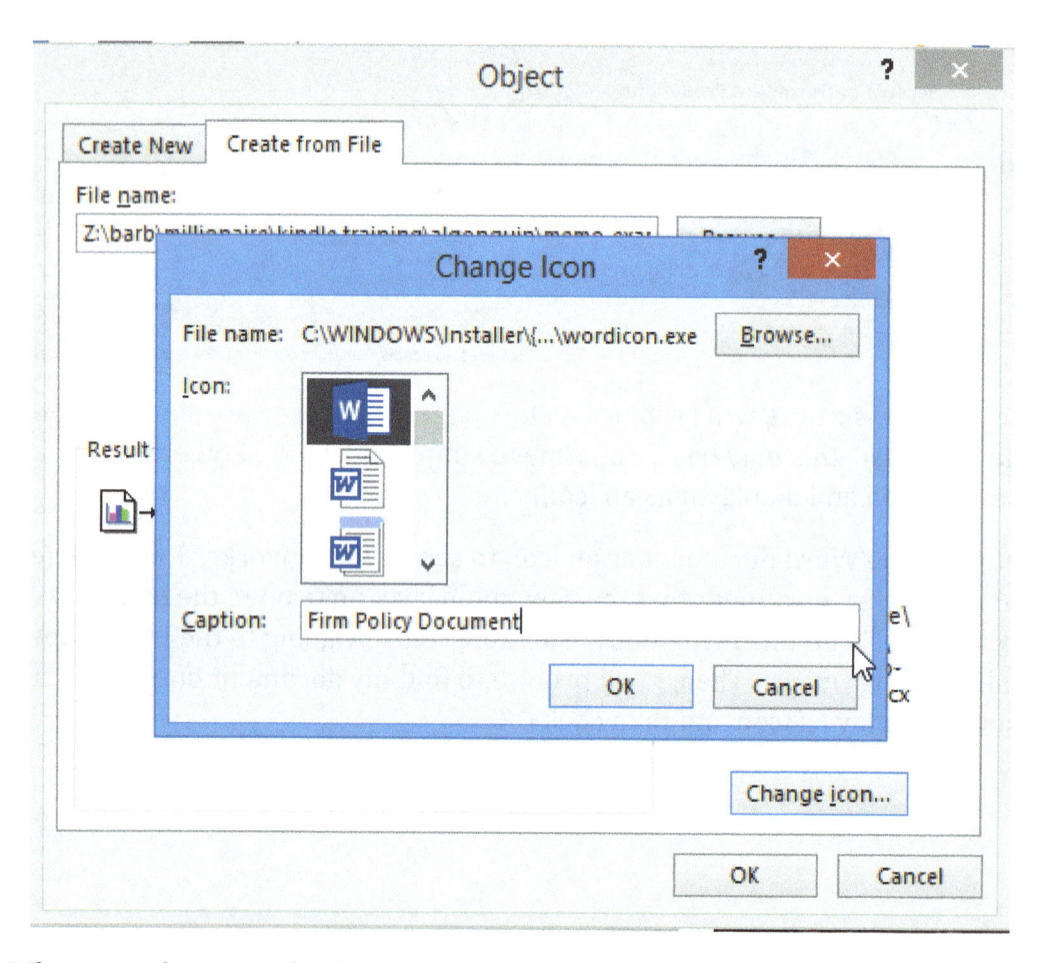

When you choose to display a document as an icon, you can choose which icon will be displayed. You can also change the Caption from the pathway of your document to a phrase of your choice. I have inserted the phrase, **Firm Policy Document**.

Here is the final product with both documents added to the Excel spreadsheet.

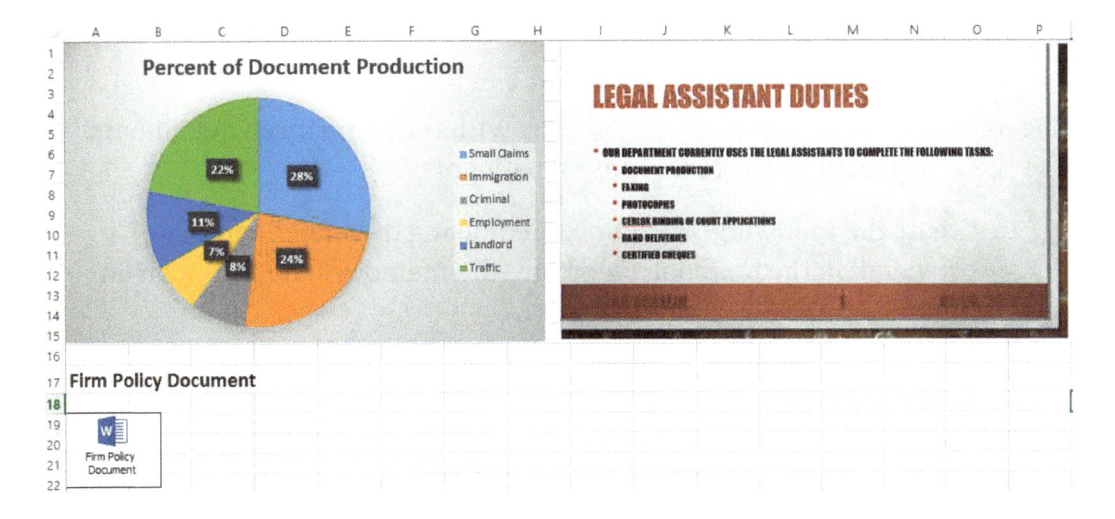

## Chapter Summary

In this chapter, students learned how to use the Object function on the Insert tab of Word, Excel, and PowerPoint to embed a document from one program into a document of another program. Six options were learned:

- Embed a Word document into an Excel document
- Embed a Word document into a PowerPoint document
- Embed an Excel document into a Word document
- Embed an Excel document into a PowerPoint document
- Embed a PowerPoint document into a Word document, and
- Embed a PowerPoint document into an Excel document.

# Exercises

The following three exercises will all start with the same three documents. Use these instructions to create those documents:

1. Create the following Word document using the memo template provided on the textbook webpage (the memo will be from you on today's date):

    | | |
    |---|---|
    | TO: | Paralegal Students |
    | FROM: | Barb Asselin |
    | DATE: | June 30, 2017 |
    | RE: | Welcome package |

    Welcome to our firm!

    We are excited to have you join the firm for your work placement. Here is a list of all of the areas of law that we practice. You can expect to work in each area during your time with us.

    We know that there are some nasty rumors out there that our students work too many hours and don't get enough sleep. We pride ourselves on having healthy, well-rested students! The following is a chart showing the average workload of our previous years' students.

    We hope you enjoy your time with us and learn everything you need in order to finish your program and become an excellent paralegal!

    /ba

Computer Applications for Paralegals

2. Create the following Excel dataset:

| | A | B |
|---|---|---|
| 1 | **Previous Years' Paralegal Students** | |
| 2 | Year | Hours per Week |
| 3 | 2000 | 52 |
| 4 | 2001 | 49 |
| 5 | 2002 | 53 |
| 6 | 2003 | 57 |
| 7 | 2004 | 58 |
| 8 | 2005 | 62 |
| 9 | 2006 | 61 |
| 10 | 2007 | 58 |
| 11 | 2008 | 65 |
| 12 | 2009 | 63 |
| 13 | 2010 | 61 |
| 14 | 2011 | 60 |
| 15 | 2012 | 57 |
| 16 | 2013 | 59 |
| 17 | 2014 | 58 |
| 18 | 2015 | 49 |
| 19 | 2016 | 54 |
| 20 | 2017 | 53 |

3. Using the previous dataset, create the following Chart and copy it to a new sheet within your file (I used the Clustered Column Chart from the Recommended Charts):

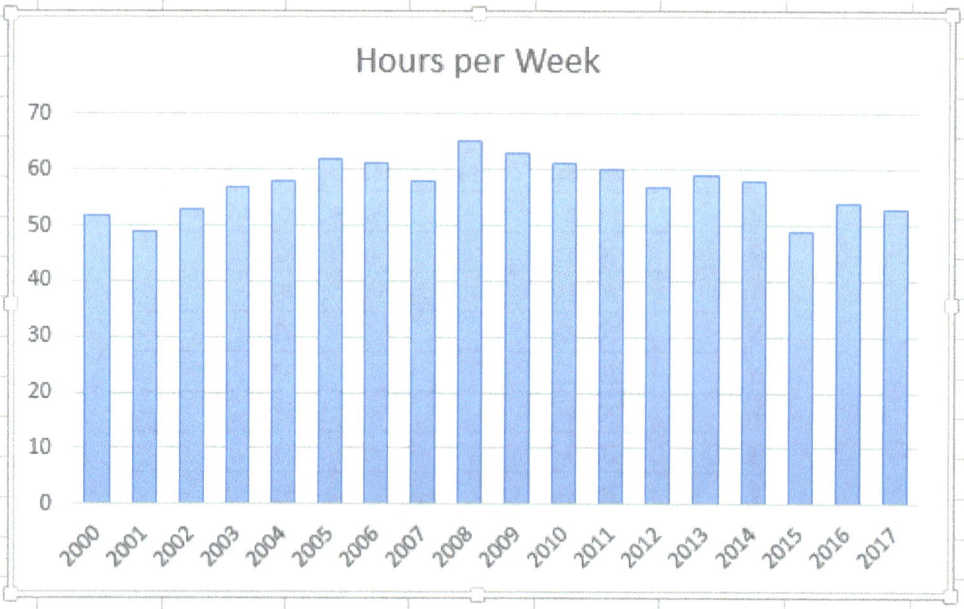
Hours per Week
70
60
50
40
30
20
10
0
2000
2001
2002
2003
2004
2005
2006
2007
2008
2009
2010
2011
2012
2013
2014
2015
2016
2017

4. Create the following PowerPoint slide (I have used the Facet design, but if you don't have access to the Facet design, please choose another one):

AREAS OF LAW WE PRACTICE
Small Claims
Landlord & Tenant
Immigration
Employment
Summary Conviction
Provincial Offences

# Exercise 7.1

**Embedding Into Word**

1. Create the Word memo, the PowerPoint slide, the Excel dataset, and the Excel chart at the beginning of this section
2. Open the Word memo and close the other two documents
3. After the second paragraph in the memo, embed the PowerPoint slide
4. After the third paragraph in the memo, embed the Excel chart
5. If your memo is a two-page memo or longer, format it properly
6. Submit your memo to your professor

# Exercise 7.2

**Embedding Into Excel**

1. Create the Word memo, the PowerPoint slide, the Excel dataset, and the Excel chart at the beginning of this section
2. Open the Excel document and close the other two documents
3. On the tab where you have saved your chart, embed the Power Point slide
4. Ensure that both of your graphics are of similar size
5. Choose a spot to embed your Word memo and, instead of having the whole memo show, you will only have the Word icon show with the caption, **Our Welcome Message**
6. Add your name to the spreadsheet
7. Submit your Excel document, all on one page, to your professor

# Exercise 7.3

**Embedding Into PowerPoint**

1. Create the Word memo, the PowerPoint slide, the Excel dataset, and the Excel chart at the beginning of this section
2. Open the PowerPoint document and close the other two documents
3. Create a title slide for your presentation called **Welcome to Our Firm**
4. Add your name to the subtitle of the title page
5. Add a new slide to your presentation after the title page
    a. The title will be **Our Welcome Message**

      b. For the content of this slide, you will embed the welcome memo
6. Add a new slide to your presentation at the end
    a. The title will be **Are There Enough Hours in a Week?**
    b. For the content of the slide, you will embed your Excel chart
7. Add a footer to the slides that includes your name, the date, and the slide number (not on the title slide)
8. Add a header and footer to the handouts that includes your name, the date, the page number, and the name of your firm
9. Print your presentation as a handout with two slides per page and submit it to your professor

# Conclusion

Congratulations! You have made it through the textbook!

I hope you have found it useful and that you have learned a lot about each of the software programs covered in this book. I could easily have written an entire textbook on each software program, but my goal was to provide students with enough knowledge of each program to create relevant and accurate documentation that would be suitable for the legal environment.

After reviewing the File Management chapter, you should be able to:

- Create an organized file management system, for both physical and digital files
- Properly organize the interior of a file, and
- Create an electronic file management system using Windows.

After reviewing the Outlook chapter, you should be able to:

- Use Outlook in a busy office in conjunction with other staff members and peers as a team
- Use the calendar feature to organize your day
- Use the contacts feature to keep track of clients, co-workers, peers, industry professionals, and personal contacts, and
- Use the task feature to prioritize your workload and keep track of deadlines.

After reviewing the PowerPoint chapter, you should be able to:

- Create a presentation that appeals to all types of audiences
- Add text to your presentations
- Customize your presentation's design
- Add various forms of content to a presentation
- Print and save a presentation in a variety of ways, and
- Give a presentation in front of an audience.

After reviewing the Excel chapter, you should be able to:

- Create a spreadsheet of data
- Manipulate your data through formulas
- Format your data for the workplace

- Use your data to create graphs and charts
- Perform a statistical analysis of your data
- Use functions to further enhance your data, and
- Answer questions about your data using pivot tables.

After reviewing the Word chapter, you should be able to:

- Create the most commonly used formats of external correspondence
- Create internal memos
- Properly format single and multi-page letters and memos
- Create a properly formatted professional report
- Use Word's templates to create fax cover sheets
- Perform a merge using Outlook or Excel and Word
- Create tables to add to letters, memos, and reports
- Create new styles and use existing styles, and
- Perform a variety of editing and proofreading techniques so that the best possible product is produced.

After reviewing the Integration chapter, you should be able to:

- Embed either a Word document or a PowerPoint slide show into an Excel spreadsheet
- Embed either a Word document or an Excel spreadsheet or chart into a PowerPoint presentation, and
- Embed either a PowerPoint presentation or an Excel spreadsheet into a Word document.

I hope you have made good use of the online resources available to you through this textbook. I hope you have used the templates and precedents that I have provided and I hope you have enjoyed the videos that I have created to further demonstrate how many of the techniques in this text are performed.

Best of luck in your future career in the legal field!

Barb Asselin

# Summary of Templates

The following is a summary of the templates referred to in the text that are available online at:

    Webpage:    http://www.asselingroup.com/paralegals

    Password:    paralegals

## Chapter 1

Halifax Office Letterhead

Toronto Office Letterhead

Ottawa Office Letterhead

Winnipeg Office Letterhead

Edmonton Office Letterhead

Vancouver Office Letterhead

## Chapter 2

University of Ottawa Criminology Acceptance Letter

## Chapter 6

Full Block Letter Example

Modified Block Letter Example

Modified Block Letter with Indentation Example

Multi-Page Letter Example

Memo Template

Memo Example

Multi-Page Memo Example

Fax Cover Sheet Template

Report Exercise Unformatted

# Summary of Instructional Videos

The following is a summary of the videos referred to in the text that are available online at:

    Webpage:    http://www.asselingroup.com/paralegals

    Password:    paralegals

## Chapter 2

Creating a New Folder

## Chapter 3

Creating a New Appointment

Creating a New Contact

Creating a New Task

## Chapter 4

Creating a Presentation

Customizing Bullets

Headers and Footers

Tables

Charts

SmartArt Graphics

Pictures

Videos

More Content

Notes

Transitions

Animations

Viewing Your Presentation

Printing Your Presentation

## Chapter 5

Creating a Spreadsheet

Formulas

Copying a Formula

Formatting

Tables

Sorting and Filtering

Conditional Formatting

Charts

Statistics

Functions

Pivot Tables

Freezing Rows or Columns

Hiding and Un-hiding Data

Showing Formulas

Printing

## Chapter 6

Full Block Letters

Modified Block Letters

Modified Block Letters with Indentation

Multi-Page Letters

Envelopes and Labels

Merging

Memos

Multi-Page Memos

Fax Cover Sheets

Reports

Templates

Tables

Compare

Find and Replace

# Chapter 7

Embedding Into Excel

Embedding Into PowerPoint

Embedding Into Word

# Also by Barb Asselin

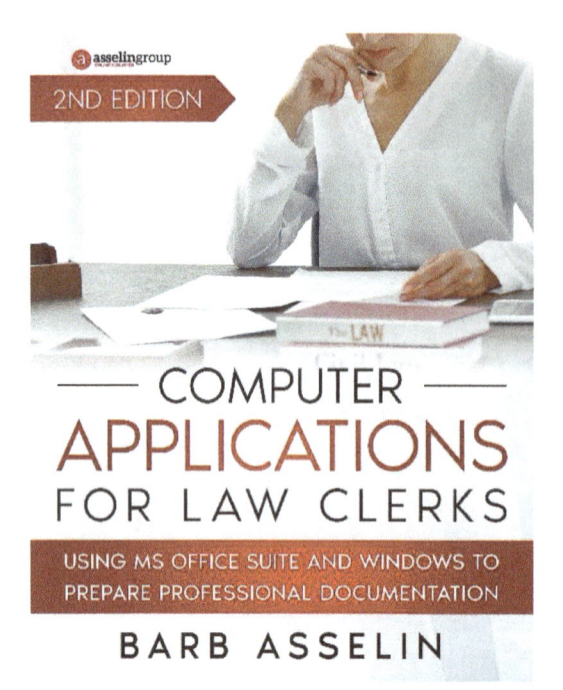

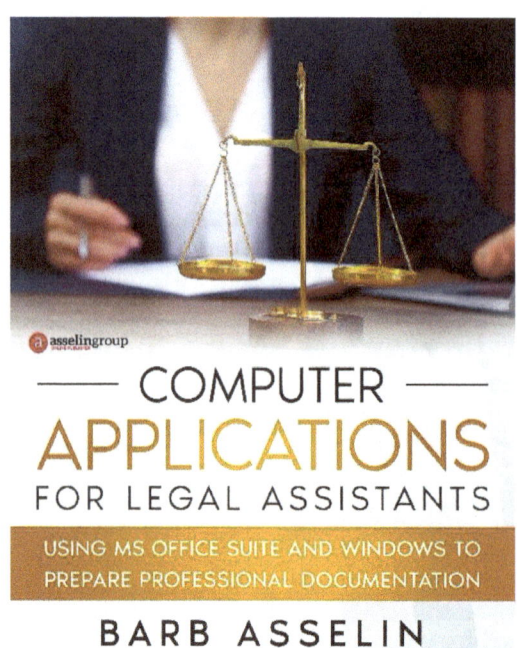

**Computer Applications for Law Clerks: Using MS Office Suite and Windows to Prepare Professional Documentation** (2nd Edition) by Barb Asselin

**Computer Applications for Legal Assistants: Using MS Office Suite and Windows to Prepare Professional Documentation** by Barb Asselin

# Notes